I'LL BE WATCHING YOU

I'LL BE
WATCHING
YOU

True Stories of Stalkers
and their Victims

Richard Gallagher

This edition first published in Great Britain in 2002 by

Virgin Books Ltd
Thames Wharf Studios
Rainville Road
London W6 9HA

First edition published 2001

A catalogue record for this book is available from the British Library

ISBN 0 7535 0696 3

Typeset by TW Typesetting, Plymouth, Devon
Printed and bound in Great Britain by
Mackays of Chatham PLC

To my father and mother,
Stanley and Ann Gallagher,
with love and many thanks.

CONTENTS

'I love thee not, therefore pursue me not'

A Midsummer Night's Dream

ACKNOWLEDGEMENTS

There are so many people who have helped. In particular I have to thank all those people who shared their harrowing experiences, including Robert Fine, Zack Green, Sarah Lockett, Gabriella Mazzalli, Tracey Morgan, and Malcolm Stewart. This short list in no way denigrates the contribution of other people I met and to them also grateful thanks is due.

The experts I have spoken to have been most helpful and I thank Parry Aftab and Jean Manley at Cyberangels, D.I. Hamish Brown, Diana Lamplugh and The Suzy Lamplugh Trust, Doctor Reid Meloy, Wayne Maxey at the San Diego Stalking Force, Lorraine Sheridan and Doctor Edward Petch.

My research has been assisted by a number of friends and professional people, among them Phil Bastable at the Metropolitan Police Service Press Office, Rachel Chadwick at Yorkshire Television, Gill Cox, Thomas Baxter at the Adelphi Theatre, Harry Fletcher at the National Association of Probation Officers, Timothy Donnelly, Philip Lowry and The Actors' Benevolent Fund, DS Neil Parker, The Theatre Museum and Amanda Skilton at Radio 4's, *Woman's Hour*.

Other people have helped by sending newspaper cuttings, by their suggestions and with their support. They are Andrew Brisbane, Kathleen Bryson, Pam Buckle, John Cooper, Michael Gallagher and Susanne Whittle, Keith Malkin, James Marriott (who was my first editor and got the project started), David Murray, Colin Richardson at *Gay Times*, Neil Roland and Sara Chanan, Kerri Sharp, and – of course – my mother and father.

While every effort has been made to contact copyright holders for permission to use quotes, this has not proved possible in all cases i.e. Chapter Four: *Between Ourselves* by Seymour Hicks, pub. Cassell PLC, 1930. Should these copyright holders wish to contact the publisher, appropriate credit will be given in future editions.

INTRODUCTION

The camera is low down, near the ground. It looks upwards, across the darkened garden, towards the lighted window of a house. The screen is framed by leaves; we are seeing through the eyes of a person who skulks in the bushes, hidden from the view of passers-by. Behind the frosted glass of the bathroom, we see the silhouette of a young woman as she prepares to undress. Our gaze lingers on innocent actions which, observed in this way, have all the erotic charge of a striptease. We know the woman thinks she is alone: she thinks her bedroom is private. We are being invited to share the voyeuristic thrill of a Peeping-Tom. We hear his breath coming quicker and quicker.

A neighbour putting the cat out sends the intruder running. We know he will be back. The woman is clearly a victim. Later in the film, a stranger taps her on the shoulder and asks her the time; or a man sits next to her on the bus and engages her in conversation – every encounter is dangerous. We know she is being followed: nowhere is safe, nobody can be trusted.

It's a stock piece from hundreds of horror films and thrillers. It's clichéd and it works. It's the filmmaker's shorthand to indicate danger and menace. Every subsequent thing which happens to the victim is now tinged with darkness.

There are other cinematic clichés which draw on our fear of being followed. For instance, there's the young male student we come to know and like, but who is maybe a bit of an oddball. He is saying goodbye to a fellow student who is female and attractive. He asks her for a date and she refuses. She does it nicely, but we can tell he is hurt. We follow him back to his rooms. He closes the door firmly, as though he wants to exclude the world from this, his private place. The camera begins to pan around, showing us his dreadful secret. The walls are covered with photographs of the girl – he is obsessed and dangerous. The woman is no longer in control of this situation: she might not realise it yet, but she has been turned into a victim. This weirdo is not going to give up so very easily. In a few well-chosen frames, the premise of the story is given.

Something within us thrills at the idea of intrusion on the screen, but when it happens for real, it's at best annoying and at worst terrifying. Many more people than might be supposed have some experience of what has come to be known as 'stalking'. It's a generalised description: so general one might argue it is meaningless. It is mostly understood to refer to an obsession which leads to prolonged pursuit or harassment.

This definition is not nearly wide enough: there are stalkers who claim they are not obsessed, there are pursuits which are not prolonged. There are cases where victims do not consider they are being stalked until it is far too late to do anything about it. There are stalkers who would claim they have a legitimate right to follow their victims. There are ex-lovers who simply won't go away; there are harrowing stories of abuse and there are sad stories of lonely people.

Some celebrities accept low-level stalking by fans and by the press as part of their job. There are also hundreds of ordinary people who have been forced, through no fault of their own, to accept a life where they must always hide, always be on their guard. These are the people who live with the fear that their stalker will one day find them again. They may have moved house, changed their jobs, altered their names but, despite this, they know someone, somewhere, has not let go of a warped fantasy about them. Given half a chance, that person will once again attach himself to their lives like a limpet.

Until relatively recently, stalking in itself was not a crime. Faced with a legal system which could do nothing to protect them, victims commonly said they wished their pursuer would do something – anything – which would be prosecutable. Since few stalkers ever give up, the only time when the victims felt safe was when their stalker was in prison (though this by no means ensured they were free from harassment).

It has been called the fastest-growing crime of our times. It is thought to have escalated as a result of easy communication, readily-available sexual imagery and a breakdown in 'normal' ways of living together. There may be some truth in all of this but, in fact, stalking has been around for centuries. It is not a single, easily pigeon-holed type of crime. Stalkers come in all shapes and sizes, they are not necessarily suffering from any mental illness and they don't always set their sights on the rich and famous.

In fact, celebrity stalking is only a small percentage of all cases: it has a disproportionate place in our minds because of the publicity it invariably receives. It is because of this publicity that, firstly the Americans and then the rest of us, decided to do something about it.

The first anti-stalking law was passed in California in 1990, after which most US states created their own variations of it and the rest of the world soon followed. In Britain, the Protection from Harassment Act was passed in 1997. The intended effects of these laws was to check behaviour before it became dangerous. As is the case with 'loitering with intent', the courts are now able to take action against repeated acts which, though legal in themselves, add up to a threat when viewed as a whole.

It doesn't entirely solve the problem. Some people stalk their victims secretly, building up a resentment inside their heads towards a person who may be scarcely aware of their existence. Psychiatrists, actors, doctors, writers, often don't know what effect they are having on their public. People whom they regard merely as 'patients' or 'fans' may very easily see them as intimates.

The stalking legislation at least goes some way towards stopping the mental torment of hundreds of people who jump every time the phone rings, dread opening their mail, wonder constantly if they are being followed or being watched. As technology becomes more and more adept at putting us in touch with people, as 'Big Brother' ceases to become our oppressor and, instead, becomes our servant (even our entertainer), it also becomes practically impossible for us to remain private. Our personal details are readily available to any competent computer user; we no longer feel surprised when we receive unsolicited mail from a company we've never heard of, addressing us by our full name and beginning: 'We know you have an interest in . . .' E-mails and web-sites carry all sorts of information about us across continents. Who knows what insignificant fact might turn a stalker's attention onto any one of us?

In writing this book I am immensely grateful to all the victims and professionals who have been willing to share their stories with me. I was made aware that stalkers often thrive on publicity and, for this reason, I have been reticent to give it to them in cases where they are not already named, and even then I have not included photographs of them. I am reluctant to make this activity seem like a path to any sort of reward.

However, it is important to understand why stalkers feel the need to pursue their victims. Psychiatrists and other professionals are still researching this difficult area. The theories I have arrived at here, unless otherwise stated, are my own conjecture, based on what I have heard and surmised. I hope they will add to the ongoing debate.

Richard Gallagher, August 2000

1. LOVE LOCKED OUT

'You teach me now how cruel you've been – cruel and false.
Why did you despise me? *Why* did you betray your own heart,
Cathy? I have not one word of comfort. You deserve this. You
have killed yourself. Yes, you may kiss me, and cry and wring
out my kisses and tears: they'll blight you – they'll damn you.
You loved me – then what *right* had you to leave me? What
right – answer me – for the poor fancy you felt for Linton?
Because misery, and degradation, and death, and nothing that
God or Satan could inflict would have parted us; *you*, of your
own will, did it. I have not broken your heart – you have
broken it; and in breaking it, you have broken mine. So much
the worse for me, that I am strong. Do I want to live? What
kind of living will it be when you – oh, God! would you like
to live with your soul in the grave?'[1]

So, at the bedside of his dying Cathy, the brutish Heathcliff
asks the reader to appreciate the depth of his love: a love so
pure, so overwhelming, that all his misanthropy, all his
violence, all his vengeful hate, are somehow purified by it. His
doomed and torrid emotions are turned into romance, and a
creature who any self-respecting female would find it difficult
to cope with for even a day, becomes a fantasy lover.

The same idea can be found throughout literature, art and
music. Millions of popular songs have unrequited love as their
central theme, and it's one we can all empathise with.

'Love,' said Quentin Crisp, 'is when you treat someone's
faults as though they were virtues.'[2] In this he was being
deliberately cynical, for he knew as much as anyone there are
many different forms of love. However, his quip accurately
describes the kind of love which, it is said, 'takes no
prisoners'. It's the kind of love which is sometimes described
as 'infatuation'; the kind of love which, when it isn't returned,
can so easily turn to hatred. This love is demanding,
obsessive, all-consuming. The lover projects an image onto his
chosen one – an image which compensates for all the

inadequacies he feels about himself. Friends laugh it off or counsel against it: such passion is not healthy, they say. Derision does nothing to diminish it; if anything, scorn only serves to make the love more urgent, more profound.

When Heathcliff says he cannot live 'with his soul in the grave', the implied idea that Cathy is actually a part of him accurately and poetically suggests one of the motivations which lie behind obsessive love. Heathcliff was a stalker.

In order for us to understand what leads one person to become obsessed with another we have to look at many different factors. The legal system has, until relatively recently, seen stalking as a component of other, more serious criminal activity – which it certainly can be. But, since a spate of well-publicised celebrity cases in the 80s and 90s, since the bringing into force of laws specifically designed to challenge obsessive behaviour before it gets out of hand, stalking is now seen as a crime in itself.

The stalker doesn't necessarily see himself as a stalker (and I say 'he' although it has to be taken into account that stalkers are by no means always male). The pursuit and harassment of the victim *may* be what he wants: he may find sufficient pleasure in knowing he has invoked fear in another human being. On the other hand, stalking is sometimes only the first stage of entrapment and could lead to rape, kidnap or murder. The stalker may be just a persistent nuisance who intends no ill-will at all, he may genuinely believe his affection is returned or will be, if he can only hang on for long enough. The nuisance-caller, the shadowy stranger who follows you everywhere, the rejected lover who won't give up – they aren't necessarily obsessed or sick, but they are stalkers.

Since 1997, any repeated activity, even if it is legal in itself, which knowingly causes alarm or distress, is breaking the law. Even if the perpetrator protests his innocent intentions, even if he believes his attentions are welcome, or if he feels totally justified because of some perceived injury to himself – whatever his excuses – he is stalking.

The popular image of the stalker is a misleading stereotype. Like all stereotypes there is a basis for it in fact. Stalkers *can* certainly be 'weirdos', frequently *are* 'loners', often *are* 'sexual inadequates', but now the behaviour has been legally defined (and in some measure, clinically), it has been seen to manifest itself in an alarming variety of people, many of whom seem outwardly harmless and normal.

This is not surprising: we all have the potential to experience desperate feelings of rejection. Most teenagers go through a stage of having a crush on an older, more attractive, more accomplished person. We've all felt that passionate attachment to someone – and how many times has rejection only served to intensify our desperate longing?

But most of us get over it.

Kenneth is a thirty-three-year-old unemployed Londoner. He saw in himself the beginnings of obsessional attachment. What he has to say is true of many:

'When I was young I had a long and miserable obsession with a fellow student. I know now – and somehow I knew at the time – that this infatuation was unhealthy. I also know now – and was repeatedly told at the time – that the person was not, in the smallest degree, attracted to me "in that way". He was two years younger than me, I am gay and he is straight. He had no problem at all with gay men – as long as they didn't cry on his doorstep and hate his girlfriends – but he wasn't interested. This didn't put me off in the slightest. If anything it made me more determined. This feeling, which I thought was love, just *had* to be real and if it was real then it had to have somewhere to go. There was only one place it could possibly go and I felt, if I persisted enough, fate would do the rest and my love would be rewarded in some way.

'It brought emotional pain to me, it brought difficulty – to say the very least – to the man I was attracted to, and it brought total tedium to my friends, but this was just like a battle that I had to fight and win. If I dug my heels in and proved myself, all the suffering, all the embarrassment, all the boredom, would somehow be turned into something wonderful. There I would be, with my lover next to me; he'd be saying something like: "Inside, I knew all along I loved you. It took your bravery to show me my true feelings." We'd walk off, hand in hand and stay together for the rest of our lives. All my problems and inadequacies wouldn't matter any more because I wouldn't be just me: I would be me and him. He was so much stronger and handsomer than I ever was. I suppose I wanted some of that for myself and the only way I could have it was by being with him.'[3]

Torrid love which refuses to be ignored, rampaging fire which consumes all and may even leave destruction in its wake – well it doesn't exactly fit in with the realities of life at the beginning of the twenty-first century, but it forms the stuff of dreams and sexual fantasy. In the 1920s hundreds of thousands of women fell under the spell of Rudolph Valentino who, as 'The Sheik', effectively abducted and presumably ravaged his woman (I think those billowing curtains were meant to indicate some kind of sexual activity). Nowadays, this film might be regarded as politically incorrect and we might even be more critical of the sort of images filmmakers eroticise. Nevertheless, there are many, many, people who find such fantasies magnetically appealing. Unbridled lust, domination and all-consuming passion are here to stay.

Such emotions can also be very dangerous. When the line between fantasy and reality is confused, or, indeed when the two things become reversed, 'the loved one' doesn't get a say in the matter. Like all unwanted attention, love can be a blight on that person's life – or worse.

Kenneth was extremely lucky. His imaginary 'true love' was patient, supportive and, he says, far more kind to him than he deserved. In time (he thinks about four years), he was able to accept his 'hopeless passion' as a friend. Thinking back over the experience, and trying to analyse what it was that changed his mind, the nearest he can get to it is that friends stopped being sympathetic and started telling him some hard home truths.

This in itself is unlikely to have been enough. To grow out of this state takes some shift within which makes the potential stalker start respecting himself. Kenneth admits he was grossly lacking in self-confidence. His father pushed him hard to achieve and he felt he could never accomplish enough: could this have been where his problems started?

In a recent television series, participants were re-introduced to their first boyfriends or girlfriends. Most found the years had diminished the attraction they felt all that time ago. Some of them had harboured a secret longing for their lost affair for years, only to meet and come away thinking 'what did I ever see in him?'

The truth is, we settle down, not with Ms or Mr Right, but with Ms or Mr Comfortable. As we mature we find our youthful obsessions were 'all part of growing up'. The desire for the extremes of emotion becomes cerebral rather than physical and we experience our deep passions in pleasant dreams as we settle down with our favourite weepy; are swept away by the closing tragic moments of an opera; or put our feet up with a Mills and Boon.

But some people, for reasons of their looks, their shyness or their social background, never graduate from the adolescent stages of desire. Among these, there are some who find partners but don't find happiness. They don't possess the maturity to value the other person for what they are. (This is the profile of the possessive lover, the wife-beater and the cheating spouse.) Others remain alone. They go through their twenties, their thirties, looking around at the couples who are their friends and wondering what it is about themselves that has condemned them to a life of emotional solitude.

A small percentage of these people never look inwards for the answer to their needs. Instead, they blame, they demand, they manipulate. While they can objectify their despair, they believe they're in control of it. They frequently experience success in many other areas of their lives. Indeed, such success is not uncommon, since they tend to overcompensate for their lack of emotional security by achieving power or skills in other fields. But the hollow inside them is never filled and, ultimately, like the alcoholic in need of a drink, they are drawn into a downward spiral: the dangerous pursuit of what can never satisfy.

J. Reid Meloy, who is associate clinical professor of psychiatry at the University of California, San Diego and editor of *The Psychology of Stalking: Clinical and Forensic Perspectives* (1998) says: 'It appears that most stalkers have had a major loss in the six months preceding the crime beginning, and are often isolated, lonely, and socially incompetent. They also typically have both a mental disorder and a personality disorder.'[4]

The loss can be almost anything, but is often a bereavement or the break-up of a relationship. Subconscious, but immensely powerful, feelings of rejection surface: the rejection felt by the child when its mother deserts it. There is panic and this precipitates desperation.

There is a good deal of support for the theory that all abnormal emotional conditions have their roots in the painful experiences of early childhood. A number of these experiences are obviously harmful and tragic, such as in cases of abusive or absent parents. Sometimes, more worryingly, a child suffers trauma from being left alone for only a minute or two. Unsure of its security, it experiences feelings of abandonment which will surface in later life and severely hamper confidence and inner well-being.

Doctor Meloy describes the projection of desire as 'a narcissistic linking fantasy'. The stalker, in his desired object, sees himself as loved, fulfilled, special. (Here, 'object' is an appropriate word since the stalker doesn't allow the victim her own personality.) He believes he is destined to be with that person and, once he is, he will be at peace with himself.

This is only the first stage. When the object of his affection proves to be less than willing, or unavailable, he experiences feelings of acute and chronic rejection. Shame and humiliation follow. These feelings are countered with rage which compels him to hurt and destroy the person who has wounded him. Once his 'loved one' is suitably terrorised, downtrodden, or even, in extreme cases, dead, he is able to restore them to the pedestal from which they've fallen. The stalker feels safe again and the object is his fantasy lover once more.

This explains the euphoric feelings the stalker feels after he has terrorised his victim. He subconsciously knows that to actually have a relationship with the person would never be enough. As idols to worship, real people are irritatingly inadequate. At every turn, they demonstrate their own needs, their own personalities and, by so doing, conflict with the stalker's demand that they must be perfect. In order to maintain his fantasy, he must devalue the actual person so they can appear to be exactly what he wants. He usually does achieve his ends, even if it's at a huge cost to himself. For the victim, being adored in this way is a sickening and dangerous experience.

John Hinckley, who attempted to assassinate Ronald Reagan in order to prove his love for the actress, Jodie Foster, wrote in a letter to the *New York Times*:

'Jodie Foster may continue to ignore me for the rest of my life but I have made an impression on that young lady that will never fade from her mind. I have made her one of the most famous actresses in the world. Everybody but everybody knows about John and Jodie. We are a historical couple whether Jodie likes it or not. At one time, Miss Foster was a star and I was an insignificant fan. Now everything is changed. I am Napoleon and she is Josephine; I am Romeo and she is Juliet; I am John Hinckley Jr. and she is Jodie Foster. The world can't touch us. Society can't bring us down.'[5]

A man who stalked a secretary for over twenty years is quoted as saying, 'I'll do my time in jail, but she'll do her time in hell.'[6]

Sarah Lockett, a newspresenter from Meridian television, described how her stalker, Jeremy Dyer, appeared to be enjoying himself immensely in court: She said '. . . it was as if he was thinking "This is my day in court and I'm going to strut it about a bit." The police said, "He's loving all this. He's got attention. He has such a nothing life – he's a nobody – this is the most attention he's ever had." '[7]

There is no all-embracing psychological definition of a stalker. S/he can be suffering from a variety of more complicated problems – schizophrenia being one. Stalking might be the sorry end to an abusive and failed relationship; there may be ulterior motives such as revenge, jealousy or hero-worship. Three main categories of stalkers have been identified, as well as three main categories of victim.

Doctor Meloy explains these as follows:

'*Simple obsessionals* are those individuals who have a prior real relation with the victim, and could range from an ex-spouse to a fellow office worker.
Love obsessionals develop a "fanatical love" for the victim, are mentally disordered, and do not have a real relationship with her.
Erotomaniacs also have no real relationship, but believe the victim is in love with them: a delusion.'

It follows, then, that victims can also be roughly categorised in three major groups. They are: prior sexual intimates (victims who have been in a relationship with the stalker), prior acquaintances (those who have known the stalker platonically) and strangers.[8]

Whilst acknowledging there may be cases which fall outside known categories the following can be said to be generally true:

- Most stalkers are men who fixate on women and would fall into the first two categories: '*Simple obsessionals*' and '*Love obsessionals*'. The first survey of stalking victims to be conducted in the United Kingdom was carried out by Lorraine Sheridan and her colleagues at Leicester University. They concluded that a significant majority of these are ex-partners who refuse to accept that a relationship has ended. These are the group who are also most prone to violence.[9]
- Ms Sheridan's research showed threats of violence being reported in just over half of the cases examined. Actual violence had taken place in 32 per cent of the cases. Doctor Meloy states there is an increased risk when the threat has been articulated. There are other, and more curious, pointers to the possible physical danger. Dr Park Dietz, a professor of Psychiatry and Biobehavioural Sciences at the School of Medicine, University of California, who is another expert on the subject, has concluded, after his analysis of various letters sent to celebrities by persistent fans, that there is more likely to be a problem when the writer has moved around the country, follow-

ing their idol. Unlike the cases where ordinary members of the public are stalked, Dr Dietz sees more of a threat in celebrity stalkers who don't articulate their violent fantasies but instead speak of love. It is these people who are more likely to feel rejected and vent their frustrations in violent activity. Doctor Meloy states: 'Most stalkers are not physically violent. If you isolate stalkers that were prior sexual intimates, then you do get violence rates that exceed 50 per cent. When stalkers pursue a public figure and are violent, threats do not occur in 90 per cent of the cases. When stalkers pursue private individuals (everyone else), threats occur at least 50 per cent of the time, and with slightly increased risk of violence.'[10]

- 'Erotomania' (also called De Clérembault's Syndrome after the doctor who first diagnosed it) is the unshakeable belief that the love you feel for a person is returned. Many celebrity stalkers are erotomaniacs; they are distinguished from their 'love obsessional' counterparts by this belief. (A 'love obsessional' acknowledges the person doesn't yet feel attraction but he believes persistence will win in the end.) Erotomania is relatively rare but can be devastating for both victim and pursuer. While there are those who say most sufferers from erotomania are women, Doctor Meloy's book says this is not supported by any evidence from studies.[11]
- Stalkers are typically more intelligent than the average criminal. In the pursuit of their victim, they often have to use extremely devious means to gain addresses, win confidences and avoid being caught. They can be fully aware of the effect their activity is having on the victim and are experts at 'turning the screw' just enough to maximise the distress without making themselves vulnerable to those who would stop them.
- They are usually 'loners' with a history of failed relationships. Their condition is directly related to the problems they have in adapting to society and the isolation they feel: the sense of exclusion.
- They may have poor communication skills and sometimes have a dependency on drugs or alcohol.

- Stalking is one criminal activity where both the perpetrators and the victims are older than average. It most often happens to people in their 'fourth decade'. There are extreme exceptions such as a nine year-old boy in Hastings, Michigan, who broke the state anti-stalking laws when he called his heart's desire – a ten-year-old girl – more than 200 times over a few months.[12] At the other extreme is a seventy-seven-year-old British war veteran from Market Harborough, who holds the dubious honour of being the oldest person to be convicted of stalking after a hate campaign directed against his ex-partner and her current lover.[13] There is new research which indicates an increasing number of instances among teenagers. Universities and colleges are focus points for the crime. Young people away from home for the first time, experiencing strong sexual and emotional responses – it's not surprising.

- It goes without saying that the stalker needs to devote a lot of time and energy to his crime. It is therefore generally true that stalkers tend to be unemployed or in part-time work.

- Ms Sheridan found that a surprising number of victims (about 40 per cent of the sample group), reported that their stalkers did not conduct their campaigns single-handedly: they were helped by family and friends.

- Stalking activity can last for months or even years. It is not uncommon to find victims who have had to put up with the unwanted attentions of a stalker for decades. Prison may stop the stalking for the length of the sentence, but the stalker is likely to carry on fixating on his victim upon release.

- Most people would imagine the driving force behind the stalker's activities is sexual. This is not the case. Most victims, like many rape victims, perceive the motivation as a desire to control. A common experience is the feeling of loss of control over your own life but, though this very often happens as a result of being stalked, the motivations of the perpetrator are more likely to be anger.

- It is common for the stalker to blame his victim entirely for his crime. 'She drove me to do it', 'she knew exactly what she was doing', 'she deserves it'.
- Doctor Meloy's book quotes an American report which indicates that eight per cent of adult American women and two per cent of adult American men have been stalked at some time in their lives. US estimates for the actual number of stalking victims give a figure of one million women and 0.4 million men. Only half of these victims report their problem and just a quarter of these complaints result in an arrest. Only 12 per cent of all stalking cases resulted in prosecution. In Britain, Sheridan's survey quotes figures from the Home Office (1999). 'In 1998, 661 persons were cautioned under the England and Wales Protection from Harassment Act. 4,298 cases were proceeded against and 2,221 persons were convicted.'[14]

Is stalking, as the newspapers would have us believe, something which has suddenly erupted at the end of the twentieth century? Is it born out of the stresses and strains of modern life, the need to succeed, the omnipresent sexual images?

We do not live in natural surroundings, we do not follow our instincts. Mankind is a hunter and, no matter how sophisticated we become, something of the animal remains in our psyche. It is the balancing of our natural instincts and our social refinement which allows us to exist together. When individuals act out of pure self-interest, in whatever way, society is diminished.

Our fabricated, human world has many, many advantages and just as many disadvantages: the false expectations we are given about what we should achieve; the pressure to conform; the taboos about aging and death; the excessive value we put on perceived notions of beauty.

The idea of intrusion is no longer unthinkable and privacy, even the privacy of the bedroom, can now be bought and sold. The tabloid press behave as though the sex lives of all of us are public property. We are invited to stand at a hypocritical distance and persuade ourselves that, no matter how we view our own messy lives, at least we haven't sunk as low as the 'Sex rat boss' or his 'kiss and tell' girlfriend on page 2.

Celebrities in particular have ceased being people who exist in another place and whose private personas can only be guessed at. Now we know intimate details of practically any star or major public figure: details which we often have no business to know and which feed our desire for more.

The press regularly stalk their targets – they make repeated telephone calls, they camp out on doorsteps, they train telephoto lenses on windows, they use various means of entrapment. This has more than once led to tragedy but it is a form of stalking we seem to accept. As buyers of the newspapers who trade in people's private lives, we are party to it. Though the press were not to blame for Princess Diana's death, it is nevertheless true that, without their unwanted and persistent trailing of her, there would have been no need for her party to have been driving at speed with an intoxicated man at the wheel.

Many people describe the tabloids as 'only a bit of fun' and claim not to believe half of what they read. We may be happy to read about kinky sexual activities or a star's secret drink problem; the ex-lover, the intrepid reporter or some professional agent provocateur get their money, but it's sobering to imagine what our 'bit of fun' may have cost the subject. Not many of us would like our secrets splashed on the front pages of newspapers.

To return to the lone stalker: in a world where, apparently, everybody is interesting, those who are not feel the rejection all the more keenly. It's like being alone at Christmas: it's worse because everybody else seems to be having such a good time. The pressure to find a partner is huge: being single is more and more suspect the older one gets. A heterosexual man who has remained single until the age of fifty is seen to be an emotional or sexual failure. A single woman of the same age is labelled as 'frigid' or 'ugly'. There is a paranoia about being thought to be gay. Princess Anne recently commented that single people were selfish.

The single person is threatening because s/he challenges the idea that we must procreate. Drama, cinema, advertising, music – everywhere there is positive support for heterosexual coupling and an implied criticism of any other state. When the young male student comes home from college one of the first questions he's asked is always, 'Have you got a girlfriend yet?' When the female in her early 20s is seen twice in the company of a youth she scarcely knows, her mother will be smiling knowingly and hearing wedding-bells.

It takes courage and confidence to fight this pressure. Some people do so and are happy without a permanent partner. Others stay single reluctantly and yearn for that time when, as the song says, 'You may see a stranger across a crowded room/And somehow you know, you know even then/That somehow you'll see her, again and again'. As has been said, there are those who never meet their soul-mate, and there are also those who choose inappropriate partners because of their desperation. Most people manage, in whatever way, with the hand fate has dealt them. A small number do not.

Stalking is one way in which the emotional inadequate feels he can become powerful. Just as we hate in others things we don't like in ourselves, we love in others things we feel we lack.

The stalker is the thief of emotions: like the burglar who excuses his crime by saying 'they have all that money and I don't have any', the stalker sees the rest of us as having an unfair proportion of security and love. A typical observation from victims is the phrase 'my life is not my own any more'. Sometimes it's not enough for the stalker to know his victim has been terrorised. He takes the view that 'if I can't have her, nobody else will' and obsession leads to murder.

When love turns to hatred, the hate can be just as powerful as the passion it has replaced. This is explained by Doctor Meloy's 'linking fantasy'. This is an experience we can all relate to in some minor degree: our relationship ends and we indulge in the pleasurable activity of sitting in a bar with friends pulling our ex-partner to pieces. We go over and over all the negative things about them in order to reassure ourselves that we were right to ditch them. When we no longer feel the need to do this, we know we are, finally, over it.

Even when you are the one who's finished the relationship, there is still a sense of rejection, a sense of betrayal. It is necessary to re-establish yourself as a person in your own right as opposed to what you were before: one of a couple.

So – imagine rejection without there ever having been acceptance; imagine the reasons for that rejection being too painful to come to terms with. Imagine the feeling that rejection is all that can be expected because you are worthless, ugly, charmless. The need to assert yourself is then not just a normal balancing – it's crucial to emotional survival. Only when the former 'girl of my dreams' has become as downtrodden as you feel yourself does it become possible to regain an illusion of self-respect.

And, of course, the underlying motive need not always be physical love, though it most often is. Robert Fine was stalked by a woman who made it quite clear she 'wanted to destroy him'. She resented him for being in a position of power over her as her lecturer at university. She resented his ability to communicate, his friends, his 'privileged' life. (See Chapter Eight.) Over a hundred years ago, Richard Prince stalked and murdered the actor William Terriss who, he believed, was occupying the space in public affection which rightly belonged to him. (See Chapter Four.) Though these, and other, cases may seem to be different from the psychological profiles we have discussed here, they are in fact very similar. 'I feel undervalued – I need the security this person has – I can't have it so I must bring that person down in order that I can be safe within myself.'

Where the emotional need is linked to specific circumstances, such as the teenager bewildered by his first, urgent sexual attractions, or the carer who, after the death of a patient, finds life is suddenly empty, there is a good chance the stalking will be a temporary aberration. When the problems are deeper and there is no compensating, previous experience of security; when the fantasy, the pain and the anger are all that's left, then the stalking can become a lifetime obsession.

We know what drives most people to stalk; we don't yet know how to cure it. There are psychiatrists involved in investigating the phenomenon, such as Dr Edward Petch at Ealing Hospital in London, who is setting up a clinic. It will be the first of its kind in this country and he is at pains to point out that it will in no way be a solution to the problem of stalking. He says:

'The clinic . . . will be designed to assess and manage stalkers and victims of stalking. Given that some of the more intrusive forms of stalking derive from mental disorder, treatment of those disorders may in some cases lead to a reduction in stalking behaviour. If the patients attending the clinic did reduce their stalking behaviour I would see this as a bonus. The primary objective has got to be the treatment of a psychiatric condition. Many victims also suffer from a psychiatric condition which is made worse by the persistence of stalking, both groups may therefore benefit if we get the treatment of stalkers right. Of course the victims themselves warrant interventions too.

'It has proved more difficult than anticipated to gain funding . . . but we will hopefully be setting up a small trial within the next few months (autumn 2000). This will be internally funded. In the meantime our project group is establishing assessment and treatment policies and protocols. We would hope to receive our first patient in the new year.

'There are many psychiatric conditions which can drive stalking behaviour. I do not believe we are able to cure any of them. Treatment is another matter and through the availability of different treatments we can alleviate some the symptoms.'[15]

Dr Petch's, Ms Sheridan's and Doctor Meloy's work (and that of other renowned professionals working in this field) would have been something of a puzzle to the general public up to only a generation ago. Stalking was thought of as a professional hazard of those whose lives appeared to invite such problems. In fact, celebrities don't make up the greatest number of victims (ex-partners do), but, as a group, they are relatively more likely to attract unwanted attention. High-profile cases of celebrity stalking have served to bring the subject into the open. For this reason, we must begin with the rich and famous. When a life is lived half in and half out of the public spotlight, those who seek to bask in the reflected glory of the stars will stop at nothing, even murder.

2. A MAN WHO WASN'T THERE

Sean was the child of famous parents. Most of the time there were people grouped around the doorway to his home, hoping to catch a glimpse of his father. This cold day in December 1980, when Sean was just five years old, was no exception. Some of them were regulars – like the two women who pointed him out to their companion – a plump, amiable-looking youth in a funny Russian hat and a long coat. Sean's nanny sometimes allowed the fans to say 'hello'. They were often almost as impressed with the child as they might have been with his father or mother.

The youth in the funny hat came forward to greet Sean. The hand that gripped that tiny fist was warm and clammy from having been deep inside the young man's pocket. The stranger told Sean he had travelled a very long way to be here – all the way from Hawaii. Then, telling the child to look after himself, he returned his hand to his pocket. As he did so, the man clutched the handle of a loaded .38 revolver.

He was Mark David Chapman. He had come to New York with the sole intention of assassinating Sean's father, his own one-time hero, the ex-Beatle, John Lennon.

The child meeting the killer: a chillingly significant moment in the cataclysmic evening of 8 December 1980 on that stretch of sidewalk outside the famous Dakota Building, on West 72nd Street.

Mark Chapman looked normal, controlled and respectable. Inside he was a screaming mess of grief and pain. He saw himself as a child in a man's body: he was, he said, 25 on the outside, but on the inside, still adolescent.

Chapman the adult may have been benign, frightened and even appalled at the crime he was about to commit but the adult was not in control. It was the child within him, shouting for release, who demanded he carry it through.

The killing of Lennon was the moment when celebrity stalking first rose to public prominence. It was the murder of the decade, some would have it the murder of the century. And yet it is an unusual stalking case. The pursuit was brief (though planned – and with some determination), the victim was not aware of his stalker and the obsession was not concerned with supposed love, but with vengeance for crimes against idealism. According to Chapman, Lennon had betrayed the message of his early career and become one of the 'phony' bureaucrats whose world he'd told his followers to reject.

Had they met at some other point in their lives, it is more than possible John Lennon would have liked Mark Chapman: most people who knew Mark liked him. It wasn't difficult, as he went out of his way to be liked. He was hard-working, intelligent, thoughtful and perceptive. He had a sincerity which, though relentless, uncompromising and often fanatical, was also self-critical and considered.

His ability to be liked was tied in with his ability to be all things to all men. He would change himself to best please the person he was with at any one time. He attacked each and every new experience as though he totally believed it would lead to his salvation and give his life the thing he felt it lacked – some true meaning. He was twenty-five years old when he became the world's most famous deranged stalker – the most hated man of his generation. By that time Mark Chapman had undergone several drastic character changes.

Friends and relatives had been alarmed when he metamorphosed from the typical high-school geek into a scary, drug-crazed hippy. They were then relieved when scary Mark changed again, this time into a fervent, evangelical Born-Again Christian. He went on through various fads from being 'artist' to 'married man', ending with the label which would stick to him for life: 'murderer'. There was no logical progression from one to the next of these roles. They were all first snatched at, then enthusiastically embraced to the exclusion of everything else and, finally, bitterly discarded.

Chapman often achieved success in what he did. Children loved him for his ability to be one of them, adults praised his industry and his dedication. He won awards as a leader at summer-camp; many people who knew him said he would go far – he was going to be a somebody.

He had grown up in an unhappy household where his mother often looked to him for protection against her husband in a marriage which was full of discord. He had, from a very early age, escaped into a fantasy world in which his room became populated by a whole race of 'Little People'. Chapman was their ruler and their god. He would use these creatures of his imagination as badly as any tyrant. When he was angry, he would blow them up by the thousand, imagining their screams of terror as the buildings he had given them fell and crushed his terrified, tiny victims.

Despite this maltreatment, his 'subjects' were always forgiving. His miniature subjects always bowed to the will of their omnipotent creator. Unlike the real people who surrounded him, they knew Chapman well enough to understand his motivations and they never complained. They would treat him with a deal of respect and a huge amount of fear. They would advise him (though he wouldn't always listen); they would praise him. They were his entertainment, his escape and the tenuous rope by which he anchored his sanity.

He would sing to them too, in his mind amplifying the childish noises with which he accompanied his Beatles albums, changing them into a powerful, thunderous broadcast which would delight his adoring subjects. Young Mark would sit, hugging himself and rocking his body to the music. Sometimes he made himself believe he was so powerful he could command armies to fight and obliterate the frightening sounds of his parents' unhappiness.

Sometimes he believed he could stand by his Mom and be the protector she wanted him to be. He was better than anybody else, even if he felt bad inside. He really understood things – things everybody else was too stupid to see.

Even as a child, Mark Chapman saw the real world through cynical and knowing eyes.

There were other famous residents of the Dakota building, but Lennon was easily the most popular. He knew he lived with the constant possibility of danger. He'd kept away from the music scene for some years but, whilst being a recluse professionally, he scorned safety precautions and led an open, approachable life in New York. Anybody could find out where he lived and could, with patience and some perseverance, easily get to meet him, if only for a few seconds. Since the days of the Beatles he had achieved a mythical status in the eyes of millions of devoted fans. He was fully aware there were people who might want him dead. He had voiced his fear of assassination but done little to protect himself from it.

Hours before he was killed, John Lennon had signed a copy of his new *Double Fantasy* album for Chapman who had acted very much like any other awestruck, worshipping fan. Lennon had left, unharmed, to go to his recording studio. Chapman, having at last met his former hero and with a signature to prove it, could have turned back at that moment. He'd come nearly this close before and had left without any harm being done.

Chapman's major problem in life was his lack of identity. He borrowed the personas which he thought might help him 'be somebody' and donned them like so many costumes. He approached each new part he played with the consummate skill of a dedicated actor. He had often shown promise and talent in the various enterprises he'd embarked upon. He was a hard worker and had various and useful skills but, ultimately, no matter where he sought it, he found no real satisfaction. Inside himself there was nothing at all. With his sanity about to collapse around him, his inner voices told him he must play one last, great tragic role. He would become the man who assassinated the greatest phony of them all.

Whether his decision to murder Lennon was born of his own free will is a vexed point. He was in control only in as much as he opened up that dark part of himself which he knew would lead inexorably to disaster. Once the possibility was unleashed, the act had to follow. He was, in some ways, a stalker in search of a victim. The woman who could have been thought to be in most danger from him – his wife – always gave him her love and unconditional support. He needed somebody he could believe had betrayed him.

* * *

The world in which Chapman grew up was equally full of both hope and trouble. The sixties saw the sexual revolution begin; people demanding their rights were at last being listened to. At the same time, there were increasing fears about the bomb and America was embroiled in the messy, protracted war in Vietnam. Americans, who had always liked things cut and dried, found they could no longer contain the anger of their young people. The sixties had begun in the spirit of optimism with the 'Camelot court' of John F. Kennedy. Within three short years he had been slain by an assassin's bullet. Three months after JFK's death, in February 1964, the Beatles, already big stars in Britain, flew into New York to take America by storm and give the younger generation its new musical heroes.

Mark David Chapman may have been young in years but the weight of trouble and hurt he carried had given him the mind of a weary man over twice his age. He was an isolated, lonely child, disturbed and unsettled by his parents' volatile marriage and unable to make friends at school because of his appalling self-consciousness. He retreated into his world of make-believe midgets where the music of the Beatles provided a backdrop for his daydreams and he, as a cross between God and Gulliver, could exercise complete control. In his imagination he could be what he could never hope to be in real life: a somebody.

His father, David Chapman, always seemed distant to him but his mother, Diane, was a dominant force in young Mark's life. Her son was a source of comfort to her. With her desperate love she unwittingly forced him into being a pawn between herself and her husband. She called upon Mark to protect her when there were fights. He often did, sometimes interposing his body between his parents.

His mother would get into his bed at nights; she would assure him she had only married his father so he could be born. Perhaps more significantly, she told him over and over that he was destined to become a great and important person. As his emotional self took shape, Chapman became confused between the super-hero his mother evidently thought he was, and the frightened, unsure child he felt inside. This was only one of many influences which split his personality, later manifesting itself as that disturbed, malevolent child hiding under the surface of the sensible, sane adult.

Sensible and sane perhaps but, for Chapman, the adult part of himself was always going to be something of a fraud – he knew the child would win in the end.

Chapman, the high-school nerd, discovered the liberating power of psychedelic drugs at the age of fourteen. The Beatles could be said to bear some of the responsibility for this change in him. No longer the lovable 'mop-heads', clean and wholesome (the image their late manager, Brian Epstein, had carefully nurtured), they were now emulating, if not leading, the zeitgeist of the late sixties: hippy freedom and a rejection of old values.

'At that time, the Beatles were no longer the same Beatles whose music I had rocked back and forth to on the couch in the den. They were no longer the Beatles whose music I had played for my Little People,' Chapman said. 'The Beatles by then were into long hair, beards, meditation, and drugs. The Beatles were into things that fit my life perfectly.'[1]

Like many of his contemporaries, who saw in the hippy movement a ready-made identity, Chapman embraced everything this world had to offer. Perhaps his need was greater than most but he was, to a large extent, no different from other drop-outs of his generation. This was not, however, some troubled youth venting his anger at the system, as was the case with other boys of his age. It was rather somebody without any sense of himself, desperately trying to adopt a personality which would make him feel part of life. When he said, as he was often quoted as saying, 'I wanted to be a somebody', it wasn't simply fame Chapman was after. It was anything that would fill the gap where his personality should have been.

As a hippy, Chapman felt he was involved with other people for the first time in his life. Forsaking his old respectable, dull, character, he grew his hair, didn't wash, donned dirty jeans and emerged as a problem teenager.

He was willing to try almost anything: glue-sniffing, marijuana, LSD. Soon the signs of his drug dependency were showing. He would laugh hysterically at nothing and stare into space for long periods. He substituted his 'Little People' for imaginary computers which would monitor his need for food, liquid or sleep.

It was substance abuse which first made Chapman aware of a boiling fury inside of him: a fury which had previously lain dormant. In *Let Me Take You Down*, Jack Jones's detailed and incisive account of Chapman's life and the Lennon murder, Chapman recalls:

'I was never one to sleep while doing acid. So I remember I was standing up in the room and everybody else was lying out, passed out on the bed. And I remember there was a knife. There was a knife in the room. Something in me, while I was tripping – I recognise it now to be a spiritual force but I didn't know it at the time – was trying to urge me to pick up this knife and stab it into these guys, into my friends. And I, of course, I had freedom of choice and I didn't do it. But it was a compelling urge to pick up this knife and kill these people. This is how these things happen when people are bombed out on drugs. They open themselves up to the bad elements of a spiritual nature and can be influenced to a point of doing some very damaging, disastrous things. Thank God I avoided doing that. But I remember getting this urge.'[2]

The void inside Chapman was being filled by powerful, negative forces. He grasped onto them and enthusiastically went where they took him. He ran away from home. He lived rough and joined in with some drop-outs on the beach in Miami. They left him when his money ran out and after a policeman asked for his ID. He then found some fairground folk who were willing to give him food in return for some light work. In this he was living out the story of one of his childhood heroes, Toby Tyler, a character in a film who runs away to join a circus.

Eventually, Chapman was lucky enough to wind up in the house of a responsible adult who suggested he should return home. He did – to a distraught mother and an angry father. He was about to enter a new phase in his life. Mark David Chapman was about to find God.

* * *

This was no clean-cut conversion. It began when he was persuaded by a classmate to go to a retreat run by the Presbyterians. It wasn't the religion which attracted him, but the fact that evangelical Christianity attracted a disproportionate number of females. Chapman was, if a little scared, nevertheless hopeful of romance.

He met a girl he'd known before when they were both children. In fact they'd stood side by side in a school photograph, one which Chapman hated because the elastic band of his underpants was showing in it – he had been acutely embarrassed at the time.

Jessica Blankenship was to prove to be a good friend to him, but she was not the most important introduction to result from his visit to that retreat. It was here he was asked to join a Christian rock group a member of which, Michael McFarland, later recommended he read a book. It was a book which eventually would burrow into his brain so deeply Chapman would think it spoke directly to him; a book which he thought guided him and eventually urged him to murder. It was JD Salinger's novel about teenage angst: *The Catcher in the Rye*.

It's a gentle, knowing story which describes the thoughts and frustrations of Holden Caulfield, a sixteen-year-old New York boy. Caulfield, having been expelled from school, wanders round the city, staying in hotels and attempting to bridge the gap between adolescence and childhood. He smokes continually, drinks, and attempts to have sex with a prostitute. He sees through the façade of those older people who attempt to give him advice and scorns the clumsy attempts of his classmates to wrestle with their burgeoning adulthood. He describes them all with a word which Chapman adopted as his all-encompassing pejorative: they were 'phonies'. Caulfield is himself a phony and, using a first-person narrative, Salinger gives a sympathetic portrayal of his character and of teenagers in general.

But Holden Caulfield didn't take over Chapman's personality just yet – that would come later. He read and enjoyed *The Catcher in the Rye* but, at this stage, the great change was brought about by Jesus.

Again, he was not unusual in this. Christianity, particularly evangelical Christianity, provides a ready-made family of warm, supportive and loving people who will welcome even the most inadequate stranger into their midst. Chapman with his history of drugs and sin was a perfect candidate, even more so because he was utterly suggestible. It was probably a mark of this suggestibility that he was able to lapse back into his hippy persona as soon as he returned to school and the influence of his reprobate friends. There was a short time when the two 'Chapmans' ran side by side. He even managed to persuade his fellow young Christians to try LSD. The result was the total disruption of a convention when one youth stripped naked and ran into a lake, shouting happy nonsense as he did so.

In the end Chapman turned completely to Christ. He renounced his long hair and scruffy clothes in favour of a severe, respectable image. He launched into his new faith with all the fervour of a true convert. His zeal was, in fact, everything you might expect from the clichéd image of a born-again Christian.

Chapman's reformed character, though it might have irritated some, at least must have seemed preferable to the nihilistic lout it had replaced. As with many other things he turned his hand to, Chapman's dedication won him friends. He even managed to recruit new converts.

His new faith also demanded a total rejection of his previous role models.

In an interview in the *Evening Standard* in 1966, John Lennon had said 'We're more popular than Jesus now; I don't know which will go first – rock 'n' roll or Christianity.' In the song 'Imagine' he invited the listener to 'Imagine there's no heaven'. Chapman the hippy might have gone along with all this but Chapman the Christian could not countenance such provocative statements and radical thoughts. He denounced Lennon as a communist and a blasphemer. His antipathy towards the pop star far exceeded normal dislike of an opposite point of view. At his prayer meetings he would paraphrase 'Imagine', singing, 'Imagine John Lennon is dead'.

It seems reasonably certain this was no more than hot air. Lennon was a star – and stars, even ones whom you find obnoxious – are untouchable and unapproachable. Chapman had not yet seriously considered Lennon in any tangible way. Besides which, Chapman, 'a man who wasn't there' as the nonsense rhyme puts it, now thought he knew who he was, he felt himself to be safe. With Jesus as his purpose in life, friends around him and even the emerging possibility of romance, he had the illusion of security. Desperate strategies were not needed.

It didn't last, of course. There was nothing genuine inside him to support it. His religious fervour was indulged by his Christian friends only as long as he was the new boy. When he found he was no longer the one who was asked to play his songs to the group and he was bypassed at meetings, Chapman began to lose interest in the whole thing. His religious passion dwindled and he looked around him to find a new person to be.

He became besotted with the works of Lennon's sometime rival, Todd Rundgren.

'Right between the chambers of your heart is how Rundgren's music is to me. I cannot overestimate the depth of what his music meant to me. I never really got into the fan-club thing. I never thought about meeting Rundgren, being Rundgren, or getting Rundgren's autograph. I went to his concerts, I bought his albums. I did it the real way, the pure way. I was into the music and I can't tell you the depth of what his music meant to me.

'To say that it defined my life sounds so shallow. It was the soundtrack to my life. More than that, it *became* my life. Those notes and those harmonies. I can't describe what it meant, it was so poignant.'[3]

Chapman at last stood some chance of mental stability. He had a balance between his now dampened spiritual ideals and his enthusiasm for a new hero. He also discovered a new enthusiasm: demonstrating a rare talent for taking care of children. He applied for a job with the South De Kalb County YMCA. He was accepted and received glowing reports from his supervisor who said he was entirely persuaded Chapman was destined for a wonderful career.

Chapman worked far harder than he need have done and was immensely popular with his young charges, who saw him as one of themselves. In fact he *was* one of them: still unable to relate properly to the adult world with its challenges and responsibilities, Chapman thrived with children who looked up to him and admired him. He adopted the name Captain Nemo after Jules Verne's character who journeyed *Twenty Thousand Leagues Under the Sea*.

Chapman found true happiness for that short period. Had he been more grounded in himself and had more confidence, he might have gone on to fulfil his supervisor's high expectations.

In this period, at the end of 1972, Chapman teamed up with his old friend from the Christian group (also a YMCA worker and one also singled out for high praise). Together they attempted to form a comedy duo 'McFarland and Chapman', satirising various public figures and politicians and gaining some success on the circuit of local churches.

After a brief visit back home to Georgia where he was unsuccessful in resurrecting an old love-affair, Chapman returned to the YMCA where he became a jack-of-all-trades: mending, gardening and administrating. He continued this promising course for a number of years. The YMCA rewarded his efforts by picking him out to go on a special overseas assignment. Along with some colleagues, he would spend that summer in Beirut.

The young team arrived to find themselves in the centre of a war zone. Their stay was cut short and they returned to America. For Chapman, it had been a disturbing experience and had left him with memories (and tape-recordings) of bombs and gunshots. The adult world was growing more and more scary but Chapman recognised his experience as important and on a bigger scale than his own, dull life.

He still had his latest identity to cling to and, as the successful YMCA worker, he was loved and admired by everyone he came into contact with. With this knowledge to protect his fragile ego, Chapman was sent to look after Vietnamese boat people at Fort Chaffee in Arkansas. Again he threw himself into his new role, emotionally and physically – and again he triumphed. The experience touched him very deeply. He really felt the pain of those in his care and his genuine humanity spurred him on to work harder and harder.

He was a great success with his bosses. He often worked double the hours of a normal working day. It was unsustainable: Chapman was finding the emotional strain of dealing with such desperate people far too much for him.

He sent his friend McManus (of the aborted comedy duo) a tape. In it, he spoke of his continued passion for Todd Rundgren's music and of the bitter suffering he saw in the faces of the refugees. He gave the tape a title: *A Portrait of a Crazy Man*.

It was during this period that Chapman lost his virginity.

For some time he had quite innocently shared a room with a woman friend. When the pair tried to find accommodation together outside the camp they were refused on the assumption that their relationship was more physical than in fact it was. Ironically, this refusal led them to end up sharing a bed. Despite his grave inhibitions, Chapman eventually gave in to carnal desire.

He was consumed by guilt. He had already promised himself to Jessica Blankenship, the young girl from the school photograph whom he had met at his first Christian retreat. She was his official fiancée, and yet he'd not been strong enough to save this most intimate of experiences for her. She was shortly to be visiting him at Fort Chaffee.

Chapman's previous sexual experiences had been adolescent masturbatory fantasies in which Doris Day had been the main focus of his erotic attention. His mother, seemingly unaware of much beyond her own distaste, would shout through the door of his room that she 'knew what he was doing in there' and later would present him with the evidence of his stained underpants. The innocent experiments thus became a source of shame for him. In adulthood, his sexual life was to remain stunted: he never felt comfortable in the act of intercourse, even with the woman he later married.

Still full of his guilty secret, he indulged Jessica during her visit and attempted to push his 'crime' into the back of his mind. The couple talked about their engagement plans and all seemed to be well. When camp finished, Chapman enrolled as a student at the college Jessica attended. His having cheated on her was something Jessica would never know, but it continued to attack his conscience.

Chapman realised he had now joined the world of adults, the world where people indulge in sex and deceit, the world where everything and everyone is 'phony'.

His confidence began to fall away from him. He embraced negativity and allowed it to swamp him. His very real achievements receded into the past, mocking him for what might have been and seeming to reproach him for not having the guts to follow them through to success and happiness. He was a nobody and he was tired of fighting fate. He would wipe out this nothing life of his: nobody would even notice he'd gone.

Chapman decided he would have one last look at the world before he left it. In 1976, the depressed twenty-two year old set out for Hawaii, planning to make it his very last adventure.

The charms of the islands washed over his depression although at first he kept his original intention in mind: he would still kill himself, but in a week or so. For a short time he allowed himself to have fun.

Giving in to reckless extravagance, a trait which was later to land him in serious financial difficulties, he booked into the most prestigious and expensive hotel he could find, the Moana. The luxurious surroundings lent him the character of the wealthy tourist – an image he could borrow only until his meagre resources were drained. When his finances forced him to move into the less palatial surroundings of the YMCA, his depression once again came knocking at his door.

He had enough spirit left to ring Jessica. She had realised she wasn't in love with Chapman and the couple had agreed to part. Now Chapman told her he wanted her back. He confessed to her his original reasons for going to Hawaii and allowed her to persuade him to come home. She let him think there was still a chance for the two of them (faced with a man on the verge of suicide, there was little else she could do). Her white lie worked: at least in so far as it got Chapman back to Georgia.

He was, he said, 'crushed' to find there was no real chance of reviving his relationship with Jessica but he pulled himself together and once again tried to settle down to life with his family. It was impossible; there were frequent rows and Chapman soon moved out again. By the spring of 1977, he had decided to return to Hawaii, but this time, he would not go there to kill himself, he would go there to escape. He planned to find a job at the Moana or some similar wonderful place and live out his days in Paradise. He was sure all his insecurities and fears would be left behind in Georgia. That original week of fun, when he'd imagined himself into a world of wealth and sunshine, would now be the blueprint for the rest of his life.

It was a juvenile notion, one which any cynical adult could have told him was bound to end in disaster, but Chapman was a spontaneous creature. Perhaps with some justification, he believed in following instinct. His naive sense of adventure left him in no doubt. Also he feared he would never be able to reconcile his troubled ego with the confusing, disappointing realities of existence. He would escape to where life was not real.

He spent the last of his savings on a one-way ticket.

Unfortunately, he could not leave his misery behind. Depression followed him into Paradise and refused to go away.

Broke and humiliated, he could no longer pretend to be the wealthy tourist. He found a low-paid, unpleasant job in the kitchens of a food factory. When he was not too dispirited to turn up for work he was able to afford a room at the YMCA, but – and it happened often – he was just as likely to find himself sleeping rough. Like a beggar at the rich man's gate, he hung around outside the Moana Hotel.

The stifling experience of being inside himself was intolerable. He was still sure he could never match up to whatever it was that life expected from him. He hated the world because it was cruel and unjust; he hated himself because he was not strong enough to cope with life. He was drinking heavily. Death became attractive to him. He talked for hours to a suicide help-line. It was one of many – Hawaii was used to Mark Chapmans.

He hired a car. After having eaten his 'last' meal (the food was included in the hire-price of the vehicle), he drove to a quiet beach where he proceeded to run a hose from the exhaust in through the windows. Feeling peaceful at last, he lay back. Closing his eyes, he waited for oblivion.

He didn't find it.

He was awoken by a fisherman who wanted to know if he was all right. The hose had melted away at the point where it connected to the exhaust. A fluke had saved Chapman. To him, this was no mere accident of fortune.

He had been saved for a reason. He didn't know what it was yet, but he resolved to find out. He said a prayer, thanking God for his deliverance and promising always to listen to Him in the future. From here on, Chapman's life was in the hands of something bigger than himself, something which would not let him down. There would, he knew, be signs to show him the path his life must take: signs that had always been there if only he'd had the sense to acknowledge them. He promised he would do so from now on.

The next morning he went to a Mental Health Centre (he'd visited it before and been prescribed medication which he'd thrown away). The psychologist who saw him immediately recognised the symptoms of severe depression and set about finding a hospital willing to admit him.

At the Castle Memorial Hospital, Chapman allowed himself to collapse for the next three days. He continued to be regarded as a high suicide risk and was watched at all times. He told his carers: 'I think of myself as a boxer in the twenty-seventh round with my face all bloody, my teeth knocked out and my body all bruised.' One of the psychiatrists who saw him is reported as having said 'I wouldn't bet a nickel on this guy.'[4]

In fact Chapman made a remarkable recovery. Soon he was chatting amiably to other patients and even singing songs to them and to staff members. Throughout his stay, he was cooperative and articulate. He appeared to have a good appreciation of what had brought him to the hospital and his problems had apparently vanished, along with his depression. On 5 July 1977, two weeks after being admitted to hospital, he was discharged.

Chapman was now transformed back into the enthusiastic mode which had given him his 'Captain Nemo' success. Latching on to the Castle as a kind of home base, he applied for a job there. The suicidal ex-patient became a popular and hard-working maintenance man.

He also found a new female in his life. It wasn't exactly the sort of affair he had planned for himself, it wasn't even a romance in the true sense of the word, but it was a close and important friendship. She was Judy Harvey, almost twice his age and a nurse at the Castle.

Harvey considered her relationship to this intense and sincere young man as being no more than that of a close friend. Though Chapman often became jealous and upset, he also could be good fun, caring, thoughtful and genuine. Through Harvey, he found himself joining in with the other members of staff, socialising and helping out with the patients.

Tragically, his chance of belonging was soon to be disrupted yet again, this time by a well-meaning but moralistic Presbyterian minister, the Reverend Peter Anderson. Chapman was a prime target for evangelicals: he was, in every way, the lost sheep, ready to be led back to the fold. He was also suggestible, confused and had a strongly developed sense of sexual guilt which could be easily manipulated.

The minister suggested Chapman should detach himself from Harvey. It was inappropriate to be fond of an older woman and it would be better to cool the relationship. Anderson then invited the repentant sinner to come and live with him and his wife.

He was doubtless very sincere, but this sort of influence exacerbated an already acute problem. Chapman had quite enough repression buried in his soul and high ideals flying around his mind. The brand of Christianity which exaggerates and encourages these was something he could have well done without.

On the surface he felt good. He was a valued member of staff at the hospital, he was living with friends and he had his faith back. In a rush of happy confidence, he announced plans to travel again. He wanted to visit the Far East, but later changed his mind and opted for a round-the-world tour. He booked through a local travel agent where he was served by a Japanese-American woman called Gloria Abe.

It wasn't love at first sight by any means. Chapman was naturally friendly and no doubt found Gloria attractive but he didn't feel any major stirrings of romance. Still, he was solicitous of his new friend, sending her notes to thank her for the services she performed on his behalf. He gave her various presents: flowers and soft toys; he flirted with her. It was pleasant and comfortable, but it wasn't the intense, burning feeling Chapman had expected. He liked her and he fancied her. She felt much the same about him – maybe a bit more.

In July, 1978, as he was about to embark on his new adventure, Chapman was surprised and pleased to find Gloria at the airport to see him off. They had grown close enough that she was able to give him a meaningful goodbye kiss. She told him how much she wished she could accompany him. In return for this display of feeling, Chapman promised to write to her every day.

His holiday was a mixed experience. His depressions were with him much of the time. He found some of the places he visited (India particularly) to be distressing because of the poverty and unhappiness he witnessed there.

In Tokyo he met a YMCA official who praised Chapman's earlier work with the Vietnamese boat-people. Chapman was disturbed to find himself suffering from compassion fatigue: the refugees had touched his heart deeply when he had worked among them, now he could raise no enthusiasm at all. Their suffering was something outside him, he could no longer relate to it. He was shocked and appalled by his own attitude.

In Bangkok he slept with a drunken prostitute. She approached him and, though he had little interest in having sex with her, he did it because it was an experience. He later commented 'It was something Holden Caulfield would do.'[5]

After visiting England (though he didn't go to the Beatles' home town of Liverpool), and a brief visit back home to his native Georgia, Chapman returned to Hawaii.

Gloria was waiting for him at the airport.

Chapman didn't hide his dark side from his new girlfriend. She seemed to be patient and supplied him with a willing ear as he discussed his hopes and fears. She even embraced Chapman's Christianity, putting aside her own spiritual beliefs (for instance such 'wicked' ideas as reincarnation).

She found his troubled soul attractive: it proved him to be sensitive and thoughtful. The couple were soon talking of marriage. At first they planned to save for a year or so but, on the advice of the Reverend Peter Anderson, they elected to tie the knot straight away.

Their marriage, founded on Gloria Chapman's genuine love for her husband and his increasing need of her, was put to the test immediately. Chapman's parents divorced and his mother, Diane, announced she was going to come and live near her son in Hawaii.

Chapman didn't like the idea at all. This was his special place where he had at last managed to find some semblance of being himself, independent of the cloying influences of his childhood. His mother's presence was intrusive and restrictive. He put up with it and, with far greater sacrifice, Gloria was forced to put up with it too.

At first, Diane's constant presence annoyed Gloria. She and Mark rarely seemed to have any time alone together and Gloria sensed her husband was torn between the two women in his life. After some time, things settled down and Gloria managed to put her own feelings into the background. This was something she was going to have to do very often throughout her marriage. She sensed Mark would not be strong enough to cope with any contradiction or argument, consequently she adopted the role which was required of her: that of the meek and submissive wife who allowed her husband to have his own way in all things.

Chapman was now seeing his identity in terms of being the 'married man'. He worried greatly that he wasn't able to live up to his own idea of what that should be. For instance, he needed to be more successful. Consequently, he abandoned his job as a maintenance man in favour of a more prestigious position at the Castle as the hospital's Public Relations Representative.

He'd made a mistake and he knew it almost immediately. Public Relations proved to be too much for him, especially now his emotional equilibrium was beginning to fall apart again. Outside work he was running up credit card bills.

In an effort to prove his standing in the world, Chapman announced to Gloria they were going to move to a better apartment. They ended up in an extremely expensive block where they took up residence on the twenty-first floor.

He had his status, but Chapman was still falling apart. He was overeating, he was moody and often disagreeable. His demands on Gloria were unreasonable but she always went along with them, even when they went to absolute lengths. Once, when he called for her after work he had to wait in the car while she finished a job she had to do. He lost his temper, stormed into the agency and yelled at Gloria's boss. It happened again and, furious that he'd been kept waiting a second time, he ordered her to hand in her notice. She obeyed.

His moods were a problem at his own place of work. When they became too much to ignore, he was asked to resign. Embracing the failure he thought he deserved, Chapman took another menial job working nights as a security guard. He'd let himself go, physically and mentally, and he was drinking again.

He had his fads. Typical of his usual behaviour patterns, he threw himself into each one before discarding it absolutely. For instance, he invested borrowed money in various works of art and painted some accomplished pieces himself. They were never good enough for him so he would carry on painting far beyond the point where the picture could be considered finished. Most of them ended up as a mess of black paint. Gloria said: 'It was like nothing he did was ever good enough until he destroyed it.'[6]

*   *   *

It was 1980.

The year, which was to end in tragedy, began with Chapman extremely depressed. He was talking to his imaginary Little People again. He was now seeing them as more mature than the creatures of his childhood. He had changed the strange autocracy he'd once ruled into a semblance of democratic government of which he was the head. He was relying on the good council of his self-created advisors to get him out of debt – a major preoccupation with him.

With perseverance and the help of his unseen ministers, he actually managed it. However, like so many of his achievements, it wasn't enough to turn his troubled mind to more positive thoughts. He found he wasn't able to work any more, so he became a househusband – like John Lennon. (There was another parallel, whether contrived or not, between Chapman and Lennon: Lennon's wife, Yoko Ono, was, like Gloria, a woman of Asian origin who was slightly older than her husband.)

Then, Chapman found the book which brought Lennon to number one on his hate list: *John Lennon: One Day at a Time*.

'I remember thinking that there was a successful man who had the world on a chain. And there I was not even a link of that chain. Just a person who had no personality. A walking void who had given a great deal of my time and thoughts and energy into what John Lennon had said and had sung about and had done – and had told all of us to do – in the sixties and early seventies, when I was growing up, when I was first trying to make sense out of a world that was so painful and hurtful and sad. I thought I love reality and I didn't want the world to be the way it was.

'I was thinking all these things, reliving my childhood, as I devoured page after page of that John Lennon book. And at that moment, something inside me just broke.'[7]

He was close to cracking up entirely. Fuelled by early-morning drinking, he was too paranoid to hold a decent conversation and, knowing this, was avoiding people entirely. He spent his days wandering around public places: libraries, court houses, parks. He knew he needed help but he was too far away from reality to ask for it. His moods leapt manically from wild enthusiasm to total despair.

He re-read *The Catcher in the Rye*. The book had stayed in his memory since he first read it years earlier, but only inasmuch as he had enjoyed the story. This time he found it profound and deeply meaningful. Chapman felt its hero, Holden Caulfield, was speaking directly to him and to him alone. He *was* Caulfield.

Chapman's tortured mind began to make connections between the various events and disappointments which had brought him to where he was. He described his emotions as being like a cyclone – perhaps an allusion to another fictional influence on his life, the MGM film version of *The Wizard of Oz*. Perhaps consciously, he allowed himself to be sucked into a spiral of chaos from which he knew he would not be able to rescue himself.

The idea of murder appeared in the middle of this storm, it came to him as though it were a means of shelter. It would be the ultimate, cathartic thing which would at long last make sense of his life. Chapman came to believe that he had to assassinate John Lennon.

Once the idea was in his mind it was not going to go away.

In those next few weeks he was visited by demons. Stripped naked and deafened by the din from his record player, he ritualistically handed over his free-will to Satan. In exchange he asked only one thing: that he would be given the strength to kill John Lennon.

He told his wife he was going to New York and he was going alone. She didn't question him but she was worried. His mother, too, sensed there was something not quite right. She asked Chapman straight out if he was going to do 'something funny' in New York. He assured her that he was not.

Just before leaving, Chapman gave Gloria a copy of *The Catcher in the Rye* and advised her to read it. It would, he said, help her to understand him better.

In September 1980, Chapman started out on his momentous journey. He'd bought a gun: a .38 calibre snub-nosed revolver. He'd managed to obtain a permit for it (he'd lied – the form asked if the applicant had a history of mental illness and Chapman had said 'no'), but he'd not bought any ammunition. He planned to get the bullets in New York, thinking this was less risky than smuggling a loaded firearm into the state.

Like his suicide trip to Miami, this was an important visit and it deserved his extravagant best. He registered at the Waldorf Hotel. On his first evening he wandered towards Central Park.

Echoes of *The Catcher in the Rye* came back to him, for Holden Caulfield describes the very same area and at the same time of year. Chapman let his mind drift pleasantly into Caulfield's character. It was Chapman's first time in the city but he had Salinger's creation as his guide.

In those first few days, Chapman behaved very much like any other tourist. He visited the sights, he went to see Broadway shows. He befriended several women whom he wined and dined and tried to impress.

Like a child who can't keep a secret, he hinted to one of them something important was about to happen. 'You're going to hear about me,' he said.[8]

He became a regular visitor to the Dakota Building where the Lennons lived. It is a large, stately edifice overlooking Central Park. Chapman made a point of getting friendly with the men who guarded the doors. He was careful to come across as sane and decent and was disappointed when he couldn't get an answer to his questions regarding John Lennon. The doormen always claimed they couldn't say whether the pop star was at home or even if he was in the city. It was obviously a stock answer and one they gave to anyone who asked.

Chapman's first attempt to get ammunition for his gun failed. He was flatly refused – it was against the law to sell him the bullets unless he was 'licensed and bonded'. He rang a friend of his in Georgia and announced an impromptu visit to his home state.

Dana Reeves, a deputy sheriff, wasn't to know the real reason for his friend's visit. Even when Chapman suggested a bit of shooting practise, he didn't think there was anything suspicious about it. Chapman's explanation seemed reasonable enough; he told Reeves he had to return to New York and he was worried about his personal safety. Reeves supplied him with what he wanted: five hollow-point cartridges. Chapman had chosen the type specially – they were the sort which would do most damage to human tissue and so bring about instant death. They would, he thought, be kinder.

He claimed it was Gloria's love which stopped him from going through with it. It might have been. Whatever happened inside Chapman's mind, it led him to ring up his horrified wife and tell her why he'd come to New York. He'd intended to assassinate John Lennon, he said, but had been saved by the thought of her. He was coming home.

This was a crucial decision. Chapman knew himself well enough to see where his points of no return were, and to realise he was getting close to one. Still screaming for revenge, the vindictive child inside him was not listened to. The adult Chapman had won a victory, albeit a brief one.

It wasn't long before his torment began again. Like before, the message which drilled into his head was clear and ruthless: 'Kill John Lennon'.

'I made a decision to be crazy, or schizophrenic, a psychopath or a sociopath – whatever it is you have to be to do such things that I did. It's a choice anybody can make,'[9] Chapman said.

It is entirely debatable whether he was quite as in control of his destiny as he thought he was. On the face of it, he had every chance of leading a normal life. He had a faithful wife who was understanding, loved him and stood by him; he had friends who cared about him; he had many and varied talents; he had a home and, though there were financial problems, they were largely of his own making and he'd succeeded in freeing himself of them before. With all this, he remained crippled inside. The demon child continued to shout for attention.

He began to 'play' at being a stalker. He would ring the pay phone across the road from his apartment. When some unsuspecting passer-by answered it, he would terrify them by saying he knew where they lived and he was going to follow them home and kill them. For absolutely no reason, he took a dislike to one of the doctors at the Castle whom he would ring up and threaten. He used a device from a joke shop to give these calls a background of maniacal laughter.

Inevitably Chapman began thinking once again of his previous potential victim. Being a murderer, he thought, would be an identity of a sort. He was not frightened of prison: part of him welcomed the idea, even if it meant an eventual death penalty. The world around him was 'phony'; he didn't want it or need it.

Once again he set off for New York. This time he would not return.

There were always fans outside the Dakota Building. Some were regulars – like the two young women Chapman befriended on a freezing morning in early December 1980. Though he was churning inside, he managed to appear normal.

When he told them where he was from, the two strangers didn't question that he'd travelled so far in order to get Lennon's autograph – to them Lennon was worth such extensive efforts. Chapman was anxious to make an impression. He offered them lunch at a nearby grill. For most of the day the fans chatted to the man who was about to murder their idol. They suspected nothing.

The two women were regular devotees and had come to be on reasonably friendly terms with the star and his entourage. They boasted to Chapman and suggested he get a copy of the new Lennon album *Double Fantasy*. 'John' was really proud of it, they told him.

Chapman's stalking of Lennon was unusual as most of it had taken place only in his mind. His actual physical presence in Lennon's life amounted to the visits to the Dakota on his previous trip and his spasmodic vigil outside the building that weekend. Was he really a stalker? He was certainly obsessed, he went to extraordinary lengths to assuage his passion.

They met only briefly before the murder when Lennon signed Chapman's copy of *Double Fantasy*. He didn't pay much attention to the wide-mouthed young man; he was used to such people cluttering up the sidewalk outside his home.

Chapman could have shot Lennon in the act of signing the album, but he was overawed in the presence of the star. Part of him appreciated Lennon was a man – a human being who had done him no harm and was willing to be pleasant, if only for a few seconds.

Had he given up his quest there and then, he would have forever buried the idea of being 'a somebody'. In his own mind he would have always been the man who went to New York to murder John Lennon and then backed out of doing it. His life would amount to nothing more than a signature on an album and a memory of something he might have done. Lennon had to return home later that evening – Chapman waited.

'It was a little kid that did that act of killing John Lennon. A little kid on his Don Quixote horse went charging up to a windmill called the Dakota with an insane, irreparable, tragic mission: to put holes through one of the sails of that windmill of phoniness.

'That's what happened. It was a child that killed John Lennon. It wasn't a man. It was a child killing his hero: the Beatles. It was a child that had been so hurt and rejected into adulthood that he had to cover up all his feelings. I maintained, I preserved my childhood. Even though I'd had twenty-five birthdays, inside I was sixteen years old like Holden Caulfield was. My only feelings were the feelings that came through that book to the sixteen-year-old Holden that was inside me – until something real finally happened.

'John Lennon was real and he was a hero. He was the hero of my childhood. But I wasn't real to myself. I was just a hulk of hurt and rejection, a confused, unfeeling defence mechanism, a cyborg. A conglomerate of adult mannerisms and jobs, but with a child's heart. That was the conflict that came crashing down. That's why I could never do anything. My child was always conflicting with my fake adult, my phony adult that I had erected around it.

'All that rage came spilling out and I killed the hero of my childhood. All the rage at the world and in myself and in my disappointments and disillusions. All those feelings I kept pent up, feelings that the child couldn't handle. Feelings that the adult was supposed to handle but couldn't.'[10]

On 8 December 1980, Mark David Chapman took a gun from his pocket and fired five shots into the back of John Lennon. Later he said that, seconds before he fired, a voice came into his head telling him: 'Do it! Do it! Do it! Do it!'

As Lennon lay dying, Chapman took off his coat and hat to show there was no further weapon hidden inside. He then paced up and down the sidewalk trying to read from JD Salinger's *The Catcher in the Rye*.

He finally had an identity which would never leave him; he was the world's most famous assassin since the sixties. His lack of control over his own life had led him to this. He had destroyed in order to survive.

Chapman was sentenced to a minimum of twenty years and a maximum of life. Today, he is held in Attica prison in upstate New York. He works as a library clerk and remains segregated from the other inmates. He is said to be a model prisoner and is a Born-Again Christian. On 5 September 2000 it was announced that the 45-year-old Chapman was applying for parole. It has since been denied.

'I had to usurp someone else's importance, someone else's success,' Chapman said. 'I was Mr Nobody until I killed the biggest somebody on earth.'[11]

3. YOU MADE ME LOVE YOU

May 1955 (the month that Chapman was born) also saw the arrival of another child who was destined to become a notorious stalker. Chapman was born on the tenth, his 'rival' followed him just nineteen days later and was to make history four months after Chapman murdered Lennon.

John Hinckley Jnr. was the child of a wealthy and successful couple from Oklahoma, John Snr. and Jo-Ann. His father had made money in the oil business and the family were the image of 'apple-pie' Americans. Mr and Mrs Hinckley voted Republican, believed in Jesus and raised their three children to believe in the orthodox values they themselves espoused.

John grew up in Dallas, Texas, under the shadow of his two handsome and talented siblings, Diane and Scott. He attended the 'right' kind of school. It was a school where success was the rule of the day; a school from which happy, bright Americans emerged into the adult world of money and power.

His older brother and sister did all that was expected of them. They were a credit to their parents and were popular, get-ahead students. John wasn't so fortunate. As he grew up, he remained apart from the people around him. Like Chapman, he began to seek solace within himself.

It was a pattern which was set early on. It seems likely Hinckley suffered from a serious psychological disorder and his solitary nature was one early symptom of it. Unfortunately, the warning signs were not heeded. Mr and Mrs Hinckley were caring and supportive parents and could not possibly have known the extent of their son's problems. Morose and withdrawn teenagers are a worry, but their behaviour is often understandable and put down to short-term causes.

John's studies at Texas Technical College, which he attended for seven years, became marked by protracted absences. He started to take a keen interest in the Nazi party and other extreme right-wing politics. Asked to choose a subject for an essay, he wrote about Auschwitz and in another about Hitler's *Mein Kampf*. His work on these unsavoury themes impressed his tutors for its thoroughness. He was awarded extremely high marks for both pieces of writing, whereas his academic work was normally not up to standard.

It was a time of rebellion: the punk revolution was upon us and young people everywhere were doing their best to express themselves in ways their parents found objectionable. John Hinckley Jnr. was just another problem kid with another perplexed Mom and Dad.

Like Chapman, he sank himself into his music; like Chapman, he was a fan of John Lennon (he was said to have been distraught at the news of Lennon's murder), he was also interested in punk rock. However, Hinckley's personality was darker than the other young man's and more obviously so – and it wasn't a novel which eventually prompted his downfall – it was a film.

Director Martin Scorsese made his name with the dark and disturbing classic, *Taxi Driver*. It was the first time the public had taken notice of the talents of its star, Robert De Niro. As Travis Bickle, a Vietnam veteran and the driver of the title, he descends into an urban nightmare: a psychological hell which is unrelenting, gruesome and poetic.

The film also featured a landmark performance by a young actress who, at the time of making it, was still a child. Jodie Foster had already appeared in Scorsese's *Alice Doesn't Live Here Anymore* and was now breaking new ground as the child prostitute, Iris, who is stalked by De Niro's character. In the film, Bickle has become disillusioned with the 'scum' of society. He becomes obsessed, first with his love for a political campaign worker played by Cybill Shepherd, then with a desire to save Foster's wise-child from the filth of the city. Bickle embarks on a crazed mission which ends in an horrific bloodbath from which he emerges a hero. Iris is returned to her parents, who send Bickle grateful letters, thanking him for what he has done for their daughter.

Hinckley totally identified with Travis Bickle. He too was disillusioned, he needed Bickle's focus, he needed a mission. He also believed himself to be in love with the half child, half adult he'd seen on the screen. From then on, Jodie Foster was his passion.

Would Hinckley have felt the same way about Ms Foster if he'd first seen her in a more innocent guise? Certainly, the strength of Scorsese's vision of hellish city life and Foster's amazingly mature performance provided a firm basis for his obsession. Foster herself happened to be of equal character and maturity to the person she'd portrayed, but Hinckley couldn't have known that. Whether or not Ms Foster resembled Iris in any way, shape or form, it's doubtful whether reality would have ever been given the chance of interfering with Hinckley's emotions. He absolutely believed he had found the other half of himself, the perfect partner, the woman whom he was destined to be with. He watched the film many times over, allowing dangerous yearnings to take root and grow inside him.

Hinckley spent the next two years dwelling on himself, on Jodie and on the Nazis. In 1978 he dropped out of college and went to Chicago where he joined the extremist National Socialist Party of America. They found his brand of racist bile too much even for them. Hinckley was now modelling himself on the ruthless vigilante, Travis Bickle. His ideas were centred on violence and death; he saw murder as a legitimate answer to life's questions and, in the end, the party expelled him.

He later joined another extremist organisation in Los Angeles, *Posse Comitatis*, who were more to his taste. They used a noose for their logo and took it upon themselves to punish those who disagreed with their ideas. One of their members has recently been involved in alleged death threats against an American woman who was trying to ban smoking in public places.

Hinckley's parents were now seriously worried about their son and urged him to see a psychiatrist, who prescribed Valium. Meanwhile, he was building up an armoury of guns.

In 1980, Jodie Foster, now a seventeen-year-old veteran of the screen with thirteen films behind her, began working on *Carny*, for director Robert Kaylor. She was again playing a runaway, this time one who teams up with two disreputable men and joins a carnival.

She was at a crossroads in her young life. She was preparing to go to university (having been offered several major placements, she finally decided on Yale), and it was to be the first time she had been separated from the forceful, guiding presence of her mother. Outwardly confident and self-assured, she was, like any other young woman in that situation, nervous and excited. Besides this, she had to cope with the stresses of being a recognised star with a new film to complete and, about this time, she was beginning to get seriously concerned about a series of letters which she'd been receiving.

Hinckley had been writing to her with some regularity, professing his love and, more than once, threatening her if she didn't respond in the way he wanted. At first, she had been able to dismiss him with relative ease. Hinckley wasn't the only nut who wrote such offensive trash and her mother had taken the precaution of sending the letters to the FBI. The Bureau had predictably responded by saying there was nothing they could do unless Hinckley broke the law. They considered him to be harmless and said it would be best to let the matter rest.

But Hinckley meant business. He turned up on the set of *Carny*. Weird and wonderful circus people had been hired as extras – it was a strange enough environment. It now contained real danger amidst the sinister make-believe. Hinckley slept in the open and hung around hoping to get near his idol.

He was arrested more than once and each time released without charge. The security guards may have resorted to physical means to deter him from harassing the young star, but he wasn't to be put off easily.

The letters continued. In 1980 he sent over fifty of them. Some were pathetic, some were malicious, some were desperate.

Hinckley was arrested in Nashville, on a charge of carrying guns in his luggage. President Carter was in town and

Hinckley later admitted his intention of killing him. He had no other reason than that he hated the President and hated himself. Fortunately for Mr Carter, one of Jodie Foster's movies was on television that night and Hinckley decided he'd rather watch that than spend the evening murdering the President. He was allowed to go free after paying a small bond which he didn't honour. As far as the authorities were concerned, he was just another harmless lunatic with a gun.

He'd toyed with the idea of kidnapping somebody. Then, after reading about John Dillinger, he considered robbing a bank. He also thought about suicide but was too 'chicken' to do it.

Foster began her student life. She asked to be known as Alicia Foster (her real name) and had her room and phone number removed from the college directory. These precautions were not taken because of Hinckley; he was not a significant threatening presence at this stage. She wanted very much to be an ordinary student, concentrating on her work, free from the trappings of fame which she had grown up with and which had previously been the only life she had known.

Hinckley soon managed to track her down. With the resourcefulness which is customary in obsessive stalkers, he found both her telephone and room number and began calling her.

It must have given him a degree of satisfaction to be able to finally speak to her in person but he found her to be less than willing to supply all of his fantasy.

He recorded the conversations. In the first one, he introduces himself as 'the person that's been leaving notes in your mailbox for two days'. Presumably he expected her to be flattered and agree to a meeting. He thought all he needed to do was persuade her of his affection and she would be bound to return it. He had a dream of their living together in the White House like Ronald Reagan, the new President, and his wife, Nancy.

Dear Jodie,
Don't they make a darling couple? Nancy is downright sexy.
One day you and I will occupy the White House and the

peasants will drool with envy. Until then please do remain a virgin. You are a virgin aren't you?[1]

Reagan had been elected President in the November of that year. It is perhaps ironic that his rise from minor film stardom to political fame had involved a battle with the Governor of California, Edmund Brown, whom Reagan had defeated in 1966 and whose place as governor he had taken. Brown was later to be hired as a legal advisor on the film *Taxi Driver*. His job was to negotiate with the child welfare authorities for permission to use the underage Jodie Foster in the picture.

In another tape recording, Foster's girlfriends are heard in the background. She tells him 'They're laughing at you'. He takes this to heart. (He was later to refer to being a subject of ridicule with her – on that occasion he said he didn't care as long as he was in her thoughts.)

She says to her friends, 'Perhaps I should tell him I'm sitting here with a knife.'

'I'm not dangerous, I promise you,' he protests.

He asks her if he may call her again during the following evening. She tells him: 'That's fine.' He makes sure she will be in and she replies 'Maybe.' He then asks her if she will talk to him when he rings and she says, 'Oh sure.'[2]

In this, Jodie Foster was no different from other victims of stalking. Hinckley was instinctively banking on certain codes of behaviour. When you're unsure who you're dealing with, you rarely risk giving outright offence by saying exactly what is in your mind. If Jodie Foster had reacted with instant anger to every unsolicited approach made to her, she would have quickly gained a reputation for being difficult and 'starry'. Also, it has to be remembered that she had been advised to treat this passionate and ridiculous suit as trivial. To receive such a call in the company of college friends, and to have a good giggle at Hinckley's expense, was one way of putting the problem – and her own fame – into perspective.

Later in the taped conversation her temper snaps:

'Seriously, this isn't fair,' she tells him. 'Do me a favour and don't call back.'

'How about tomorrow?'

'Oh, God. Oh, seriously. This is really starting to bother me. Do you mind if I hang up?'

'Jodie, please!'[3]

Hinckley's misplaced adoration of Jodie Foster eventually brought him to his most desperate attempt to win her admiration. He described it as 'a historic act' which he intended would prove his love for her.

At the end of March, 1981, Hinckley waited outside the Washington Hilton Hotel where President Reagan had been speaking to an audience of trade unionists. Reagan was about to get back into the presidential car when Hinckley fired six shots. The President slumped to the ground as security men rushed to arrest the would-be assassin.

James Brady, Reagan's Press Secretary was crippled by one of the bullets and two other people, a police officer and a secret service man, were injured.

Jodie Foster received the news at university. She was horrified.

From that moment on, the name John Hinckley Jnr. became a continual blight on her professional life. For years after, references were made to the incident in nearly every interview with her. She refused to offer any comment herself and tried in vain to keep news reporters focussed on whichever film she was making at the time but, perversely, Hinckley had succeeded in permanently infiltrating himself into her life.

The following letter was found in his hotel room. It had been written only two days before he made the attempt on the President's life.

Dear Jody [sic]
There is a definite possibility that I will be killed in my attempt to get Reagan. It is for this very reason that I am writing to you this letter now.

As you well know by now I love you very much, the past seven months I have left you dozens of poems, letters and messages in the faint hope you would develop an interest in me.

Although we talked on the phone a couple of times, I never had the courage to simply approach you and introduce myself. Besides my shyness, I honestly did not wish to bother you with my constant presence. I know the many messages left at your door and in your mailbox were a nuisance, but I felt it was the most painless way for me to express my love for you.

I feel very good about the fact you at least know my name and how I feel about you. And by hanging around your dormitory, I've come to realise that I'm the topic of more than a little conversation, however full of ridicule it may be. At least you know that I'll always love you.

Jody, I would abandon this idea of getting Reagan in a second if I could only win your heart and live out the rest of my life with you, whether it be in total obscurity or whatever. I will admit to you that the reason I'm going ahead with this attempt now is because I just cannot wait any longer to impress you. I've got to do something now to make you understand in no uncertain terms that I am doing all of this for your sake.

Jody, I'm asking you to please look into your heart and at least give me the chance with this historical deed to gain your respect and love.

I love you forever.
John Hinckley[4]

Predictably enough, Hinckley's trial was a cause célèbre. The world had been denied the chance of its first big stalking trial when Mark Chapman had pleaded guilty to his crime (God had told him to plead this way, he said). In Hinckley's case the obvious defence was brought: that he was not responsible for his actions because of his state of mind. The greatest evidence in support of this was his unshakeable and abiding obsession with Foster.

It must have been a disappointment to him and an enormous relief to her that she was not required to appear in the courtroom. Instead, she gave her evidence on a video film. After long deliberation, the jury accepted the defence and Hinckley was sent to a secure hospital where he remains to this day.

* * *

In a bizarre and frightening twist to the story, Foster found herself the victim of another stalker. He was a man who saw Hinckley as a role model and was just as obsessive – and just as dangerous.

Foster was appearing in a play at Yale: *Getting Out* in which she was cast as an ex-prostitute. Towards the end of the run, a young man called Edward Michael Richardson appeared on the campus. His behaviour was almost a copy of his predecessor's. He wrote to Foster, he pushed notes under her door: he was determined to make contact. She had ignored many of his messages, thinking they were from Hinckley and no longer being inclined to subject herself to the stress they caused. The one she did eventually read terrified her. It plainly stated Richardson's intention to kill her.

Jodie Foster showed her tough, resilient side when she bravely elected to go on appearing in the play. She wasn't going to let these 'nuts' constrain her life and, despite the advice of her friends, she thought she would be safe enough on stage in front of an audience.

One night, however, her new stalker was a member of that audience and he had a gun. He settled down in the dark, planning to state his love for the actress before killing her and then shooting himself.

She was immensely lucky. Faced with a real, live Jodie Foster, Richardson was overwhelmed. She was too wonderful, too beautiful a young woman for him to kill. Unable to do what he had set out to do, he left for New York.

Later, the emotions which had prevented the murder faded in his memory. He became disgusted with himself for being so weak. He had to make some kind of gesture in order to associate himself with his film star, even if it was a hoax. He rang the university and told them a bomb had been planted which he would explode unless Hinckley was immediately released from custody. He then placed another call, this time to the White House, where he made threats against the President. The call was easily traced and Richardson was arrested. He was sent to prison but was freed only a year later.

In May 2000, at the St Elizabeth's Hospital, nineteen years after his attempt on Reagan's life, the 44-year-old Hinckley, who had been allowed to make escorted trips into Washington, applied to be allowed to go out without his guards. Permission was refused when it was discovered he had racist material in his room. He had also smuggled in a book about Jodie Foster: he is still obsessed with her.

A hospital spokesman was quoted as saying: 'He has blown it now. He is forbidden from having any kind of material connected with Jodie Foster.' As a result Hinckley was ordered to remain on his ward twenty-four hours a day.[5]

Eighties America was to see more horrific incidents, like the attempted murder of actress Theresa Saldana who, in 1982, was stabbed ten times by a Scottish man, Arthur Jackson.

Jackson had used a circuitous route to get to his prey. He had pretended to be a reporter when he'd spoken to Saldana's agent, and then had pretended to be an agent when he'd managed to contact her parents. Saldana's mother believed him when he said he represented the director, Martin Scorsese. She swallowed his story that he had a marvellous part for her daughter and so gave him Theresa's address.

'Theresa Saldana,' Jackson wrote, 'is the countess of Heaven in my heart and the angel of America in my dreams. Theresa Saldana is a soul mate to me. I have psychedelic fantasies of romance about her in springtime – enchanting visions of our walking together through the gardens of magnificent palaces in Heaven.'[6]

Saldana, who had appeared in the Martin Scorsese film *Raging Bull*, was rescued by a passer-by and later recovered from the serious injuries she had sustained. Jackson, it transpired, believed that by killing her he was in some way liberating her. He himself wanted to die but had not found the nerve to commit suicide. Instead he would kill his 'goddess'; he would be electrocuted for his crime. They would, he believed, unite in Heaven.

He was found guilty of attempted murder and sentenced to twelve years. His release became a subject of concern for his victim since he has never relinquished his intention to kill Saldana and had expressed his regret that he hadn't managed it in the first place. He was, he said, 'the benevolent angel of death'.

Because of Saldana's persistent campaigning, Jackson was convicted of sending threatening letters to the actress and given an extension on his sentence of five years and eight months. While in jail, he confessed to murdering a man during a bank robbery in Britain in the sixties. On his release he was extradited to England where he was charged with that crime.

Saldana's experience with her stalker, and her subsequent setting up of an organisation to help other victims, is documented in a film in which she stars as herself, *Victims for Victims: The Theresa Saldana Story* (1984).

In July 1989, Robert Bardo, who was only nineteen years old, murdered Rebecca Schæffer, the 21-year-old star of the American situation comedy, *My Sister Sam*.

The programme had launched what promised to be a wonderful career for the young actress. She was soon well on the way to fame and fortune after having been completely penniless for nearly four years.

Her beauty was part of her success story and also partly why Bardo decided he must end her life. Two years before he killed Schæffer, Bardo had journeyed to Warner Brothers studios to try and see her. He had a huge collection of tapes of her show but his adoration had turned to anger when he'd seen her having sex in the film *Scenes From a Class Struggle*. As a thirteen-year-old teenager, Bardo had stalked the singers Debbie Gibson and Tiffany, and had run away from his Tuscon home to Maine to get to Samantha Smith, a teenage girl who had got into the news by writing to President Gorbachev about world peace. He'd had a troubled and isolated childhood. He described his parents treating him as if he was their cat: he was given food and left to himself.

He'd obtained a signed photograph of Schæffer and had kept it close to him, believing it to be a personal message from the star. His bedroom was a shrine to her. Following the same methods he'd read Arthur Jackson had first used in his attempts to get to Theresa Saldana, he found Shæffer via the services of a private detective. He paid just $250 dollars for this man to trace her via the Department of Motor Vehicles.

Carrying the photograph with him, he called on her. The intercom wasn't working and she answered the door herself.

At first he allowed himself to be dismissed. He paced the street for about an hour, letting the anger build inside him. She'd told him he was wasting her time. That, he thought, was a callous thing to say. He called again. This time, as she answered the door, he shot her once in the chest. Some reports say he was laughing as he did it. At his trial he described how he had tried to shoot himself immediately afterwards so his body would fall on top of hers. They would be together in death as he could never hope they would be in life.

In fact, he left Shæffer dying on her own doorstep. He caught a bus to Arizona where he confessed to his crime the next day.

For America, he was one stalker too many. The time had come to wake up to the problem. The first law was passed against the crime in California in 1990. Other, less famous victims soon started speaking up for themselves. Inevitably, the rest of the world followed America's lead.

Because of these and similar shock cases of the eighties, it was generally supposed the problem had sprung up almost overnight. In fact stalking had just been given a name – it has always been with us. Even where celebrity is concerned, we can go back over a hundred years and find the envious and the envied, the loveless and the loved, the nobodies and the somebodies.

David Copperfield muses on 'whether I will turn out to be the hero of my own life, or whether that station will be held by somebody else . . .' The stalker can never hope to be the hero of his own life, but many are content to be included in the index of somebody else's biography – as the villain.

4. THE HERO OF MY OWN LIFE . . .

Fame may be a curse, but it's a curse many wish to have visited upon them. Among stalkers of modern celebrities, there is a common desire to associate with the fame of the star. It is, if you like, as if name-dropping has been taken to a distorted extreme. The stalker, feeling himself to be unimportant, seeks a vicarious renown by standing close to a personality.

When the celebrity already has a partner, that partner is often the focus of the stalker's jealousy and hatred and can be at risk of violence. The stalker may believe that, but for the presence of this troublesome third party, they would achieve their objective. Some stalkers believe their celebrity has been tricked or coerced into a relationship which they now need to be 'rescued' from.

Nowadays fame is more powerful than ever before, but it has always had a strong pull. Long before the media created any of our modern-day celebrities, even before the talking pictures or the silent flicks before them, there were stars and there were sex-symbols: people whose faces were known across the country, people whose names set hearts fluttering. Just like today their personalities usually bore only a fleeting resemblance to their public personas – but not in the case of the actor William Terriss. It could be said he was, both in his life and in his art, the stereotype of the dashing hero.

We are going back almost exactly one hundred years before the stalking law was passed in Britain. This stalker, who displayed many of the symptoms of erotomania, was not a man consumed by passion for another person. His 'object' was the theatrical profession itself – he stalked it relentlessly for most of his life, haunting theatres, never accepting the constant rejections he suffered, sure that he would, in the end, gain recognition. He never bestowed his affection upon another human being: Richard Archer Prince made the theatre his true love and, whilst receiving not a glimmer of real hope, he refused to believe his devotion was not reciprocated.

If the theatre was Prince's fantasy lover, it could be said that lover had already chosen her partner. The unwitting focus of Prince's jealous venom was Terriss, a man upon whom the theatre had showered her affections. He was all the things Prince was not: handsome, popular, happy, rich and talented.

At the inquest into his death, William Terriss's grieving son testified that 'he had not an enemy in the world'.

William Charles James Lewin (his stage-name was said to have been arbitrarily picked from a street directory), was born on 20 February 1847. Apart from its tragic end, his was to be a charmed life. His family were well-off and, after an early life which reads like something from *Boys Own*, he entered the theatrical profession.

He graduated from being the second lead to Henry Irving at the famous Lyceum Theatre to becoming the star at the Adelphi, where the melodrama was becoming an immensely popular alternative to the classical play (and the new Gilbert and Sullivan operettas across the road at the Savoy). Terriss, playing the kind of young heroes whose daring escapades he'd emulated in his early adventures, rapidly became the darling of the West End public.

His was a familiar kind of success story; it shows how fortune smiles on her chosen few. Despite their youth, inexperience, faults – despite everything – they are guided along their path and unfailingly achieve all they set out to do.

Others are not so fortunate.

About ten years after Terriss made his London debut another stage-struck young man attempted to take that first step along the road to theatrical success. His story is as different to Terriss's as it's possible to get. His name was Richard Archer (he changed it later, adding and sometimes substituting 'Prince'). The son of a poor Scottish farm labourer and his second wife, he had a brother who was born insane and Prince (as we shall call him) himself was to show acute signs of mental instability from early in his life. His mother described him as '. . . a bad-tempered boy, (who) would get very angry. He was not very fond of play.'[1]

She gave her son's date of birth as 1858, but on an application he made to the Actors' Benevolent Fund he claims to be seven years younger. Either way, we can estimate his age as being mid-to-late twenties when Terriss first began to attract nationwide fame.

Prince began his working life as an apprentice to a shipbuilder in his hometown of Dundee. At some point in his youth, he became infatuated with the theatre. The gaudy, exciting world of canvas and greasepaint must have seemed to him like a door leading into his real self.

Once smitten, he was never to let go. From that moment on, he was to stalk the profession. He considered any energy expended elsewhere to be wasted. This was more than misplaced ambition. It was born of that same unshakeable belief that others like him have had in their infatuations with people. Unable to accept himself for what he was, he decided instead to live in a fantasy wherein he'd already gained the love of his audience and the praise of his peers.

There were two theatres available to him in Dundee: Her Majesty's and the less auspicious Theatre Royal. In both, he managed to get small, non-speaking roles for which he was not paid. One can suppose he took these with good grace, 'knowing' he was on his way and would soon progress to bigger and bigger parts.

This was to be his 'courting' period and, for a time, he was content to let his true love play hard to get. Had he been able to see his chances objectively he would have been cruelly disappointed; as it was, and throughout his life, he retained an image of himself as a supremely talented artist – the perfect groom for his chosen bride. It wouldn't be long before he'd begin to blame others for his lover's indifference.

Prince's half-sister figures largely in his sorry story, though she is rather an elusive person. She called herself 'Mrs Archer', but this is thought to be a cover, most probably for prostitution. She lived in London and Prince's parents eventually moved south to join her. Prince himself soon followed. Blissfully unaware of the mediocrity of his talents, he dreamt of the rapid rise to fame which would result as soon as his obvious genius was recognised – as it surely would be.

It isn't stretching the 'lover' metaphor too much to say that the theatre 'led him on'. Considering his lack of talent, he should have been applauded for getting the small amount of work he did. After all, he possessed no charm or easy nature; he had 'an accent you could cut with a knife' and his half-crazed notions and his rantings would have been difficult and embarrassing to deal with. Nevertheless, he found himself treading the boards as a 'super' (short for 'supernumerary'), or 'extra' as we would say today. This humble work had another Victorian sobriquet: an 'Adelphi guest'.

Sadly for Prince, his entire theatrical career was to prove so insignificant nobody bothered to record its details. The name appears occasionally but no one is entirely sure it refers to the same person. If he *was* the 'Mr Archer' who was listed in the programme, it is possible his native brogue was something of an asset in such parts as 'First Traveller'. Also, if he was 'Mr R. M. Archer' we can suppose he made a passable stab at Irish in such parts as 'Sligo Dan'. Whatever the case, he was an actor few people would employ more than once.

Prince's desperate need to achieve recognition overrode every other aspect of his personality. His sights were set much higher than he was able to reach and failure hit him very hard. The nagging doubts which he surely had (at least subconsciously), must have been increasingly difficult to keep at bay. He needed a scapegoat, a way of explaining his lowly status. He often made reference to some dark plot against him.

It was important for him to distinguish himself from the other 'supers'. He would parade his delusions of grandeur, oblivious to the derision he earned as a result. He was, in fact, a 'dressing room butt'.

George Rowell, in his book *William Terriss and Richard Prince – Two Characters in an Adelphi Melodrama* gives us an idea of what Prince's colleagues thought of him:

'He thought himself a great actor, simply because once or twice he got a couple of lines to speak, "My lord, the carriage waits", and that class of work. Wanity, disappointed wanity and ambition – that's what I calls the reason of it.'

'He possessed a great histrionic ambition . . .'

'While in a small part in *In the Ranks* he complained to me twice that another actor was trying to "queer" him.'[2]

Though it is unlikely Terriss was very much aware of him, Prince appeared in several of Terriss's greatest successes at the Adelphi, including *Arrah-na-Pogue*, *Harbour Lights* and *The Union Jack*. These plays have not survived like those of Wilde or Shaw (who wrote *The Devil's Disciple* with Terriss in mind), but they were not exactly ephemeral either.

It is difficult to translate the extent of Terriss's popularity into modern terms. British people outside of the capital would only have known him by reputation; even so, it was a mighty one. Aided by his undoubted physical appeal it was quite sufficient to warrant him heading the bill when the company toured to the United States. He was, to all intents and purposes, a household name. He was given affectionate nicknames as a tribute to his free-spirit and his considerable achievements – 'Breezy Bill' and 'Number One Adelphi Terriss' – Prince, on the other hand, was commonly known as 'Mad Archer'.

In 1888, Prince's mother returned to her native Scotland. There is no mention of what happened to his father but we know his half-sister, 'Mrs Archer' continued on in London as, for a while, did Prince himself.

He had recently finished playing 'Diego' in *The Silver Falls*. It isn't a part that figures at all in the script, but George Rowell supposes it to be one of a crowd of onlookers at a wedding. It was his last engagement for some time.

In 1890, two years later, Prince first sought assistance from the Actors' Benevolent Fund. This may have been a crushing blow to his pride but he was to overcome his feelings of ignominy. In fact, within seven years, he was to be 'practically living out of the fund'.[3]

Rowell also points out that at this point, round about the late 1880s, 'Mr Archer' first became 'Mr Prince'. He appears to have decided to hone his technique, maybe out of necessity, more probably from affectation. Thus, he discarded his Scottish brogue in favour of 'a slight foreign accent'. Forced to seek work outside the theatrical profession, he'd been a valet to a guards officer. Rowell proposes his new vocal technique was an attempt to imitate 'His Master's Voice' and this is entirely probable. Whatever the case, it's fairly certain 'Mr Prince' sounded nothing at all to others like he sounded to himself.

He was able to capitalise upon his Adelphi experience with a CV which was more impressive on paper than in reality. He turned away from London and sought work in the provinces, ending up in the northwest. Here he appeared for JF Elliston, a Bolton-based tour manager, who employed him in, among other things, the one-time Terriss hit, *The Union Jack*.

In this, very inferior, northern production, Prince was given a modest promotion from 'super' to 'Sergeant'. The experience might have served as a difficult, but profitable, lesson for him: had he reduced his monumental ambition he could have enjoyed a degree of success in minor provincial tours.

Needless to say, this was not to be. His fantasy-self, the great West End actor, now slumming it in the provinces, was becoming more and more real to him. He blamed Terriss for his fate. If Terriss wasn't around he, Prince, would occupy that cherished place in the public's affection.

He 'claimed an intimacy with the Prince of Wales and spoke of himself as brother-in-law to the Emperor of Johore. . . . He would sit at the piano and sing stupid songs to the most discordant accompaniments, and give imitations of actors he had seen . . .' He also threatened 'If a man did me an injury, I would rip him up.'[4]

'For a period of six years, Prince was under engagement with JF Elliston, the well-known proprietor of theatrical travelling companies, and during that time played small parts in *The Union Jack* and *Alone in London*. Whilst with Mr Elliston, Prince wrote the most extraordinary letters, demanding more important parts to play, and on many occasions went so far as to threaten Mr Elliston with bodily harm if his requests were not complied with. When *The Union Jack* company was at Dundee (in 1893) some of his letters to Elliston were of such a character they were handed to the chief constable there, but upon receipt of an abject apology the prosecution was withdrawn.'[5]

Prince was not able to subsist on the wages he earned. In 1895, his colleagues generously (or perhaps with some relief!) collectively paid his fare back to London. Unable to find any employment there, Prince attempted suicide by jumping into the Regent's Canal. If it was a cry for help it didn't work, for nobody appears to have taken very much notice. He was eventually forced to return to Dundee where he swallowed his monumental ambition sufficiently to accept a job in an ironworks.

His behaviour was becoming more and more erratic:

'. . . he used to think (his mother) doctored his food. He had told her he himself was the Lord Jesus Christ and that she was the Virgin Mary, and had charged her with adulterating his tea. When he was affected with what (she) described as "his turns", he would sing songs and hymns, and his eyes would stare out of his head. . . .'[6]

His temper boiled into rage at the slightest provocation. He nearly killed his brother Harry by attacking him with a knife and poker. Harry and his mother were forced to hide from Prince's wrath in a neighbour's house.

The word 'blackmail' was one Prince was extremely fond of using. At his trial, there was some doubt as to whether he meant the same thing as others mean by it. He often accused Terriss of trying to blackmail him – in this and other instances, he used the word as one might use 'undermine' or 'defame', Rowell suggests 'blackball'. The reports show a man on the edge of nervous collapse, a man who reacts violently when crossed, a man who is ridiculed so often it can only be a matter of time before his sense of humiliation demands satisfaction.

Prince was a regular among the theatregoers at Her Majesty's, Dundee. Here, as elsewhere, his peculiar mode of dress and his eccentric behaviour marked him out. He would sport a 'tricoloured sash' over his velvet jacket. Claiming distinction as an ex-member of the Adelphi company, he would demand the best seat in the house. When he succeeded in getting it, he would applaud at all the wrong moments and attempt to strike up a conversation with the characters on stage. On one occasion he was evicted from the theatre after having brandished a revolver and threatened to shoot one of the actors.

William Terriss featured highly on his list of 'enemies'. In fact, it's extremely unlikely Terriss had given him a second thought since the run of *The Silver Falls*. Even during the time they 'worked together' they could only have had the briefest of meetings.

Prince made occasional attempts to ingratiate himself with the profession but most of the time he was sinking further and further into madness. Both his actions and his letters show the conflicting sides of his personality. On the one hand there is a man who, though humbled, still wants to associate with the famous people he has brushed against, on the other is a man who sees these same people as unworthy, antagonistic, in league with each other to rob him of his rightful place in their midst.

Once again, he took the long journey to London, arriving towards the end of 1895. He asked his half-sister for help. We must thank George Rowell for steering us towards a story which, but for his having unearthed it, would probably have been forgotten. As he says himself it is an 'episode of which not one word was spoken at the trial, nor a whisper leaked to the press, yet which led directly to disaster'.[7] Rowell's account is corroborated in a book of memoirs published in 1930 by Terriss's son-in-law, actor and writer, Seymour Hicks.

'Mrs Archer' (as we shall continue to call her) was one of a frowned-upon set: 'a woman well-known to be a frequenter of the then notorious Empire promenade'.[8] The Empire in question was the theatre in Leicester Square and there are no prizes for guessing which sort of women used the promenade outside it. Mrs Archer, who by Hicks's account 'was by no means an unattractive specimen of her class', had a regular gentleman-friend whom Hicks tactfully refers to as 'Mr A', but whom Rowell believes to be the actor WL Abingdon. 'Mrs Archer' persuaded Abingdon to help her strange brother, and as a result Prince landed a job as a 'super' in Hicks's play, *One of the Best*. Abingdon, as was usually his lot, played the villain and Terriss, needless to say, was the hero.

The hero was a 'dashing Highland officer'. It wasn't long before Prince, who had absolutely no lines in the play, was seeing himself in the role – and of course he would play it so much better than Terriss could ever hope to. This ridiculous notion was aided and encouraged by Abingdon.

Abingdon saw in Prince an opportunity to have a laugh at the expense of a gullible, suggestible eccentric. It's easy to see how a bit of unkind, but seemingly harmless, goading got out of hand. Hicks again:

'He (Abingdon) lost no opportunity of making the man believe that if he (Prince) ever got the chance of appearing in the part Bill Terriss was playing in *One of the Best*, . . . London would be at his feet and the name Terriss would be relegated to the limbo of forgotten men for ever.'[9]

Abingdon entertained Prince's sister in his dressing-room and often invited Prince to join them. One can assume from this that 'Mrs Archer' was in on the joke and maybe had even suggested it. The 'fun' pretty soon spread throughout the lower orders at the Adelphi. Prince, blissfully unaware that he was an object of universal derision, could always be relied upon:

'. . . Prince's fellow-supers, with whom he dressed, little realising on what thin ice they were travelling, encouraged him for their amusement to talk more grandiloquently than ever of what he would do should his great day ever arrive.

'To please Prince (Abingdon) had the part of the hero, the part Terriss was playing, typed for him to learn and, indeed, even went so far as to have what to him was a comic rehearsal called and, with the assistance of the extra people in the piece, had a hilarious hour watching the miserable weakling make a complete jackass of himself.'[10]

Hicks sets much store by this cruel but hardly surprising ribbing. He was not alone in blaming Abingdon for making Terriss the focus of Prince's hatred:

'James Beverage and Charles Somerset, two of William Terriss's oldest comrades, years afterwards informed me of the terrible interview they had with (Abingdon) the day after the funeral, for when telling him that they laid their friend's death at his door he completely and utterly broke down.'[11]

Which is not to say he was guilty. Since Terriss was the leading actor at the theatre where Prince did most of his work, he was always going to be the likely recipient of Prince's spleen. Had Prince been a 'super' at the Lyceum, who knows but that Henry Irving might have not survived into the early twentieth century?

One of the Best ran to packed houses for a year and half. At the end of it, Prince found himself out of work again. Hicks suggests it was because not many 'supers' were needed for the following production; Rowell disagrees saying that *Boys Together* had 'elaborate crowd and battle scenes'. It's likely that the Adelphi 'let him go' because of his unruly behaviour and disruptive influence.

He was soon in dire circumstances. His sister and her gentleman had tired of their joke – in any case they could carry it no further now the management were aware of Prince's problems. If either of them had any genuine charity, neither showed it. The theatrical grapevine has always been fast and wide-ranging and it's likely that Prince's reputation at the Adelphi precluded him from getting employment at any of the other West End theatres. What could he do but take the long trip by boat, back to Dundee?

Not for the first time he signed on for manual labour – this time at the Wallace Foundry. At his trial, a foreman, Alexander Husband, said Prince had showed him a letter in which Terriss gave permission for Prince to use his name in his search for an engagement. Prince, he said, had interpreted this generous act as blackmail.

At this point, in the summer of 1897, Prince had one of the very few sparks of good luck that came his way, career-wise. Arthur Carlton, the manager of the Crown Theatre in Stoke, was in Glasgow with *The Union Jack*. Even by provincial touring standards, Carlton's company was 'third rate'. Now, because of emergency recasting, he had no choice but to scrape the very bottom of the barrel and offer the part of the villain to 'Mr Prince, late Adelphi Theatre'. It's unlikely that Prince had persuaded him of his abilities. No doubt Carlton was very stuck indeed and took the strange man on trust. If he thought Prince's inflated view of his talents and experience was even partly justified, he was sadly mistaken; Prince was dismissed in the autumn. He avowed darkly that the reason for this was that 'he smoked a clay pipe instead of a cigar', adding a paranoia about his social class to his list of excuses for misfortune.

Prince once again found a management who needed somebody quickly. He had to descend still further in quality, but it was nevertheless incredible good luck. A north-east-based touring company took him on. Ralph Croyden, his new employer, was required to give evidence at his trial. His report shows the extent to which Prince, once just a conceited no-hoper, had become a crazed obsessive.

Croyden told how, in October, 1897, he was at Newcastle with his company. Prince wrote to him in answer to an advertisement. He was fond of writing letters and, in them, equally fond of making much of his inauspicious career. Though it's excusable for Croyden to have seen him on the strength of the letter, he must have been very desperate to employ Prince after seeing him audition.

True, Prince was engaged to play only very small parts. He told Croyden the public must not know he was playing minor roles: he'd been playing 'a large part' at the Adelphi in *The Union Jack* and would be still in the West End if he had been treated justly. He asked for 30 shillings per week, and was given 25 (a perfectly respectable wage – 10 years later 21s 8d was considered the subsistence level for a family of 4).

As Prince had no firm base in Newcastle, Croyden and his wife invited him to tea, along with other members of the company. It was a difficult evening. At first Prince was simply over-the-top and Croyden supposed him to be drunk or simply over-dramatic. His Scottishness was a source of great pride to Prince and, though still south of the border, he entered the room with the loud announcement, 'my foot is on my native heath and my name MacGregor!'

Prince made another reference to the curtailment of his career at the Adelphi, saying that although his name was MacGregor, he would smoke his clay pipe if he wanted to. He said he'd only left the Adelphi through one man and he might have starved but for the Actors' Benevolent Fund. He added 'I will be even with this man some day'. He didn't, on this occasion, give his mysterious enemy a name but we can be sure he meant Terriss. He pointed out a picture in a magazine claiming, 'That's my sister. We are considered the handsomest family in Scotland.' Hinting at some unknown tragedy in his life, he excused his own physical appearance by saying, 'It's only this secret sorrow that has made me what I am.'[12]

On the following morning he joined the train for the nearby town of Hetton where they were to open two days later. Even for this short journey some members of the company chose to leave the compartment Prince was in. On arrival they went to the theatre where the new company member became impossible.

To his dismay, Croyden found Prince was unable to rehearse at all. He knew nothing of his part and, even if he had, what should have been obvious from the start was glaringly evident now: Prince couldn't act to save his life. Croyden told him that it was a direct swindle for him to have taken the engagement in the first place. Prince responded by claiming to be ill, he said his 'brain had gone' and he couldn't think. He asked the company to close up the theatre for that night, and re-open later to give him time to recover. Croyden flatly refused – it was an absurd suggestion, Prince was only playing a very small part and would just have to get to grips with it.

'I now have got two enemies,' Prince replied. 'One here, one at the Adelphi.'[13]

Croyden left Prince in the hands of the stage manager. On his return he found the man could do nothing with him, and the rehearsal had been stopped. Prince was fired yet again.

On the following morning he turned up at Croyden's lodgings asking for his money. Not surprisingly, Croyden refused to give him anything at all. Prince then repeated his statement about having two enemies. When asked the identity of his other 'enemy', he said, 'Terriss, that dirty dog.'[14]

Croyden's wife, in an unladylike demonstration of candour, told Prince he was mad. 'Yes,' he agreed. 'And the whole world will ring of my madness yet.'[15]

Humiliated and without any firm means of support, Prince once again decided to try his luck in London. He arrived by boat on 28 October.

Here we take up the testimony of two people: the first, Mrs Charlotte Darby, was a bus driver's wife, who had rooms to rent at her home in Eaton Court, Buckingham Palace Road, Victoria. She let a back bedroom, furnished, to Prince at four shillings a week. He took possession that evening, excusing his lack of luggage by saying the rest of it was still on the boat. (He'd left his trunk as surety for his unpaid fair.) He offered Mrs Darby two shillings up front, which she declined as insufficient. Eventually, she agreed to accept three shillings, providing Prince paid her the remainder on the following Saturday. He showed her what appeared to be a Post Office book to prove he had access to more money. He was given the absolute basics: a cup and saucer, a plate, knife and fork, a coffee-pot, and hot water.

Prince existed during this time on a diet of bread and milk. The small table-knife he had been given was not practical for slicing his bread and it was possibly to obtain a knife for this innocent purpose that he visited the cutler, George Lauberg, in Brompton Road. Having said this, Brompton Road was sufficiently far away from Prince's lodgings for there to be doubt about his intentions: one would normally purchase such necessities closer to home.

'It was a butcher's boning knife,' Lauberg said at the trial. 'About the end of October I had similar knives in my window for sale. The price varied from 9d to 2s 6d. This one would be about 9d. I don't recollect selling this particular knife. At about the end of October we did sell one to a shabbily dressed man. It was between six and seven in the evening. I don't recollect seeing him before.'

Prince helpfully jogged his memory: 'There was a lady there and you asked me to buy a shilling one. I said *that* was large enough to cut bread. That is all that passed.'[16] (my italics)

To Prince, knives already had an unhealthy significance. In his last, inauspicious appearance, as the villain in *The Union Jack*, he had been called upon to stab the hero – a part created by William Terriss in the Adelphi production. Also, during a break in the disastrous rehearsal at Hetton, a member of Croyden's company had produced a knife to open a tin. Prince had asked him to remove it as it made him uncomfortable. Later, he'd picked up a prop-dagger and commented on how 'a man would not want that stuck in many times'. The landlady, Mrs Darby, remembers seeing the knife Prince had bought lying, quite openly, on his dressing-table and, at the time, she thought little of it.

He had told her he was a 'pro' and out of an engagement. She allowed his arrears to mount up and said he behaved '. . . quite like a gentleman. He appeared in very cheerful spirits until his rent was due.' Later she said, 'He spoke about a sister who, he said, was well-to-do but would not assist him. He said she kept her servants while he was starving in a small back room. He also showed me a photograph and said it was of his sister, adding that he expected a letter from her, and it would be one way or the other. I asked "Mr Prince, what do you mean?" he said, "That is best known to God and Man".'[17]

The reference to his sister's rise in social status was not imagined, and she did have servants. One of them, Mary Waller, testified at the trial that Prince had been in the habit of calling. Two days after Prince's arrest Mrs Archer had vanished and Mary Waller had no idea where she was.

Prince was to spend eight weeks with Mrs Darby, dividing his time between writing letters and wandering the streets. Many of the letters were to the Actors' Benevolent Fund.

In order to qualify for relief, the Fund then required the applicant to have a letter of recommendation from one of their subscribers. Having been given a form, Prince chose to approach none other than his 'enemy at the Adelphi'. Terriss readily confirmed in writing that he knew Prince as 'a hard-working actor' and had done so 'for many years'.[18] Seymour Hicks's account ignores this letter and suggests that Prince approached Terriss for money some weeks later when he was given a sovereign. This incident, if it happened, was not reported at the trial.

Prince's letter of application for relief was dated 9 November 1897. It stated that he'd lost his last engagement through no fault of his own and referred the committee to Terriss's endorsement. On that occasion he was given a pound.

His financial troubles were obviously real and pressing. Mrs Darby noticed his clothes were disappearing and she guessed correctly he was having to pawn them. He applied again and again to the Fund, at first suggesting he was confident of getting theatrical work before long but soon admitting 'I shall not get an engagement in London now'. In this letter he asks for money to take him home: 'the fare is 15 shillings and I will go from London today if you can get the money'.[19]

This promise is forgotten in the next letter which reads: 'Two of the best agents in London are doing their best to get me an engagement and I think I shall get one very soon. If you will only help me once more I shall not trouble the Fund again until I pay back what you so kindly lent me.' He adds that he 'could have got an engagement yesterday, only I had not got the wardrobe required for the part'.[20]

As Rowell says:

'With a mind as confused as Prince's it is impossible to decide how serious was his search for work. He certainly made contact with R St John Denton, the actor he had dressed with in *Harbour Lights* and now a theatrical agent, who reported his coming to his office "in a deplorable state". Denton did what he could, fixing him up for a pantomime chorus, only to learn he had been turned down "because of the cast in his eye". He also obtained for him the part of Lord Mountsevern "in a small production of *East Lynne*", but this too was withdrawn because "he had no frock coat".'[21]

Another letter asks for a further ten shillings, claiming his name had been placed for a production of *Julius Caesar* and saying he had the chance of chorus work in a tour.

Yet again, he writes, and yet again promises this will be the very last time he has to ask for money 'if I have to die'.

'The only thing I can say in the matter now . . . is what a poor part I am playing in the eyes of my brother actors.'[22]

On this last occasion, the committee turned him down. The Secretary, Charles Ismay Coltson, deposed they might well have given Prince further assistance but at that particular time there were more pressing cases and he'd already had more than his share. In fairness it has to be said the charity could not be expected to support an unfortunate colleague indefinitely, and they had done all that could be expected of them. It's also very likely they were aware of Prince's sorry prospects and were hoping he would do as he'd promised and go back home, where he would become somebody else's problem.

It was 16 December 1897 at a little before four o'clock in the afternoon. The committee meeting, headed by the celebrated comedian, Edward Terry, had just finished. Prince, anxious to know their decision, turned up at the offices. He was not allowed to see anyone other than the clerk who gave him the bad news. Seymour Hicks's later account suggests Prince asked who the chairman was and, given the name 'Terry', possibly misheard it as 'Terriss'. Contradicting this, the clerk stated at the trial he 'mentioned no name at all'. Whatever the case, it seems Prince accepted the news calmly. He left the office without a word.

He had repeatedly stalked the Adelphi stage door. The doorkeeper, Henry Spratt, knew him as someone to be wary of, even though he (Spratt) had only worked at the theatre for sixteen months. He'd become used to Prince hanging around for half an hour or so at a time. On the previous evening, 15 December, Prince had asked if Mr Terriss was in the habit of leaving the theatre by means of the stage door. Spratt, being cautious and well-used to having to protect his actors from nuisance fans, had said 'yes'. This wasn't in fact true.

The Adelphi was considerably altered in 1901 but the stage door area is still very much as it was in 1897. The building backs onto Maiden Lane, a thoroughfare leading from Bedford Street to Southampton Street, running parallel to the Strand. Though undeniably a back street, it boasts, amongst other establishments, Rules Restaurant where Edward, Prince of Wales, used to dine with his actress friends. In fact, apart from that which carried Royalty, the road was then closed to traffic. The Adelphi's actual stage door led out into a narrow passage which joins Maiden Lane to the Strand. Terriss, however, invariably used a private entrance in Maiden Lane itself.

This had been constructed as a convenient way of slipping Royalty into and out of the theatre. (Thirty-five years earlier, when Queen Victoria paid her last visit to a public theatre to see *The Colleen Bawn*, she had used this door.) The entrance led through to a staircase which, in turn, led to the Number One and Number Two dressing rooms. Terriss was one of a few privileged people who had a key.

It was still early when Prince turned up in Maiden Lane. He went to his reluctant agent, St John Denton, who had offices there. He was turned away empty-handed and so made his way into the Strand and there, by chance, he met his sister, Mrs Archer.

After his arrest, Prince asked, 'Will you please be kind enough to acquaint my sister with my condition? . . . There is no occasion to break it to her gently. I met her in the Strand about an hour before. She was accompanied by her husband. I asked her for assistance. She said she would rather see me dead in the gutter than give me a farthing. Had she given me a half-sovereign this would never have happened. It was all through her.'[23]

We don't know who the 'husband' was. Had it been the actor, Abington, as George Rowell hypothesises, it seems likely Prince would have had something more specific to say about him. In other accounts, he states the meeting wasn't in the Strand at all, but at his sister's house.

An immediate solution to his desperate money problems wouldn't necessarily have calmed him enough to send him home. He had good reason to be in Maiden Lane, given that his agent was there, but he would have been there anyway: he couldn't keep away. He was carrying a knife, he might have had any number of reasons for doing so: self-defence, morbid fascination. Or maybe he had gone out that evening with the sole intention of committing murder.

After his sister rejected him, Prince went back to Maiden Lane and, though his usual habit was to wait in the alley by the stage door, he took up a vantage point in the shadows just opposite the private entrance. Inside the theatre, Terriss's leading lady, Jessie Millward, was preparing herself for the evening's performance of the American play *Secret Service*. She had left Terriss at her flat, playing cards with his friend and godfather, John Henry Graves.

Millward had been ill at ease for some weeks past. She'd had dreams where she found Terriss in great danger and had been worried by the presence of a strange man with a squint who haunted the stage door.

Terriss arrived, along with John Henry Graves, just after seven o'clock. He told Graves to wait a minute while he produced his key. As he was unlocking the door, Prince rushed at him and stabbed him twice in the back. The attack was so quick and so unexpected Graves didn't at first realise what had happened. Terriss made the fatal mistake of turning to face his assailant whereupon Prince plunged the knife into his chest.

As Graves described it: 'Poor Terriss then said "My God, I am stabbed!" and backed. I followed him (Prince) instantly and seized him by the arm. I don't remember which arm. He still continued backing and I heard cries of "Murder!" "Police!" I do not know who uttered these cries but it was not Mr Terriss. A constable came up and I gave the man in charge saying "I charge this man with having stabbed Mr Terriss." The constable took the man and I looked round and saw Mr Terriss lying huddled up at the left side of the stage door. I was unaware until then that he was stabbed mortally.

'The constable and myself took the man to Bow Street police station. He went quite quietly. We did not know what weapon he'd used on Mr Terriss and the constable and I were taking care. I had fancied at the time the blows were struck that I saw a glint of something. On our road to Bow Street I turned round to the man, Prince, and said "What could have induced you to do such a cruel thing?" and he said "Mr Terriss prevented me from getting employment and I did it in revenge" or "to be revenged" – I'm not sure which expression was used. I'm perfectly certain he used the word "revenge".'[24]

Today there is a plaque to mark the place where William Terriss fell. His fame might not have survived the demise of the melodrama; he is remembered simply as the actor who was murdered at the stage door of the Adelphi Theatre. Back then his popularity was legend. Thousands paid their respects at his funeral, lining the route from Chiswick to Brompton Cemetery in West London.

Prince, who tried to enter a plea of guilty 'with great provocation' was deemed to be a criminal lunatic, ending his days in Broadmoor in 1937. He survived nearly all the actors in a tragedy in which he'd at last played a leading part.

5. POISON IN JEST

Jeremy Dyer was fond of TV presenters; there was a new one on Meridian, his local channel. She was smart and good-looking – as were her colleagues of course – but perhaps it was her voice which attracted him most. Beautifully articulated Standard-English vowels delivered with an easy, fluid efficiency. In Sarah Lockett he saw a woman who knew her own mind; a woman whom he might respect in one way but whose confidence was also a challenge to him.

First things first. Jeremy Dyer made his initial approach by writing Sarah Lockett a fan letter:*

Dear Sarah
I don't want to offend you but your new haircut makes you look like a boy. Oh well, it will grow back in a couple of months so don't panic. I hope this letter does not offend you too much as the aim of it is to invite you out for a drink etc. I have already blown my chance probably. My name is *Jeremy* so remember it. I am 28 am English and am a freelance writer on economics related things. I will ring you at Meridian (Maidstone?) soon to invite you out. I am assuming the Meridian show comes from Maidstone but could equally likely be beamed in from Spain I suppose. If it is, why don't you have a sun tan? Oh dear, I am insulting you again. While I am writing this letter I am watching you with the sound turned down as I am listening to England v Morocco football on the radio. But with your new haircut you can become a footballer!
    Yours sincerely,
    (Signed Jeremy D)
    Jeremy[1]

---

*The letters have been edited slightly. I have retained some of Jeremy's idiosyncrasies (such as writing 'abit' and 'alot'), but have corrected some minor spelling mistakes and typing errors. I have mostly retained Jeremy's original punctuation but have added some upper case letters where appropriate.

Over the next year, 'Jeremy' was to bombard Sarah Lockett with letters and small gifts. His correspondence is fascinating: mostly juvenile prattle, often schoolboy smut and occasionally sick fantasy. He is evidently intelligent and is objective about himself. He clearly knows what effect his letters might have. However, he carries on regardless, sometimes acknowledging that Sarah Lockett probably wants him to stop and may be frightened by what he writes. At the very least, he knows she must consider his letters a nuisance. He often takes a tone which suggests he believes he has a 'right' to stalk Sarah.

If you picked up one of his letters at random, you might believe he was writing to a pen friend – or a girlfriend he'd been out with for just one date – until a paragraph suddenly hits you and you wonder, as Sarah did, 'Is this man as dangerous as he seems?'

Jeremy Dyer often refers to himself as a 'good stalker' a 'guardian stalker'. He sees himself as quite different from the 'sad' types who usually indulge in this 'pastime', but whether or not this is true is open to debate. I will let his letters speak for themselves.

Jeremy's hair was thinning and he wore thick, pebble glasses but, behind them, he had very piercing eyes which were unusual enough to arrest the attention. It was his personality which let him down, for as soon as he began to speak, he betrayed himself as 'a weirdo'. He'd had various fads: chess, stocks and shares. Now he had decided to try his hand at stalking. He would do it properly and devote all his energies to his new hobby.

The programme Sarah had started working on that day was to give her the kind of celebrity which many of her better-known colleagues might have envied. She would be recognised as an old friend by the people of Kent but was anonymous in London. She did not, however, resent the former or hanker after the latter. She is realistic about the work she does and takes the well-meant intrusiveness of her public as being a part of the job she is paid for.

'I do get letters from people who are perfectly well-meaning: "Oh we do love you on the TV" – that kind of thing

– perfectly nice, but you occasionally get one who's a sandwich short of a picnic. They can be odd in a perfectly nice way. I remember a very nice woman at a day-care centre who latched onto us. You come into contact with a cross-section of people and some are going to be less than a hundred per cent. I'm talking directly to the person at home, I'm not directing what I say at other actors. There's no side to you. If you have an ad-lib or a funny story, that's genuinely your personality. You're coming over very directly as yourself: more so than an actress does. So, if someone is a loner and they haven't got many friends – which was certainly the case with Jeremy – you're the only person who talks to them on a daily basis – actually talks *to* them. You're the only company they've got.'[2]

Jeremy wasn't the first 'sandwich short of a picnic' who'd worried Sarah sufficiently for her to consider getting the police involved. A man had sent what she understatedly describes as 'saucy' postcards. They contained hardened, offensive, sexual references which were far more worrying than the initial letters Jeremy sent. It was obvious this man was getting a thrill out of describing his fantasies. One example was during a very hot summer when Sarah made an off-the-cuff remark, joking that they needed hosing down. Her mystery correspondent wrote saying that *he'd* be willing to hose her down. He called her a 'saucy cow' and added childish sound effects: 'Slurp, slurp. Gasp, gasp!' It was disturbing but it wasn't until later when he sent a booby-trapped box of chocolates that she alerted the police. The chocolates turned out to contain a harmless toy snake and she was advised not to take it further. She agreed.

When Dyer wrote his first letter on 27 May 1998, Sarah found it 'creepy', but there was no great cause for concern. He waited just under a week before he wrote again. This time more fully (two pages). He compared the Meridian news with that of its neighbouring company, Anglia. He advised Sarah her next career stop was London Weekend Television or Carlton and went on to say:

> You seem to get a fairly good deal at Meridian anyway as I don't see you on at weekends – so you can stay in bed all day.

I won't charge you for this valuable/useless (delete as applicable) careers advice. Even if I did charge you, you could pay in other ways than money (see previous paragraph) i.e. spending the weekend in bed (as long as you don't expect any action during world cup matches).[3]

'I don't think he wanted to terrorise me or frighten me,' Sarah said. 'I think he wanted to go out with me and be my friend. Maybe I'm being terribly naive. He had this double side to his personality and when he was in a pleasant mood he'd write all this nice, positive sort of stuff.'[4]

In the third letter, dated 4 June 98, Dyer first gave Sarah the nickname, 'Pocket Lockett' which he used frequently from then on. He asked how tall she was and, supposing her to be short, he described her as a 'Miniaturised Super-Sonic Pocket Lockett'. Towards the end of the letter he said:

You can up the flirting on Meridian a notch. So far you use different voice tones, stick your chest out every now and again, that's about it. Meridian seems to keep an informal ship. Why don't you show your bra every once in a while, or lick your lips suggestively etc. Do you dare do this on TV?[5]

Letter number four begins in a chatty, jokey sort of way. It gives snippets of news and bits of information about himself. He asks why Sarah hasn't got pierced ears. He jokes that he's never seen any alcohol on the newsdesk – he supposes she must have a quick drink during the advert breaks. He had been thinking of doing a PhD in psychology but never got round to it. He admits to being fully aware of Sarah's probable reaction to this unsolicited correspondence:

As you don't know me I'll have to be careful what I write as you may think I am writing to you from Prison? Hospital? Mental hospital? and am not a very nice person. If I was going to send you death threats or other stuff I would have done it by now. Okay so now and again I write some sexy stuff to you but this is fairly normal. If I didn't think you were worth it I wouldn't waste my time writing to you.

Be rest assured you would probably be quite pleased if you saw me as I'm okay. I'm someone you would flirt with if I caught your eye in a restaurant. That kind of thing. I have quite a high opinion of myself and I get the impression you have a high opinion of yourself. This is good. I really have got two degrees you know. Not that that probably impresses you. I think I am a great lover and good with women, your still not impressed?[6]

At first, he would sign himself more or less anonymously as 'Jeremy'. The letters were typed on his computer. Most fans would have included a full name and address from day one, but Jeremy knew this would result in a standard letter back which would curtail the correspondence. He didn't want Sarah to write back, he wanted to imagine she was compliant in an imaginary two-way relationship which was gradually allowing him to trawl the depths of his sexual fantasy.

Sarah: 'He said "I'm a nice stalker – aren't you lucky that you've got a nice stalker who sends you presents and who has only your best interests at heart?" And he did send me presents and chocolates and things, not that I opened any of them – and a mug. I put them on the communal table in the office and I said, "These are from Jeremy and anyone who wants them – you're very welcome." Of course they all went – because people are suckers for chocolates aren't they? In a way, it gives you some feedback about what you're doing as a job. At the beginning he would say things like "I didn't like you in that blue jacket." In a way, during the early part, it was like a bit of conversation when I'd had a letter from Jeremy.'[7]

The conversation was entirely one-sided but that didn't stop Jeremy inventing Sarah's part of it. The following 'script', for example, is taken from letter number twenty-three, dated 9 August 98:

Question and answer sheet
Sarah asks –   Why do you send me all these letters and
                   present when you don't even know me?
Jeremy replies –   Because I think you're attractive and I'm
                   interested in you.

Sarah asks –   Will you ever ring me or come to
                     Meridian studios?
Jeremy replies –   Yes. The idea is to take you out a few
                     times and get to know you. Maybe over a
                     drink. Or cinema, whatever.
Sarah asks –   But you'd probably want a relationship
                     with me and it would be embarrassing
                     and it would all go wrong
Jeremy replies –   I just think your a nice enough person to
                     want to spend some time with. Not
                     necessarily anything further.
Sarah asks –   But why would I ever go out with you,
                     you might be dangerous?
Jeremy replies –   Well I'm not. Of course your safety is of
                     paramount importance to you, but you
                     could bring someone with you or check
                     out who I am beforehand or even tell the
                     police where you are and who you are
                     with incase you're worried
Sarah asks –   But you write all this sexual stuff. You
                     must be weird.
Jeremy replies –   You're attractive. That's a good enough
                     reason to write sex stuff. I can't just write
                     you things like what library books I have
                     read recently, that's boring.
Sarah asks –   Why don't you ever give me your
                     surname or address?
Jeremy replies –   What's the point? You don't need to
                     know them.
Sarah asks –   Will you stop stalking me?
Jeremy replies –   No. I haven't even managed to find
                     Meridian studios on a map yet. I know
                     it's somewhere near New Hythe train
                     station I think. Anyway I'm a nice guy not
                     a criminal.
Sarah asks –   Are you really a fantastic lover?
Jeremy replies –   YES!!!!
Jeremy asks –   Sarah, do you deserve someone as
                     fantastic as I am?

Sarah replies —   YES!!!! I'm attractive and I've got a nice
                    figure[8]

There were more of these 'conversations' to come. They not
only represented what he hoped or imagined Sarah might
think about him, they also gave him the chance to plead his
case. He considered himself to be a good catch, attractive and
he insisted – despite certain other things he wrote – harmless.

The first explicit sexual overtures were contained in an
undated postcard. It was in an envelope which warned:

'There is some sex stuff in here, so beware. (Not much but
a bit.) Dare you read it? You might like what you read.'

The card, which is handwritten, contains a poem which
ends:

> Remember me without ill thought
> And I'll remember you
> To stalk you is a pleasure
> And I hope you think so too

In a boxed-off paragraph he says he is writing at 3.10 a.m. He
is trying to finish an assignment:

> I still have 1,000 words to write. I have less than 9 hours to
> hold my life together. I don't even have time to write on
> this card. My worlds are colliding. Remember Sarah, you're
> my biggest secret.

On the reverse he asks if being stalked sexually excites Sarah.
He 'hopes so':

> . . . After all you might as well enjoy being stalked. I'll be
> coming home soon anyway so you can get yourself wet
> then. And you can wear the jacket that shows your tits at
> their best with your bullet nipples.[9]

He apologises for sending a card which she might think crude
but says he is just in the mood to write this kind of thing.

* * *

His next letter contains some candour but it is superseded by what he has previously admitted is his 'arrogance':

> Not that I probably match up to any of your requirements. Too short, wear specs, English. If I market myself differently it is not so bad. Intelligent looking (i.e. with my sophisticated glasses), average height, well developed muscles (don't get your hopes too high I am not a Gladiator), English like you, that is something in common, masters degree in economics from the best business school in Britain (okay so it's top two or three, that's the same thing), also I have spoken to Rudiger Dornbusch over the phone. He is the top economist in the whole world and works at MTT [sic] in the states. This is my name-dropping claim to fame. (It impresses some people some time.) Also, some of the articles I have written and worked on are published in journals held in the library of the Bank of England this is good I think.
>
> Also I am someone who thinks he is great with women and they all want him (this is probably a delusion). Fantastic personality.[10]

He was now behaving very much as if *Meridian Tonight* was being screened for his personal benefit and Sarah was performing especially for him. He talked about the way she swivelled round in her chair; he said this was good because he could see how big her breasts were. He fancied himself as something of a romantic and obviously thought he had a disarming way with words:

> When I see you smile I wonder if your heart is as pure as your teeth are white. And you can wonder if any man in the world could make love to you more sweetly than the man who wrote these words to you.

At the tail end of a long and chatty letter he told her he was waiting for the Meridian news to come on the television:

> Are you on? The adverts are still on so I'll wait and see. La la la, dum dum dee dum tru lu la etc etc.

I was just humming while I was waiting for the news. There is a Nescafé advert on now, now a trailer for a show about sports or holidays here we are . . .

It's Alan Rook, not you.

Wherefore art thou Pocket Lockett?

Maybe you've been sacked for being late or being drunk on tv or you've run away to join the circus or you're ill. Or you kicked the bucket at the weekend. Oh dear I will come to your funeral if you are dead and will put your present (*one he has recently bought for her*) on top of your coffin before they fill you in. On the other hand you're probably sitting in the Meridian restaurant – too lazy to be bothered to present the news . . . Get off your lazy butt and start presenting. Or rather, sit on your perfectly proportioned rear end and present me some news.[11]

While Sarah was on holiday, Dyer diversified by writing to her colleague, Natasha Kaplinsky. He had mentioned her several times in his previous letters, sometimes saying she was attractive, at other times (here included) claiming he didn't want to make Sarah jealous. He described her as:

. . . the prettiest flower in Sarah Lockett's garden . . . but I'm sorry to disappoint you that I am only interested in Sarah Lockett. Being the second most attractive female presenter at Meridian should be enough for you, Natasha.[12]

He occasionally did this: gave other female presenters praise in an attempt, it could be supposed, to make Sarah jealous. Much later on, he enclosed a 'photo sheet' of six women, Sarah and his own ex-girlfriend included. He gave each marks out of ten in various categories such as 'sex appeal', 'person-ality' etc. He didn't give Sarah 'full points'. In fact, his ex-girlfriend was his favourite, Gabby Yorath (the presenter of the television programme, *On the Ball*) next and then Sarah. '. . . Just trying to keep you on your toes' he told her.[13]

His belief in himself as an attractive and eligible young man wavered only slightly from time to time. Mostly it was sure and constant:

My fantastic lover ego trip comes from
1. a fantastically attractive girl I once went out with . . .
   who has boosted my ego quite a bit (a woman I would
   marry in one second if she asked me)
2. my fantastic love-making abilities (which I will not
   disclose to you as you are still a perfect stranger to me
   and this is very private stuff) also because it would only
   be explainable in explicit detail which I will not write
   you, you will just have to guess the reason why I could
   be a fantastic lover
3. my own belief that most women fancy me as I look so
   great (e.g. muscles and looks)

Believe or disbelieve whatever you want or don't want from
the above. You will definitely meet me sometime anyway
when I get bored of letters etc.

He didn't always play the 'hopeless romantic' card – as one
would have expected him to. He writes later in the same
letter:

. . . You will also notice that I have never mentioned love in
my letters to you. This is quite deliberate. I would never tell
you 'I love you, Sarah' or write it to you as I have never met
you and therefore, how can I love you? But I do fancy you
abit and would probably love you if I ever got to know
you.[14]

Late one night in August, Jeremy cycled to the Meridian
studio and managed to get into the building. It was surprisingly easy: he simply waited for the cleaners to arrive and,
when the security guards buzzed them in, he followed along.
It was a disappointing visit since he didn't get any further
than the reception area. He spoke to the security guard,
boldly admitting that he was waiting for Sarah. He wasn't
allowed any further into the building. He tried to speak to
Sarah's colleague, Sue Kinnear:

. . . but she didn't want to speak to me. Infact I think she
was abit scared. She asked one of the security guys to walk

her to her car. This is not the idea or image I want to put across. I don't think I will visit the studio again.

He was evidently not pleased. Taking the rejection as a personal insult his tone is injured when he writes: 'Not that it is easy to get to the bloody place anyway. I had to cycle ages to get back to Maidstone East station . . .'

In fact he did come up twice more and was threatened with arrest if he didn't remove himself. He asks:

Do you like having someone giving you this attention? Like I am. Every celebrity needs a stalker. Oh well, there are good stalkers and bad stalkers and you my dear, are lucky enough to get a good one who sends you nice presents and writes you nice things. This is very much an interactive stalking case. With these letters etc. It doesn't do your image much harm to have someone stalking you like this. Maybe the other presenters are jealous because no one stalks them around.[15]

He eventually discovered that Sarah lived in Hastings. He wrote saying maybe he would come and visit her there. He continued:

You know the Perry Southall case? You mentioned it in your 'Headlines' bit on *Meridian Tonight*. Apparently Perry Southall (a Pam Anderson look-a-like) was stalked by a black psychopath who threatened her with a hammer and said he'd kill her. Also he sent her love letters and 'unwanted' presents.

I send you presents and letters. Oh no! Help!

Don't worry Super Sonic Pocket Lockett. God gave you a nice face and a nice stalker. So you are really quite lucky. I suppose I must be stalking you. I don't know.

(This doesn't stop us socialising together though.)

My uncle is a solicitor. Maybe I will ask him about the law as regards this situation.

. . . You are kind of like my project. Not a girlfriend . . . or a friend . . . but someone I'm interested in. Like maybe a girl

I would see at university but not know her, but still fancy her from afar and wait for an appropriate moment to approach her. Instead of seeing you in a lecture or at lunchtime I see you on tv. There is no real difference really.

He describes seeing a girl in his home town of Ashford who looks like Sarah adding: 'I will investigate her further, she may do as a Lockett substitute for a while, who knows.'[16]

Jeremy might even have had moments when it all seemed hardly worth the bother. He was about to go to university in Coventry to do a teacher-training course. 'This will mean I won't see you ever again. Or until I move back to Kent (if I ever did).'

. . . I suppose this is the best way to part. There is no point in me writing to you from somewhere else in Britain if I can't even see you on TV.

. . . You will probably know that I spoke to (the Senior Editor of *Meridian Tonight*) on Tuesday. He seems a nice enough guy. I said I would ring him back on Thursday to find out whether you would be willing to speak to me.

This sounds far too complicated for my liking. It was not my intention to really involve other members of Meridian in the contact I have with you. I certainly don't expect to have to go through the editor to find out if I can speak to you. He seemed to know all about me talking to your security guard. This was funny rather than anything else. Maybe everyone in the Meridian office has read all these letters. That is a good reason for not personalising them with my name and address.

I don't believe for one minute that you could be worried by someone posting you things like I do. As I've said and I'm sure you're aware, many women are terrorised, humiliated, assaulted, raped etc. . . . you really do feel threatened by me you might send the police round to my house. Even though I haven't done anything wrong. This makes me vulnerable. . . . it is not my intention to hassle you at all.

. . . Now for another question and answer session.

Sarah –   Jeremy, I am concerned by the unwanted letters you send me, infact I am abit worried. How long are you going to write to me and will you stop?

Jeremy – If you are worried, you shouldn't be. I just fancy you. It's not that amazing is it?

Sarah –   But it's not very normal to keep sending letters and presents is it?

Jeremy – Of course it isn't. But then I only see you on tv so what else can I do? If I worked near you or lived near you I could just talk to you but I don't. And if you are not around when I ring Meridian how can I talk to you apart from coming to the studio.

Sarah –   If I spoke to you on the phone would you stop contacting me?

Jeremy – If that's what you wanted. Of course I would stop writing. But if I can't talk to you how do I know you don't like the letters or gifts? And how do I know that you wouldn't want to meet me?

Sarah –   So what are you saying exactly?

Jeremy – Basically I am saying that I will continue to ring you and write to you until I get a chance to speak to you. Then I will find out one way or the other if you appreciate me contacting you or whether you would prefer it if I didn't contact you. If I rang Meridian and asked to speak to you and you told me that you definitely do not not [sic] want me to contact you again then I would stop immediately. On the other hand we could arrange a time to meet if you wanted that.[17]

Jeremy was bright enough to have made a success of teaching, but his tutors worried that his lack of communication skills were going to severely handicap him. Privately, he was still intent on becoming a stalker. There was a point where he considered Gabby Yorath as a suitable victim but he later wrote to Sarah, explaining with audacious pragmatism he could only be expected to stalk one person at a time:

I think she [Gabby Yorath] does her shows from Nottingham which is too far to go. Also I am too busy to spend all this time on her. However, she is veryyyyyyyyyy sexy. At the moment I am remaining faithful to you (in stalking terms anyway).[18]

Coventry is served by Central Television. He watched it, hoping to find a suitable victim nearer to his studies but none appealed. In this he displayed objectivity about his mental condition. Though it didn't override his genuine obsession with Sarah, it gave him the illusion of control over it. He was a stalker because he'd decided to be, not because he had a fixation. Sarah Lockett was just the most practical person to go for: it was always easy to have her reassuring image on his television screen.

Just before he left to begin his course at Warwick University, he wrote, ostensibly for the last time. He included his address and phone number. Sarah was relieved:

'I thought, if he does anything dodgy in the future, we know who he is,' she said. 'So I felt a lot more reassured. I sent him a letter saying "thank you for your interest in the programme. I hope you don't mind if I ask you not to contact me again, we're a very busy newsroom." He wrote a letter saying "Fine, it was a bit of fun. I hope you didn't mind. I won't write to you any more." '

He didn't write for three months and Sarah could have been forgiven for believing her nuisance 'fan' had given up. Then came the Christmas break and Dyer returned to his parents' home in Kent. He immediately began his campaign over again.

'Dearest Sarah . . .' (he resumes in a handwritten and hefty missive.) 'Do you know what I did yesterday?' (Here he digresses as he has, he says, seen a 'totally gorgeous woman' who he describes in some detail.)

'What he did yesterday' was buy a pocket TV on which, he writes, he's just watched the 2.35 news. He can now watch Sarah when he's 'out and about'.

He later explains:

. . . The reason I haven't written to you for so long is basically because it is good for me to separate my course —

(i.e. now/Christmas) – being silly writing you letters/
sending presents etc. Do you see now? You are kind of my
holiday project. As I have two weeks off from my Warwick
course I can spend time writing to you etc.

He says he can't be bothered to write to her during the time
he's at University: '. . . If I can't see you on Meridian then it
is as if you don't exist I suppose.'

He again makes reference to a celebrity stalking case, this
time to Martine McCutcheon who was was then playing
Tiffany in *EastEnders*. She had been terrified by an escapee
from a mental hospital. Jeremy comments:

> . . . He claimed to have sent her 'telepathic messages'
> advising her about her career, and is now demanding
> money from her for his services . . . This is such a cliche,
> wanting to kill some poor woman or extort money. That is
> why are so lucky having me as your 'guardian stalker'.
>
> Maybe you think I'm a real sad case. I don't know. It is
> not for me to tell you that I am not. Although I would
> accept conventional wisdom that most 'stalking case' seem
> to revolve around unemployed/mentally ill/social rejects.

He goes on to distinguish himself from these types, reiterating
that he has a degree, is doing well on his new course and has
written articles which have been published.

> . . . Anyway I see my contact with you as something that
> has perspective. It also lacks *aims/goals* which means it is
> continuous rather than discrete. It is something which is
> fun/ challenging/a test of ingenuity etc.
>
> . . . I do have an obsessive personality (which you have
> no doubt realised) at the moment at least. The interesting
> thing is that I have found it difficult to cultivate obsessions
> with some other women. I really like Gabby Yorath . . . This
> obsession never really developed properly though. So I
> have gone off her. I never got to writing to her or trying to
> contact her, only you!

. . . I went to Maidstone yesterday (where I posted the sweets to you from). I have decided to write the rest of this in the form of a *fictional story*.

One day a man went to Maidstone with a pocket tv and his little binoculars. In Maidstone he bought some chocolates which he posted to a pretty lady who was a tv presenter. Anyway, realising that she would be presenting the 10.15 news on 22.12.98 he thought up a plan of how to see her without disturbing the pretty lady. So he got on the choo choo train to New Hythe and pedalled off on his bike in search of her when he got off the choo choo train. After about 5 minutes he arrived at Meridianland. It was about 5 to 10. He knew the pretty lady was close by so he hid somewhere in case she saw him and told Mr Clark [Sarah's co-presenter] the evil king.

He was well prepared with his pocket tv and binoculars to see the pretty princess when she left Meridianland after the news.

After waiting awhile in the secret place, watching the princess on his pocket tv, he saw her come out of the Meridianland palace and walk across to her little black sports car. Then she zoomed off as quick as can be. The man then talked to the sentry at Meridianland briefly before biking away.

What do you think of the story?

OK so I was being abit devious, but never mind. At least I am keeping you fully informed. You see, this is a two way exchange. You know exactly what I'm up to. Anyway it was abit cold so I wont do that again. Also I had to cycle for *ages* to get back to bloody Maidstone. At least it didn't rain much. However, it was a total success. As I was undetected by *anyone*. How much can I trust you darling, to tell you all this? Please don't let me down pocket lockett as this just a bit of fun.

The pages which followed contained a map of where Sarah's car was parked with details of her movements from the studio. The map also showed where Jeremy Dyer hid and ended by saying the 'data' he had given her must be treated as confidential:

. . . ONLY TO BE DISCLOSED TO SARAH LOCKETT AS
PART OF LOCKETTWATCH BRIEFING. *NO ONE ELSE!*[19]

The next letter was handwritten on 22 small pages torn from
a pad his parents had brought back from holiday. Included in
these are the following passages:

> . . . I haven't decided whether sending you stuff/stalking
> you is emotionally fulfilling for me. It requires planning so
> that I don't make an idiot out of myself or humiliate myself.
> So far it's gone really well.

And later:

Sarah ~~writes~~ /– says	um, well, oh dear, . . . hello Jeremy how are you? Thanks for your new letters and all the other stuff.
Jeremy says –	I'm fine. Hope you like the chocolates.
Sarah says –	Yes they were very nice but you really don't need to send me things or write to me, even though i'm very flattered
Jeremy says –	I know I said I wouldn't write again after September . . . but . . . well
Sarah –	What are you going to do next?
Jeremy –	I don't know. Anyway, have faith in me pocket Lockett. Have I ever let you down.
Sarah –	I suppose not. But i'm still abit concerned about you, you must be a bit dodgy
Jeremy –	oh thanks, insult me why don't you. Let's up this conversation to a higher level. Most people who write to celebrities do it for a very short time or have a more sinister/disturbing motive such as threats etc or they are stalkers. your average stalker would want to sap your strength, wear you down, frighten you, upset you, humiliate you, attack you. This is all designed to empower the stalker at the expense of the victim.

continued 8:10 p.m.
Where was I . . .
Basically stalkers want 'power' over their stalkee. This is a fairly common if cliched characteristic. I don't have a problem with you (in contrast to most stalking experiences). Wow! Two *nice* girls have just sat near me in the bar. On the other hand maybe they're not that nice.
Anyway, I don't want power over you Sarah, my life is going well. That's why I can only stalk you part-time at the moment. As i've said you're kind of my holiday project. Anyway I see you as a *valid* part of my life.
1 My course is no 1 in the country
2 I went out with a girl – easily supermodel standard
3 my 'stalking victim' i.e. you is a beautiful girl
So, Sarah, I consider you good enough to bother about.
Sarah says: Yeah, but why should I think that you're good enough stalk me?
How can I answer that? Except that I've probably got more degrees than you. I'm a *great lover* . . . I'm sophisticated enough to make this work!

Giving the page the title,' philosophy' Dyer muses about wild animals which have become extinct. Does it matter, he ponders, when we have them on film? After all, this is the only way most people would ever see them anyway. He uses this proposal as another tenuous link to his favourite subject, Sarah:

what about your own situation? Appearing on tv. Do you see it as an invasion of privacy? That people might keep you on video for the next 1,000 years? I suppose it is the same for anyone as far as photographs are concerned. But for you it's a more thought provoking situation.

The letter is rambling, some of it is written after an evening in a pub. He signs off in poetic style (using a phrase he has used before and boasts he's quite pleased with): 'I'll write again, before the brightness of the sun can compete with the brightness of your smile.'[20]

In his next letter he says he has decided to write once a week on Saturdays (he didn't stick to this idea for more than a couple of weeks). He continues:

> . . . Now I will get back to dodgy stalker stuff (after I get a new lager from my cupboard). Here we go, yeah, basically if I write stuff to you about my life it should be reassuring to you. In other words, the information I give you necessarily constrains me. I.e. I have alot to lose. This creates an equivalence in this stalking situation. It creates balance. On the other hand my course finishes on July the 2nd so I can devote the summer to you (apart from looking for a job that is). I don't yet know how important you are to me that I would choose a job specifically in the Meridian region 'just to see you' I don't know yet. In that sense I will find out things about myself at this later stage.

He then indulges in some juvenile smut, saying a particular jacket she wears shows her 'tits' well. He goes on at some length on this subject. Later, he includes this list:

Advantages of having a stalker
- they send you nice presents
- they flatter you with nice letters
- you can see having a stalker 'as a status symbol' of your celebrity level
- you can brag about having a stalker and make others jealous if they don't have one
- you can rely on them to protect you where necessary

Disadvantages of having a stalker
- they may send you offensive/threatening letters
- they may send you presents such as dead animals, razor blades, broken glass, etc.
- they may plan to kidnap/rape/kill you
- they may try to get you in trouble with your work
- adverse publicity damaging your image/career
- they may burgle your house
- they may insult/humiliate you to your colleagues

- they may follow you around making scenes in public etc embarrassing you

Bugger, I have just notice that there are more disadvantages than advantages to having a stalker. Oh well never mind, as I've said before you have a good stalker (as in the Wizard of Oz, there are good witches and bad witches).

It does you no harm at all to remind you how nasty some stalkers are. In fact it should make you please that you have such a nice one.

. . . Always remember the golden rule of all stalkers (which I have just invented) – 'If your stalker walks during your sleeping hours, is he your dream or your nightmare?

If you can choose, then be sure to kiss him goodnight before you go to bed and he will be your dream'

. . . for as long as you continue to kiss him goodnight.[21]

The new year, 1999, looked set to be one where Sarah would continue to be plagued by Jeremy. His letter of 23 January says:

. . . Maybe you have someone advising you on how to handle situations of unwanted attention or stalking. I don't know. The probable advice you would receive would be to be polite at all times . . . to not get involved in any way with the stalker . . . to not react to things they ask you to do, or react to things they do. Is this true or not?

It is difficult to know how best to handle this sort of situation. Bearing in mind that whatever you do, you stalker will probably not go away. In some sense having no contact with your stalker may encourage your stalker because

- a stalker is someone who usually seeks your attention in some way and therefore will try even harder to contact you meet you etc. If they are thwarted at most attempts
- the nature of stalking is one of a lack of relationship with the person you are stalking. What I mean by this is e.g. if I saw you each week or met you regularly I couldn't send letters or write the things I write etc. because I would

have some (social) relationship with you. I don't have
that with you which makes it easy to carry on like this.
Do you understand what I mean?

Whatever the situation I will find out which jacket shows
your breasts off best and write to you at Easter. Then you
can decide what to do. Whether to wear it or not. You see,
you get choices here . . .

He goes back to his earlier assertion that he is a 'good stalker':

. . . Proper stalkers would want to intimidate or frighten
you. This is primarily done by devious or random effect.
I.e. you never know what is going to happen next. Or bad
things happen to you. By now you should be pretty relaxed
about getting letters/parcels from me.

In the next letter he sends, he decides he will include some:

. . . sexually explicit stuff and put it in a sealed envelope (so
you can decide whether you want to read it or not). You see
I even protect your delicate little eyes from potentially
offensive stuff so you can't moan that I'm a sicko type.[22]

Towards the end of February, in another of his longer
communications, (the one in which he considers stalking
Gabby Yorath as well as Sarah,) he assures his victim:

Anyway you know by now that I'm not dangerous to you.
Otherwise I would have done something by now and I
haven't. Anyway I'm too professional for that rubbish. I see
you on telly enough (when I'm in Kent) so I don't need to
see you in real life too much by following you around all
the time. I just need to [be] obsessed with something in my
life as I am an obsessive person. I could try and become
obsessed with work and reading etc for my course but that
doesn't work. So far nothing has gone wrong in our
relationship.

I think you are quite a stable person which is good. Just
ignore me Sarah. No don't ignore me I've changed my

mind. If you meet me you might be quite angry with me I suppose or scared I might do something to you. I hope you don't think this. After all prison is not my idea of fun and I'm not an idiot. I'm just a bit dodgy that's all. But nothing you need to worry about. I enjoy stalking you and I hope you enjoy being stalked. When you asked me not to ring you at work – I haven't done since, have I. So who is doing the controlling here. You are. You asked me not to ring you and I haven't. Because you've got work to do and phone calls from a stalker are annoying and unprofessional.

. . . I've already been such an idiot by sending you my address, telling you university stuff, signing letters etc. This is called incrimination evidence I think. If you choose to call it that, Sarah. So basically you already have enough information about me to prove I'm dodgy and that I'm harassing you/stalking you.

But on the other hand, I would like to think that everything I have sent you is acceptable to you. Not ringing you up is something I have agreed to do. That is what makes this such fun. You can consent to being stalked and I can stalk you darling.

Because you know you are perfectly safe as I was such a twat to give you my address etc. Oh well, never mind. As I have said all along, have faith in me. I can be obsessed with you while retaining the *important* principle of not compromising you etc.

In fact it is even nicer that you can accept what I am doing. It makes it even more exciting. We can explore the boundaries of stalking, together, without anyone ever knowing – unless you want them to. We can both get some sexual kicks from the danger (or at least I can). I want this to remain at a professional level and for you to accept that I am obsessed with you, but conversely, to accept that I have a structured and disciplined enough life to channel things into positive but nonetheless satisfying directions.[23]

The body of most of these letters are not offensive, do not refer to his stalking and are not sexual in content. There follows an example which is fairly typical. As Sarah herself says, it appeared he wanted her most of all as a friend and confidante; he just wanted someone to share his thoughts with:

My parents rang me at about 6 p.m. today.
(If you were a stalker you could start putting some pieces of information together here).
1 Jeremys parents probably aren't divorced
2 Jeremys parents are both alive
3 Jeremy has a good relationship with his parents
The list is endless, darling, you just have to think abit.
   Anyway, of course all these things are true. Excuse me while I go and get an apple pie (a Mr Kipling individual one if you're really nosy).
   Who the hell is Mr Kipling anyway? Did he invent apple pies or something? Did he start the company? I don't usually buy them but you get 8 for the price of 6 so I did.
   Getting back to my parents (I will have to go to Tescos soon before they shut at 10 p.m. – just up the road as you already know) they are well, didn't have alot of news. My sister is visiting them tomorrow.
   You have at least one sister don't you. I remember you saying on M Ton sometime. Does she look like you? Do you have brothers? What about your mum and dad? Are they in telly?
   My sister has a brother (ha ha)
   I'm not going to go to Tescos now. I'll go tomorrow.
   You see what you're doing to me. Wrecking my life by stopping me buying beer and muffins and other junk.[24]

In a letter which he admits was written when he was drunk, but which he decided to send anyway, Jeremy says he is getting bored with stalking Sarah. It is, he says, getting to be nothing but a one-sided routine.

   . . . There is no interaction between us. Just watching you on telly and stalking you part-time.

He reiterates he doesn't want to go to prison. Sex with Sarah, he says, would mean nothing if she wasn't a consenting partner.

> . . . if I say Darling Sarah, your safety lies in the law (and me not wanting to go to prison), you should at least believe this. I question whether I love you or if I could. It is probably a bad point in my character that I could be obsessed with a woman I have *still* never met.

He acknowledges Sarah might well be questioning his state of mind and goes on to list points about him which he invites her to categorise as negative or positive. 'See which predominates.' Most of these are the usual boasts about his love-making prowess but number seven gives cause for concern:

'I have fantasised about becoming a serial killer.'

And the last, number 14 says:

'I'm probably sociopathic (look it up in a book)'.

A separate note is enclosed which reads:

'Sarah, If you don't want me writing to you any more . . . wear your blue jacket with the split down the front on Friday 9th April . . . or you have me for life.'[25]

8 March 1999:

> Hi!
> Guess what?
> I've just discovered an interesting thing about your name.
> If you reverse the name Sarah it becomes . . .
> Haras.
> That's only one letter away from the word harass as in Harassment.
> Reading it out loud sounds exactly the same.
> haraS Sarah.
> My true purpose is finally revealed to me. Harass Sarah[26]
> . . .

At Easter Jeremy was back in Kent. Because he was able to watch Sarah on the television again, he saw this as the resumption of their 'liaison'. He was away from his computer and was writing by hand on lined paper:

My parents are *so* supportive of me pocket Lockett. Put it this way, I'm 29½ and I've never done a decent days work in my life, *ever* . . .

Okay, lets have a strategy meeting. How is our stalking experience going?

what do we want out of easter?

1 Re-establish our relationship
2 launch 'operation Lockett watch – Easter'
3 Send some letters, presents etc
4 watch Sarah on M. Ton.
5 other

Another idea I had was to give you an opportunity to get rid of me. This is your chance to get rid of your 'annoying stalker' or to show you 'don't mind' me writing to you etc.

> so, if you (Sarah Lockett) wear your blue Jacket with the split down the front on meridian Tonight on Friday 9th April – I (Jeremy) will stop *all* contact with you . . . forever. If you don't wear it I will continue to write . . . forever

Underneath is a childishly drawn picture of 'Sarah thinking' and a 'thought bubble' which says:

Hmm, what does this mean? Is Jeremy serious, what shall I do, *wear the jacket* and reject him completely, risking turning him into an 'evil stalker'. *Not wear the jacket* and have him continue stalking me, *wear the jacket* and risk being controlled by a stalker. *Not wear the jacket* and appear to be encouraging him to stalk me. *Wear the jacket* and Jeremy might keep writing – making it a waste of time

He goes on:

This is the essence of clever stalking, Sarah. Think of it like a chess game. In chess this is calle [sic] Zugzwang (forcing your opponent into making bad move).

It's not that I'm forcing you to make a bad move (as there can never be bad moves for us darling) or that I'm even forcing you to make a decision.

All I am doing is giving you an opportunity to decide things for yourself. Your views are valid and to be respected, as are mine.

Okay, that's the end of our strategy meeting.[27]

Monday 5 April 12.10 a.m. He tells Sarah he's now 'very obsessed' with her: '. . . if obsession is something you can do to "very" levels, that is. The obsession I have with you is positive at the moment. However, I don't know where it is going.'

He warns her he will be 'bombarding' her with letters over the next couple of weeks and adds a note in the margin: 'as all good stalkers should do'. These dubious comments are submerged in innocent chit-chat in another handwritten letter. He once again proposes to visit the studio. He also makes one or two references to being Sarah's 'guardian stalker'.

Then, in the last paragraph he tells her he might borrow his father's car in which he would be able to follow her home from work – if only he had a driving licence. It could be read as a joke; it might be a threat.

Finally he writes he's going to employ someone in Kent to video Meridian News for him and post it to Coventry. He'll tell this person he needs the tapes as part of his studies – a ruse, he says, they're bound to fall for.

'Darling pocket Lockett this just gets better and better.'[28]

In March 1999, Sarah became engaged to her boyfriend, Peter. Seeing her wearing a ring was a major shock for Dyer.

I am questioning whether I want to continue contacting you. Especially as I noticed a ring on your (engagement?) finger. Are you engaged or was it a wedding ring? Or is it some other kind of ring? It seems things have changed since christmas.

If you have got engaged or married I suppose congratulations are in order. Even though it depresses me to think of you with a man.

You will have children I suppose and be happy. Maybe it is the right time to stop contacting you. The fact that you may be engaged or married changes the situation greatly.

It depresses me to think that you would have sex with a man. Even though I don't know you. Ultimately your life is none of my business whatsoever though. This is the mind of a stalker. Everything I have ever written to you is irrational I suppose. So this is no more so.

Think of these words and think of me feeling sad:
For nearly one year I have love every inch of you
But from today I will always hate one of your fingers
The finger that holds your ring.

This isn't supposed to be a poem or have any literary merit it just lets you know how I feel.

I will console myself with watching Man United play Juventas tonight.

What is your husband or husband-to-be like?
I wonder.
what does it take to make love to you forever?

I have just rung Meridian. Your switchboard man has told me you got engaged a couple of weeks ago. I expect you will marry in the summer.

That was written on Wednesday 7 April at 4 p.m. At 11.30 on the same day, Dyer was still brooding:

. . . I guess you will no longer be presenting the late Meridian news. This saves me the bother of turning up at Meridian studios again.

Maybe I will give you my Kent phone number/address or the same for coventry. As I have said I am getting bored with this abit. No 'relationship' can be a one way street indefinitely.

He tells her he went to the studios the previous Tuesday night, even though he was aware she was not working.

. . . it is no coincidence that we have never met Sarah. I know when you present and when you don't present. I saw you leaving the studios at Christmas (as I wrote to you at the time) from my 'stalking centre' at UK paper across the road from Meridian studio.

He managed to get inside the reception area but was almost immediately challenged by a security guard. Although he gave a false name, the guard soon guessed who he was. Jeremy was asked to leave and did so without very much fuss. It seems he did all this simply to demonstrate that he could.

He closes with a PS with some crude observations about Sarah (he refers, as he has frequently done before, to her 'jelly bumps'). He signs off: 'And remember, you look much more beautiful when you're not wearing that ring.'[29]

Sarah's engagement had certainly not put Jeremy off his 'project'. Two days later he was musing on whether or not she actually wanted him to stop. He noted she didn't wear her blue jacket on the Friday night (his proposed 'signal' that Sarah wanted him to cease communication). He was aware enough to wonder if this was because of a prerecorded section in which she had worn a black jacket which she then had to keep for continuity.

He rang the Meridian newsroom with a story, as he later explained to Sarah:

The story was about a woman called Sarah from Maidstone who had got a piece of metal stuck on her finger. I'm not sure if the woman got the joke (i.e. your engagement) but I said my name was Jeremy and she said she would pass the story on.

The characters he goes on to introduce could easily be the product of any youth who has read too much 'action' fiction. When they represent the alter-egos of a disturbed man, it is foolish for anyone to believe his assurances that he is 'not dangerous'.

I am considering some aliases for myself. Here they are

Name	Definition/Description
Jeremy	Me in reality
Mr Chuckles	A lunatic. Has a warped fascination with clown as sinister rather than fun individuals. Dangerous.
The Cleaner	Not 'domestic staff' but an assassin. The Cleaner refers to his ability to eliminate people efficiently. A James Bond character – but on the wrong side.
Mr John Charles	Similar style to the Krays. A London East-end gangster type. He is 'thick' but people respect him for his charity donations. He's nice to his mum.

Summary – and points out of ten for each characteristic

	Fear factor	Intelligence	Sex appeal	Mentally ill
Jeremy	3	9	9	0
Mr Chuckles	9	2	0	10
The Cleaner	6	10	10	0
Mr Johnny Charles	8	0	2	4

I am probably closest to The Cleaner. Who would you be?
. . . This is the sort of message The Cleaner might leave:

> What do you do If you don't
> have the key to a door?
> Answer – make sure you're
> already on the inside
> when they Lockett.

This is the sort of message Mr Chuckles might leave:
What's the difference between blood and a milkshake?
Answer – I don't like milkshakes.[30]

This provoked a response from the regional editor of *Meridian Tonight*. Without seeing any contradiction in his actions, Jeremy replied, not to the editor but to Sarah:

> I am only in Kent until the weekend anyway. After that I return to Coventry. So I will cease my letters to you.

. . . Enjoy the summer Sarah. I can't promise you that I wont surface somewhere in the summer. As I say I have things to work on. Au revoir Sarah, rather than goodbye.

. . . When it is time for me to forget you Sarah I will, until then I can't.

By the way, before I forget, I will be employing someone in Kent to post *all* your April, May, June *Meridian Tonights* to me in Coventry. I will tell them it is for a University of Warwick news database. They will never suspect a thing. I will tell the person we need a regional news contributor (News Gatherer) to cover the Kent region.

Mr Chuckles and The Cleaner send their love.[31]

Like a tedious guest who is reluctant to leave, Jeremy waited for five days before saying 'goodbye' yet again: 'This is the last letter I will ever write to you Sarah'. He then adds the word 'probably' in parenthesis. He is aggrieved at having received the letter from the regional editor. He seems particularly worried at the suggestion that, should he persist, the company would not hesitate to involve the police.

What's the worst thing I have ever done to you anyway?
Sent you unwanted stuff (letters, presents, etc.)
Rung up now and then
Turned up abit at Meridian studio (without a scene ever occurring)
Mentioned jelly bumps etc
That's it really. Do you really not want me to write to you?

Before you turn me over to the police – to get life in prison – for posting chocolates to a lady remember you will be *wrecking my whole life completely*. As I say, I have never done anything malicious to you because that is not the purpose of writing to you. I am not a proper stalker I just fancy you abit. I thought you understood that most of what i wrote to you was tongue in cheek etc. I thought you were a nice person (and still do).

Maybe I will write (to the Editor) explaining things.

He goes on with his usual affable ramblings and includes another, typical, sexual reference. He says he can't guarantee

Sarah won't hear from him again 'sometime ... somewhere ...' He points out that she is one of the few people at Meridian he hasn't actually spoken to:

> You have remained as elusive and as difficult to catch as a butterfly.
> Like I say Sarah, I am involved too heavily with you to just 'drop you'. It will have to be a gradual process if at all. I wont go into any details yet.

Despite the statement at the top of the letter, he then declares (with a 'Hooray!') that someone has just rung him about 'the job' (taping Meridian shows). He thinks this is a 'foolproof plan' and says he will let Sarah know when he receives the first tape.

> ... Now I will address the issue of the letter sent recently by (the regional editor of *Meridian Tonight*). I have thought this through for a while and here's my proposal.
> What Jeremy will do from now on
> - write to you occasionally at Meridian
> - read papers etc to find out more about you
> What Jeremy won't do from now on
> - phone Meridian
> - Fax Meridian
> - post you parcels
> - post you letters with things written on the envelope e.g. pictures or words (e.g. jelly bumps)
> - turn up at Meridian studios*

> The criteria above are intended to provide you with some control of this situation. Unless you choose to tell them, no one will know that I am still writing to you. This is intended as a *genuine* compromise with you. Think about it Sarah.
> You can ring me on (*gives number and adds a handwritten note* 'please do not release this number to others') (evenings

---

*This last was handwritten – maybe as an afterthought.

and weekends) this number gets you through to my bedroom via the university switchboard.

if you need to 'in an emergency' (sic). I would appreciate you not writing to me at the Kent address again.

Please do not abuse the information you have about me.

As I say I was very disappointed in you. It wasn't very nice to receive a letter mentioning the police. Infact I will send you a copy of the letter incase you didn't see it.

He adds a handwritten page which says he's thinking of sending Ian (the person he goes on to call his 'stalker's assistant' who is able to tape the Kent news), to Meridian studios: '. . . to meet Sarah Lockett. "To obtain photos and publicity material for use as apart of a Warwick University database" I may get him to go there pretending to be Jeremy (I will tell him he must pretend to be me as I can't go in person).'[32]

On 26 April came the tragedy with which Sarah's case was linked in all subsequent press reports. *Crimewatch* presenter, Jill Dando was shot dead (*see* Chapter 6). To Jeremy Dyer it was enough that it was a newspresenter who had been killed. He often seemed to feel the need to discuss his thoughts on the subject:

My feelings are that if the murderer was a contract killer he behaved quite bizarrely. Hanging around for about 1 hour before hand. Also why does he have to be a contract killer to shoot her through the head? Any idiot could do it (e.g. The Cleaner, who I told you about!)

Maybe it was a stalker. But psychologists have said stalkers *never* kill their stalkee. Or if they did they would do it in a more passionate/emotional/frenzied way. This is probably true. Why shoot someone through the head? Who knows. I can't say I would ever want to stalk Jill Dando. She wasn't anything special to me.

. . . you looked abit miserable on the Monday show. I supposed you would be considering Jill Dando just got her brains blow out by a probable stalker.

Oh well, never mind, as they say.

The inferences people would be bound to draw from what he writes suddenly occur to him. A complete non-sequitur on the last page reads: 'Sarah – If anyone ever contacts you asking about me – deny all knowledge of me. It should be impossible, as noone knows about you (so this is just precautionary).'

He then writes about what he calls 'Serial Killer Olympics': he lists Sarah's name, his own and his 'aliases' but gives up, saying he will continue in another letter. He adds a hand-written P.S.:

By the way, I have worked out a theory on why Jill Dando was murdered.
1. Jill rhymes with kill
2. Dead rhymes with head
3. She used to read news BULLETins

Simple, when you have the right kind of mind. 'Kill Jill Dead with a Bullet through the Head'[33]

He was reported to the police immediately and Sarah recalls how they blanched when they first saw the Dando references. However, Dyer was eliminated from their inquiries and was left to carry on his harassment. In court he said he'd assumed Sarah would be interested in Jill Dando's murderer and was simply sharing that interest with her.

One of Jeremy's 'jokes' followed. It's a typed letter, purporting to be from a 'Sandra Evans' who says she hopes Miss Lockett doesn't mind her son, Jeremy, writing 'but he's been in hospital recently'. 'She' says she's a lecturer at the university and letters for 'Jeremy' can be sent to her address. Enclosed is another letter written as if from a child:

Dear Sarah
I am five years old. I like your jelly Bumps. My dad likes your jelly Bumps too. My Mum doesn't like your jelly Bumps though.
I went to scool today and played with my toys when I got home.
I did sums at school $5 = 7 + 12$

I am good at sums. I saw you on tv. My dad says he'd make you come but I don't know what he means.
Love from Jeremy, age 5.[34]

The Jill Dando references persisted. On 17 May, in a boxed section (because 'it's sick so I have put it in a box to separate from the rest of this letter'), he writes:

> Jack and Jill went up the hill to fetch a pale of water
> Jack fell down and broke his crown
> And Jill got shot by stalker

He says he has been accessing some pornographic websites on his flatmate's computer (which he lists). Then, after several pages, he ends with:

By the way I have found another really good porno web site. It is of a woman in a red jacket sitting with her mouth slightly open. She has a cheeky 'Take me here, Take me now' look on her face. You can see that she has very good skin and that her breasts would be delightful to caress. She is wearing red and black, the two colours of sex.

Does she sound familiar?

I don't know, this kind of perverted filth should be banned from the internet it just encourages stalkers and lunatics like that to become obsessed with vulnerable little ladies who can't help sticking their tits out or wearing provocative clothing whenever they get the chance on tv. encouraging these people even more.[35]

Sarah's co-presenter received a letter headed 'Southern Area Recreation and Humour Ltd. An Associated Company of Pocket Toys Inc. . . . Chuckle House' (and a London address). It pretends to be offering a free gift on behalf of this 'major supplier of jokes, toys and magic tricks'.

If you reply to this letter within seven days we will send you a free saw, as used in several of our tricks including the famous sawing a persons head off trick. You will also receive a free red clowns nose.

Why not get a presenter colleague to practice the trick on you?

Please don't blame us if they get the trick wrong and really do saw your head off though![36]

The letter is signed 'Simon Talker'.

As if this constant barrage wasn't enough, Sarah Lockett's fears escalated one day in June '99 when she arrived home to find one of Jeremy's letters on her mat. For the few sickening moments it took to discover otherwise, she believed Jeremy had at last found where she lived. In fact he hadn't. He'd sent the letter c/o Sarah's old university who had forwarded it, together with a compliment slip assuring her that no personal details had been divulged and asking if she would prefer not to receive any other forwarded mail. The letter itself is oblivious to the reactions Jeremy has encountered. Its implied purpose is to demonstrate his ability to find new ways of getting to her. It's short and, as had so often been the case before, appears to be an innocent communication from an old friend:

Dear Sarah,
Hope you get this letter! Give me a ring soon and we can have chat. I don't have a forwarding address for you so this is the easiest way to write to you. I haven't seen you for so long. Did you end up working in television? Are you still a chocolate addict?
Best Wishes
Jeremy.[37]

It was now June, 1999, almost a year since Jeremy Dyer had first contacted Sarah. The police were increasingly concerned about the possible outcome of Jeremy's 'project'. He then wrote:

I am enclosing some stalker stuff from the net. Hope you find it interesting reading. I have concluded that you don't really mind having me around. Good. As I have always said you have nothing to worry about from me. Just don't write anything horrible to me or call the police and everything will be lovely.

. . . I have just heard on the radio that police believe the gun in the Jill Dando murder was purchased in a Midlands pub. Oh no! The police are onto me.

[Then, immediately afterwards] Did you watch the euro song contest? I did. What a sexy blonde baby the winner was . . . the relationship we have is strictly Stalker/victim rather than boyfriend/girlfriend

. . . As I have said I enjoy having you as an obsession. Someone to stalk etc. Whether you like this or not is really irrelevant. Stalkers are selfish of course and are motivated by self interest.

This doesn't mean that I will want to insult or hurt you. I don't. I like you. I wouldn't become a malicious stalker as this means I would be wasting time and money contacting someone I hated. If I hated you I would not bother to contact you at all.

The bottom line is that even though I write you nice letters and send presents etc. You can never afford to take me for granted. Ultimately you are dependent on my maintaining good will towards you. There is no reason why I should lose this though. It is for you to make sure that you do not upset me as I have not intention of upsetting you. Even though we may be stalker/victim I like to think you are happy enough with me and that you can enjoy being stalked abit. I am sure you prefer being stalked by man rather than a woman. If a woman stalked you how would you feel?

Please don't write to me further even though you have addresses *unless* you are sending me a nice letter or photo. I regret giving you the opportunity to get rid of me over easter. As I have said I cannot stop writing to you easily so please don't ask me to. Try to enjoy these letters and J-re-y. Life is too short for everyone, to be miserable.

I hope you enjoy reading the serial killer stuff. I will write the one for The Cleaner soon. If you think it is sick, well never mind IT IS SICK! And so am I. But what do you expect from me.

Just be pleased that I am not malicious towards you and that you can continue with your life in perfect peace.

Jill Dando's death seems totally pointless. If I was stalking Jill Dando I would have KIDNAPPED HER OR DONE SOMETHING ELSE TO HER RATHER THAN SHOOTING HER THROUGH THE HEAD [*The upper-case portion is written in 'Dingbats': a font which uses symbols and pictures instead of letters and thus serves as a makeshift code.*]

How can you enjoy shooting someone in the head? Unless you hate them of course. It seems a waste of a victim if you ask me. He could have used her before killing her e.g. by RAPING, ASSAULTING HER. [*In Dingbats again.*] Getting his moneys worth as it were.

This is as honest as I can be Sarah, telling it as I see it.

He then includes a couple of pages of a 'Serial Killer profile' – 'No 2 – Sarah Lockett'. It is mostly pornographic imagery, describing necrophilia in prurient detail. He gives 'ratings' out of ten for various aspects of his character's personality: then he switches back to chit-chat, enclosing a map of Strathclyde University.

So you can see where I studied my masters degree . . . Coincidentally the maternity hospital (Rotten Row Maternity Hospital) where Ian Brady (as in Ian Brady and Myra Hindley) was born is featured in the photo. My label 'Brady born here' shows the building. You will notice it is quite an old building unlike most of others in the surrounding area.

Even when I tell you normal things it seems we can't get away from mass murder.

This thick envelope also contains scribbled notes, presumably the ones Jeremy made to remind him of what he intends to include in his letters.

One of them refers to Sarah's fiancé, Peter. It says: 'Ring K.M. – I worked with him. What company does he work for now? Can I find him (on) Reuters Business TV link . . .' From this it can be supposed that Jeremy is planning to track Peter down under the pretence of being an ex-colleague.

There is also the draft of a letter to the regional editor:

I was interested to receive your letter [it begins]. It may come as a surprise to you that I have never actually met Sarah Lockett in person or ever spoken to her on the telephone.

I hope not meeting me and not speaking to me on the phone has not caused Sarah too much distress. I have not attempted to meet Sarah in person, although I have had the opportunity to. I have not rung Meridian and asked for Sarah personally since I received a letter from her dated 7th September 1998. This is because Sarah asked me not to in the nicest of all possible ways.

He quotes from Sarah's letter which politely says 'I am always pleased, of course, to know that viewers enjoy my contribution to the programme, especially when they contact me to say so', and he goes on:

Of course I can read between lines and am obviously aware that Sarah did not ask me to start writing to her. However, since I have been writing to her I have not been aware that this was a necessary concern of hers. I have attempted to reassure Sarah, through my letters, that I have only the most positive of thoughts towards her.

Then more notes:

In the summer I promise to come and visit you somewhere.
I'm looking forward to the summer . . .
I will return . . . definitely
In the summer I will /come looking for you.
Finders keepers
losers peters
Come summer 99, you're mine
When I come back with my chalk,
I'll teach you a lesson[38]

Jeremy Dyer had gone too far and for too long. He was arrested shortly after this last letter. The police raided his digs in Coventry. In his bedroom they found a kitchen knife, a legal textbook on harassment and a guide he was writing – on how to be a stalker. On 10 January 2000, he was sentenced to two and a half years. He was released in September, 2000.

Sarah Lockett has left Meridian Television and is now freelancing.

6. NOT HIMSELF

In Crookham Road, Fulham, his neighbours knew him affectionately as 'Mad Barry'. They coped well enough with most of his eccentricities, though Queen, his favourite rock band, playing at headache volume, did prove to be something of a trial. He also had a worrying habit of patting females on the bottom and asking them to kiss him: somebody should have had words with him about that but, well – Mad Barry was harmless enough.

It was easy to have a laugh at his expense: like when he donned his 'Freddie Mercury' string vest and danced up and down Crookham Road with a fake microphone; or when he marched around in a fluorescent jacket with a walkie-talkie, pretending to be a traffic warden. Local children took malicious delight in his regular appearances in combat fatigues, when he would wield a toy gun and chase them on his roller skates.

Mad Barry lived in a squalor that belied the extravagant lies he told about his past exploits and the famous people he was related to. The local authorities had known about him for fifteen years and saw no special reason to be concerned. As everybody knows, London is full of his sort.

In 1991, he was using the name 'Barry Bulsara'. He was about to become famous throughout Britain as the man who shot Jill Dando.

Jill Dando was hugely popular: a 'household name'. Physically, she bore a passing resemblance to the late Diana, Princess of Wales. As a BBC television presenter, her friendly, reassuring good looks and easy style had endeared her to millions. Most recently she had been the co-host of the *Crimewatch* programme in which real-life crimes are represented by actors and appeals are made in order to help bring the perpetrators to justice.

At 11.30 a.m. on 26 April 1999, Ms Dando arrived back from a brief shopping trip. She was about to open the front door of the house she was selling in Gowan Avenue, Fulham. Things were going from good to better for her. That very week she was launching her new series, *Antiques Inspector*, and in the autumn she was planning to marry gynaecologist Dr Alan Farthing. At 38, she was successful, fulfilled and happy.

In only a few seconds her life was taken from her. Someone put a gun to her left ear and fired a single shot; the bullet ripped through her head and lodged itself in a flowerbed. The killer then walked away, leaving Ms Dando's body to be discovered some fifteen minutes later by a neighbour. As the woman frantically called for help, Ms Dando's mobile phone rang from inside her bag. It was a call she would never answer.

In May 2000, just over a year after Ms Dando was shot, Bulsara, under his real name of Barry Michael George, was arrested and charged with her murder.

In George's early life, a familiar pattern may be discerned: even before he was born, his parents' marriage was on the verge of collapse. George was the youngest of three children and had to learn bitter lessons early; his mentally retarded elder sister and his parents' unhappy union were always going to stand in the way of his own need for attention. Though there were danger signals, his mother and father had neither the expertise nor the necessary support to enable them to help him. Awaiting him was a downward spiral of lonely, desperate fantasy mixed with frustration. Barry George was never going to be the hunk he'd always hero-worshipped. He was never going to be able to live up to the ideal of aggressive masculinity that he saw in his father. Instead, he created an imaginary world where these things were possible. Indeed, Barry George could be said to be another Mark Chapman; the similarities between the two men's stories are frighteningly obvious.

He was born on 15 April 1960 to Margaret and Alfred 'Paddy' George at Hammersmith Hospital in West London. The family had only just moved into an unwelcoming block in Creighton Close, only a minute's walk from the BBC's headquarters in White City. Paddy, a truck driver, was at that time a volunteer 'special constable' in the Metropolitan Police

Force. He was also an army man. Barry's grandfather had served with T.E. Lawrence, better known as 'Lawrence of Arabia'. A photograph, which Barry loved, showed Paddy as a toddler, sitting on the very motorbike on which Lawrence was eventually killed. Paddy presented himself as masculine through and through: a 'hard man'.

This macho image was something the young Barry fervently wanted to live up to. Paddy George left his family in 1967 and, for Barry, nobody would ever fill the gap he left. Though he continued to see his father at weekends, the effects of his parents' divorce were evident. He couldn't settle to his studies and, as a result, attended three or four different primary schools in succession. At the tender age of ten, he was expelled for hitting a teacher. This incident has been held up as evidence of his latent violence but, as the teacher in question had just given George a caning, it could with equal justification be interpreted as a show of spirit.

His parents had always been aware that he was a slow developer. His father freely admits that his son was 'two sandwiches short of a picnic'[1] but blames Barry's later social and sexual deviancy on medication taken to control his epilepsy. This may have some validity but, at the very least, George's increasing and overwhelming desire to be tough, manly and important compounded his problems. The reality of his dull, underachieving self was too much to bear.

He was sent to a 'special' school for 'maladjusted' boys: Northcroft in Shepherd's Bush. Not yet a teenager, Barry George was already a social outsider.

Some of George's displays of aggression were more worrying than others. He once attacked his sister, Susan, and was dragged off her by other members of the family, who thought him quite capable of killing her. (As well as her mental problems Susan was, like her brother, an epileptic. When, in 1986, she died as the result of swallowing her tongue during a fit, George was heartbroken.)

Adolescent anger might give parents and teachers cause for concern, but it isn't exactly uncommon. Most young men, and it is more often males, grow out of such thuggery and settle down to become normal, responsible members of society.

True, there are those who take their time about this but they are rarely seen as psychotic: it's hardly surprising that George's darker problems went unnoticed and uncured.

Even so, it was evident he needed help. It was provided in part at Heathermount, a boarding school in Sunningdale, near Ascot, which catered for boys with emotional and behavioural difficulties. It was as good an example of its type as you might expect for the period and, by all accounts, much better than most. The less academically able pupils were encouraged to find fulfilment in sports, crafts, practical pursuits and performing. It may have been here that George developed his desire for celebrity and realised his need to show off in public. However, in his day-to-day school life he was an outcast: a lost child who followed one of the matrons around like a lost lamb. In his fantasy he became the rock star Gary Glitter. The other children made fun, but that didn't deter him. He called himself Paul Gadd, Glitter's real name, and completely immersed himself in glam rock.

Children's cruelty towards the weaker members of their group is well enough acknowledged to be something of a cliché; the damage it does in later life can be easily imagined. Round about the mid-teens, damaged children turn into damaged adults and are no longer absolved of responsibility for their actions. So, the abused turns into the abuser and the broken psyche, which has corrupted an innocent victim, is forgotten or ignored. They are 'old enough to know better'.

The school's staff recognised George as an easy target for bullies and did their best to protect him. He was put in a class of children younger than himself where they hoped he might be safer. This may have prevented physical abuse but it didn't save him from hurtful taunts. Because of his bulging eyes and harelip, George, or 'Gadd', was nicknamed 'Frog'. One of his contemporaries there maintained he was never seriously bullied but admits George was often laughed at.

He left school with little to show for his years of education and went back to live with his mother. Shortly afterwards, fate allowed fortune to smile on him, albeit extremely briefly: he was given a menial job at the BBC. He may have been just a general dogsbody, but the thrill he felt whenever he saw a famous face in the corridor gave him a real sense of importance. It was a feeling he quickly became addicted to and an image of himself as a 'friend of the famous' started to form in his mind. Sadly, his contract at the BBC lasted only a few months. It turned out to be the only period of real employment George ever experienced.

He left his mother's house and set up on his own, not very far away, in a high-rise council block overlooking the Shepherd's Bush traffic roundabout. He wasn't capable of looking after himself and his new home soon became disgustingly filthy; it smelt and was cluttered with rubbish. George was a horder; he especially liked to keep back issues of magazines, including *Ariel*, the BBC's in-house free-sheet, and various publications for gun enthusiasts.

His father had remarried and emigrated to Australia when George was thirteen. By the time he arrived back in Britain some eight years later, his son's life had all but fallen apart. George's fantasy world was gradually taking hold.

At first the make-believe was harmless enough: he invented Xanadu Constructional and Mechanical Engineers. He decided Jeff Lynne, the lead singer of the Electric Light Orchestra, was one of the managers of this mythical outfit and had no shame about advertising this fiction in the music press.

At the age of nineteen, despite his complete lack of academic qualifications, he applied to join the Metropolitan Police. They rejected him out of hand but, by now, tedious reality wasn't going to be allowed to spoil his dreams. He used the logo on the rejection letter to forge a police identity card. It may not have stood up to close inspection but it was enough for George. Posing as a police officer, he intervened in a quarrel between a couple in the street. Incredibly, the woman gave him her address. When George turned up on her doorstep the next day, he was unlucky enough to be confronted by her son who immediately called the real police.

He was arrested and charged with impersonating a police officer.

It wasn't the nondescript Barry George who stood before Kingston County Court: it was Paul Gadd in all his glittering finery. His long hair fell 'seductively' over his eyes; he wore a sparkling 'showbiz' jacket with the sleeves rolled up. He told the court he was an out-of-work musician, gave himself a fictional CV and claimed to have been the managing director of a company with three rock bands on its books. This time, Jeff Lynne was given the dubious honour of being his cousin. It was outrageous and the local press loved it. At last George was receiving the attention he'd craved since childhood.

The woman whose home he'd visited had had a lucky escape. George never understood the meaning of the word 'no'. It is possible he imagined she would be so grateful for his 'public service' that she would agree to have sex with him. In the more likely event of this favour being denied, he almost certainly would have tried to force himself on her. His attempts to ingratiate himself with the opposite sex were frequent, disturbing and always utterly hopeless. Most of them must have been extremely unpleasant for the women involved.

Meanwhile, the mythical action-man inside him was demanding acknowledgement. His first documented attempt to prove his masculinity was ludicrously transparent. He presented himself at the offices of the *West London Observer* looking plausibly like a martial arts enthusiast. This version of 'Paul Gadd' was a karate champion: he had, so he said, broken a world record by splitting forty-seven slate tiles with a single blow. He produced his trophy and was photographed holding it aloft, his face creased in a proud smile with just a hint of modesty hovering over it.

It didn't take long for the paper to smell a rat – for one thing, the trophy wasn't even engraved. Without much effort the paper to exposed 'Paul Gadd' as a fake. Barry George would have to seek elsewhere for the hero inside himself.

So occurred one of the most remarkable fantasies in his mind's repertoire, remarkable in that he actually did what he set out to do. He had no skill, he had no training and, it would seem, not even the remnants of common sense, but he persuaded himself he was a successful stuntman. His latest name, Steve Majors, was an amalgamation of Steve Austin and Lee Majors, the former being TV's *The Six Million Dollar Man* and the latter the actor who played the part. George arrived at the Long Eaton Stadium near Nottingham boasting an impressive list of action films he'd supposedly worked on. He offered to perform a daredevil leap, on roller skates, over four double-decker buses parked side by side.

It was a popular event. A huge ramp was constructed in order to give 'Majors' the speed he would need to clear the waiting vehicles. Hundreds of tickets were sold and, of course, the local media were keen to interview this intrepid young man.

If there was any skill to be demonstrated it would be in the landing: the leap itself would be the inevitable result of hurtling down a forty-foot slope ending abruptly in nothing. George can be credited with a huge amount of bravado for having suggested and executed this bizarre display, but skill was not on his menu. He landed badly, breaking bones and dislocating his spine. Nevertheless, he'd done what he said he was going to do and, for a brief time, he could bask in the minor glory of local fame. What the organisers of the event didn't know was that 'Steve Majors' had a three-month suspended prison sentence hanging over him.

George needed a relationship with a member of the opposite sex, but he hadn't even the most rudimentary social skills or any idea of how to initiate a meeting. He felt he had to impress in some way: by being a policeman; by having an exciting career; by being related to a famous singer. After Jill Dando's murder, a note penned by George was found in his flat. It describes how he has difficulty handling rejection, how he becomes angry, which sets off a chain of events beyond his control.

Rejection often came his way; approaching complete strangers and asking them for a kiss is not the easiest path to emotional fulfilment. In June 1981, three months before his leap over the buses, he'd met a civil servant in Kensington and asked her for a date. She tried to ignore him but became alarmed when he followed her back to her car and clumsily attempted to force himself on her. She resisted, but he took hold of her breasts and groped her. He might well have gone further had she not managed to escape. Some time later, his victim recognised George at the Department of Health and Social Security, where she worked. He was promptly arrested and charged. This wasn't the only serious incident involving Barry George and women he didn't know.

The lift at the block of flats where June Elvin was living in 1981 was only large enough for two adults and the weird man who deliberately squeezed in next to her gave her the creeps. She was a one-time star of the Ealing Studios and a former member of the cast of the popular television series *Z Cars*, but that was some time ago and this man didn't seem like an autograph hunter. Her instincts proved exactly right: she'd just had the misfortune to meet Barry George. He brought the lift to a halt using the emergency button and put his hand up her skirt. Ms Elvin managed to get the lift moving and her screams brought a neighbour to her rescue. George escaped; no charges were brought against him for this incident.

His victims cannot be expected to view him with anything other than contempt, but this was a drowning man who had no one to save him. He hadn't the wherewithal to know how to begin a healthy relationship; these violent, disturbing attacks were his only way of expressing a bewildering, powerful urge that was increasingly taking control of him.

That winter, the winter of 1981/82, three separate complaints of harassment were made against him. George was becoming a stalker.

He was still attempting to make something of himself, trying to make the reality fit the image. He applied to join the regular army and was summarily sent on his way. Instead, no doubt buoyed by his double-decker bus stunt, 'Steve Majors' joined the voluntary Territorial Army. He was with them for eleven months during which time he learned how to assemble, strip and fire rifles and guns. He was a boy playing at soldiers – he was in his element.

During his time with the Territorials, his most serious sexual assault took place. One day in February 1982, an attractive young student was seeing her boyfriend on to the tube at Turnham Green station in West London when George arrived. He waited for the woman's partner to be safely on his way before he sidled up to her. He began chatting and found out she was studying languages. He was able to manage a sentence or two in German, intending to impress her – it didn't.

Her parents lived in Acton, a short walk away. George dogged her footsteps until she was nearly home and his optimism finally evaporated; she was not going to respond to him after all (he might have guessed this earlier: she'd already told him to 'Fuck off'). His initial hope, his 'friendly' approach and his persistence had all come to naught. He panicked; she was just like all the others. He couldn't be left alone again; he *must* have her!

She had reached a deserted stairway, seconds away from her parents' front door – it was there he pounced. Clapping his hand over her mouth, he pushed her arm behind her back and shoved her to the ground. According to his victim, he then raped her. When at last ran he off, he shouted back that he was 'sorry'.

Almost a year later, on the 10 January 1983, the Royal Parks Police discovered a strange figure skulking in the bushes outside Kensington Palace, the then home of Princess Diana and Prince Charles. It was George, carrying a vicious-looking knife and fifty feet of rope. He was arrested for trespass. It wasn't long before one of the detectives who was questioning him realised this could be the same person who had assaulted the student in Acton. He remembered the rapist had spoken to his victim in German; when he tried a few words, George promptly responded and the detective was certain he'd found his man. George was charged with attempted rape and subsequently sentenced to thirty-three months, three of them being the suspended sentence he had received previously.

While in prison he metamorphosed yet again. Stuntwork had evidently lost some of its appeal: this time he renamed himself 'Thomas Palmer'. The real Palmer had led the SAS team which ended the siege of the Iranian Embassy in 1980. In adopting this identity, George was demonstrating his perturbing fascination with firearms. Having recently been turned down for full membership of the Kensington and Chelsea Gun Club after only eight provisional visits, and with his brief Territorial Army career fading into the past, George's fertile mind had again provided him with the heroic persona that reality denied him.

He was released from prison in 1985 and went to stay in bed-and-breakfast accommodation in Gloucester Road. Like many largely genteel areas of London, it has its sores but hides them well. The overall Victorian splendour masks the dilapidated conversions in which the poor are tucked away; this might well be a breeding ground for despondency and resentment. During his time there George kept a small collection of firearms, among them an imitation machine gun, a handgun and a small silver Bruning starting pistol which he wrapped in tissue paper and kept in a shoebox. The following year, he reported this as having been stolen; it has never been found. Had it indeed been stolen? Or had it 'vanished' for some other reason?

He was hardly a responsible person where firearms were concerned; he treated them as toys and loved frightening people with them. A family he'd met at the Gloucester Road hostel found this out when they were forced to dive for cover after he barged into their midst and fired what turned out to be a blank round. George, who'd dressed for the part in army combat gear and balaclava, was delighted with the result of his 'joke'.

By 1989 he'd moved to Crookham Road, not four minutes away from Jill Dando's house in Gowan Avenue. While there he met Itsuko Toide, a Japanese woman some four years older than he was. Apart from an apparent penchant for blonde women, George had always lusted after Orientals; since being a child he'd apparently harboured a secret passion for Yoko Ono. In Ms Toide, he thought he'd found the perfect partner at last.

Employing his usual 'bull in a china shop' methods of introduction, he followed her – stalked her – but this time he achieved results. Ms Toide was vulnerable, having been sexually assaulted by another man; also, she didn't speak English very well and desperately wanted a British passport. She believed Barry George's persistence to be an indication of sincerity. She saw in him a caring, concerned benefactor who would be a friend to her and provide her with support. So he was – at first. On 2 May 1989, after knowing each other for only five months, the couple tied the knot at Fulham Registry Office.

Their miserable marriage didn't have a hope. The new Mrs George did her best to acquiesce to her husband's endless demands. She was expected to provide virtually everything: income, domestic services, emotional support and sex. Meanwhile, George wasted his days away in solitary depression. When Mrs George came home from work (usually exhausted), she would have just about enough energy to prepare a meal for them both before going straight to bed. This wasn't enough for George: isolated, lonely and unable to consider her needs, he frequently resorted to violence in order to get attention or sexual relief.

Though he often behaved appallingly, he was something of a Jekyll and Hyde in that he could also be caring, considerate and gentle. His convenient excuse was the medicine he took for his epilepsy which, he claimed, robbed him of self-control. On one occasion he stabbed his wife in the side with a bamboo stick; on another, he raped her.

She was a compassionate and amazingly understanding woman but, even so, she was surprised and unnerved when, after each display of loutish wrath, George dialled 999 and reported himself to the police. Reflecting later, she wondered if this was a Freudian link to his father, the policeman: he wanted this brief attention; he desperately needed to be taken seriously by figures of authority. Whatever the reason, it was George, not his wife, who phoned for help.

The marriage rapidly fell apart. Itsuko eventually reported her husband for assault, though she withdrew the charge before it went to court. Whatever had happened on that occasion transpired to be the final straw; they were divorced in August 1994.

George continued to bark at society's door without ever being allowed in. In 1991, the singer Freddie Mercury died of AIDS. Mercury was everything George could never hope to be: as the genius behind the rock band Queen, he was successful, talented and handsome. His charisma overflowed, flooding into the hearts of millions. For George it was like picking a personality off the shelf: he decided to be Freddie Mercury's cousin.

Mercury's original name was Farookh Bulsara; Barry George became Barry Bulsara. On the first anniversary of the singer's death, he drew up outside Mercury's former home in a hired limousine; he signed autographs and left flowers, 'From your cousin, Barry Bulsara'.

He invented Bulsara Productions Inc. and had visiting cards printed. Never one to let facts interfere with a publicity opportunity, he produced one of them at the London office of a Japanese newspaper and suggested they interview him. They refused.

'Freddie Mercury's cousin' also often logged on to a Japanese website for fans of Queen but he was exposed as a fraud; the site warned other visitors to have nothing to do with him.

George's stalking of female strangers continued unabated. He took nearly three thousand surreptitious photographs, though he never developed any of them; he kept notes of car registration numbers, Princess Diana's among them; he observed and recorded the daily habits of hundreds of unsuspecting women.

It's easy to dismiss this man as an eccentric menace. It's perhaps equally easy to blame the social services, the medical profession, his teachers or his parents. The truth is, people like Barry George continue to live in our midst. The most common reaction to their odd behaviour is to look the other way and hope they go and bother someone else. When they overstep the mark we protest: we ask why something wasn't done about them beforehand. What? When?

* * *

In the months that followed Jill Dando's murder, there was a media frenzy. There was talk of a contract killing, that the culprit was an ex-lover; even the Russian Mafia were suspected. Inevitably, there was much speculation that a stalker could have been responsible. The police had little to work on: the bullet had been tampered with, possibly to lessen the noise. It was an amateurish job but showed the murderer had some rudimentary knowledge of firearms. There were no other obvious clues.

Even taking account of the 'professional hazard' element, Ms Dando had attracted more than her fair share of 'weirdos'. One man, whose home was later raided by the police, had created a shrine to her, papering his room with copies of her picture. He had admitted his obsession in a series of e-mails. The woman he'd sent these to had become alarmed when they stopped on the day Ms Dando died and she had contacted the police. Another reported incident tells of a man who pretended to be Ms Dando's brother. He had tried to have her electricity, gas and water bills charged to his account. There were others – detectives said that 1,800 people were suggested, the majority being quickly eliminated from the inquiry. Sir Paul Condon, who retired as head of the Metropolitan Police in January 2000 and who was a friend of Ms Dando, said he believed the murderer to be a stalker who, having vented his anger, was unlikely to kill again or be caught.

Meanwhile the public, led by an outraged popular press, demanded a reason for this tragedy. However warped a mind, however malevolent a criminal was responsible, it couldn't simply be that Jill Dando had been murdered by an unknown person and for no apparent reason.

As George lived so close to Ms Dando's home it was inevitable someone would put his name forward as a possible suspect. Ever since his arrival in Crookham Road, he'd made himself conspicuous as an eccentric and, more relevantly, as a nuisance to women. Even so, when a neighbour reported a certain Mr 'Busara' [sic], whom she knew to be unstable and to possess air rifles, he wasn't included on any of the high-priority lists.

Mr Ramesh Paul, the controller of a local taxi firm, had already told the police of a man, agitated and sweating, who had been with him at 1.15 p.m. – an hour and three-quarters after the time of death. The day after, the same man turned up again; he wanted Mr Paul to recall exactly what he'd been wearing on his previous visit. Mr Paul couldn't and the stranger became extremely agitated. He'd been 'wearing yellow like the colour of the sun,' he said. Mr Paul 'must remember'.

Also the local community centre, known as 'Hafad' (the Hammersmith and Fulham Action for Disability), reported that George had behaved oddly on 26 April 1999. He had been keen to establish at what time he'd been with them and had said he would be suspected of Ms Dando's murder as he looked like an e-fit of the man wanted for questioning yet, at that point, no e-fit had been released. Just over two weeks later, a woman on a bus found herself sitting next to a peculiar man who said he was Freddie Mercury's cousin and he was en route to a memorial service for Jill Dando where he was to give a reading. By this time, an e-fit *had* been published and this man looked very much like it. The woman told the police.

Despite all these pointers, George was not regarded as high priority and it was to be over a year before the police reconsidered the possibility that he might be the man they were looking for.

By the spring of 2000, the massive investigation had failed to produce anything concrete. Detective Superintendent Hamish Campbell had decided the popular theories regarding professional hitmen and organised criminals were unlikely; he instructed his team to re-examine old leads. Hence, almost as a last 'stab in the dark', DC John Gallagher (no relation to the author) looked again at Mr 'Busara' – finding him to be 'Bulsara': Barry Michael George.

George's police record attracted Gallagher's attention. The card index kept at Hammersmith police station stated that he'd regularly followed women for no apparent reason and was 'one to watch out for'. George's flat was searched on 17 April 2000; his collections of guns, photographs and news-papers were discovered. The find might easily have confirmed his guilt in the eyes of the police but they knew it was not nearly enough to prove their case. George was kept under close observation for the following four weeks, during which time the police were further persuaded when it became apparent he was growing a beard. Was this a feeble attempt at disguise? Was George anticipating being placed in an identification parade?

When his flat was searched a second time, forensics were able to identify a microscopic particle of lead – invisible to the naked eye -in the pocket of his coat: it matched other particles found in Ms Dando's hair. Furthermore, a fibre found on a pair of his trousers matched another on Ms Dando's coat. George was brought in for questioning.

He did himself no favours by being able to recall exactly what he had been doing on 26 April 1999. Not unreasonably, the interviewing officers presumed he'd been expecting the interview and drew their own conclusions as to why.

On 2 July 2001, George was convicted of murder by a verdict of ten to one – the twelfth juror had been excused because of bereavement. The prosecution's evidence was largely circumstantial and, if viewed as separate contentions, would not have been nearly verifiable enough to prove their case. However, it was alleged that considered together, his behaviour, his reactions to police interest and, most of all, the forensic evidence, were enough to damn him.

Dissenting voices say this is entirely untrue: he knew the police had reason to suspect him; as soon as he heard that a famous television personality had been murdered so near his home he would of course have felt the need to invent an alibi, especially if he'd happened to be near Gowan Avenue at the time of the incident. This could also explain his change of appearance, his subsequent claim that he'd no knowledge of Ms Dando (which was clearly a lie), and his denying any experience of firearms. The coat in which the particle of gun discharge was found had been taken to a photographer's studio before it had been examined; there was therefore every possibility that it had been contaminated. The fibre on his trousers could have come from a variety of sources; it was not conclusive proof of George's having been near Ms Dando at any time.

Itsuko Toide maintained her ex-husband couldn't possibly have been responsible. George's hands, she recalled, trembled so violently he had problems even putting coins into a purse, the idea that he could have aimed and fired a gun accurately is ludicrous. Furthermore, if by some miracle, he'd managed it, his movements were so laboriously slow that a crowd would certainly have gathered before he reached the end of the path.

Was Barry George, as has been suggested, an erotomaniac whose fixations included successful, confident blonde women? At the beginning of that fateful week in April 1999, did he perhaps see the cover of the *Radio Times*? On it, Jill Dando, the efficient, clean-cut 'girl next door', stands provocatively in front of a flashy car, her arms folded and her legs set squarely apart. She is wearing sexy, tight black leather and has a half-inviting smile on her lips. Did Barry George see this image as his Madonna turned whore? Did he find the image unbearable?

Or had he always seen Jill Dando as his ideal woman? Did he hope to know her? Did he try, in his blundering, aggressive way, to introduce himself and was he dismissed without a second glance? Did the bitterness and isolation of years suddenly overwhelm him, driving him to murder?

On the other hand, was he a convenient local 'nutter'? Was he a convincing enough 'patsy' for a jury to be persuaded of his guilt? Was he the victim of the public demand for somebody – anybody – to be held to account for this ghastly crime? Did the police grasp at a plausible and available result?

If we're to assume the jury were correct and George is guilty, he's extremely unusual in that he's consistently denied it and continues to do so. Stalkers who kill celebrities generally have a strong desire to bask in their notoriety, to link their name with that of their famous victim. Of course, George may be far more devious than he's ever been given credit for, but his protests could also be legitimate: he could well be an innocent man.

In December 2001, Barry George was given leave to appeal against his sentence. The grounds were possible contamination of evidence (the particle of discharge in the coat pocket) and the questionable relationship between a witness and one of the police officers who worked on the case. Whether or not his conviction is quashed, we may never know for certain whether this strange and lonely man murdered one of the most popular and successful television presenters of our time.

7. WHO DO YOU THINK I AM?

When a stalker fixates on a celebrity the fantasy created is partly the figment of the stalker's imagination and is partly derived from the star's public image. Famous people have a version of themselves which they present to the public and it's not surprising that fans are apt to buy into this totally. It's not unknown for the public (not necessarily just stalkers) to treat the fictional character an actor plays as a real person. Funeral wreaths flood into the studio when a popular soap character dies; hate-mail is sent to villains and love letters are sent to heart-throbs. Soap stars, in particular, are regularly hailed by the name of the person they play and given unsolicited advice in the supermarket about his or her problems.

It doesn't have to be soaps, however – and the actor doesn't have to be famous . . .

Sir Gideon Petrie, philosopher and campaigner for peace, is a man of high principles. He bears some resemblance to the late Bertrand Russell. His home is the retreat, Shrivings. It's open to all, regardless of their political persuasion, religious beliefs or antipathy to Sir Gideon's pacifist views. When Susan first saw him, she wanted very much to meet him. In Sir Gideon, she'd found a man who would help her realise her purpose. He was unique and exciting. From the first time she heard him speak, in the back room of a pub in Birmingham, she was utterly persuaded by the deep, important truths Sir Gideon seemed to know. She could cope with his evident flaws; they only served to make him more human.

There was only one problem: Sir Gideon didn't exist.

He was in fact a character in Peter Shaffer's play *Shrivings*. It was first performed (as *The Battle of Shrivings*) in 1970 at the Lyric Theatre in London, where the part of Sir Gideon was taken by John Gielgud. Coincidentally, Shaffer began working on this original script from a small room at the top of the

Tracey Morgan

Above and Left
Entrance to the Dakota
Building, New York,
where Mark Chapman
shot John Lennon
© David Murray

Opposite, top left
Bull Inn Court, off
Maiden Lane by the
Strand – site of stage
door to the Adelphi
Theatre, 1897
© Richard Gallagher

Opposite, top right
Private entrance to the
Adelphi Theatre, where
Terriss was stabbed
© Richard Gallagher

CITY OF WESTMINSTER

WILLIAM TERRISS
1847 – 1897

HERO OF THE ADELPHI
MELODRAMAS

MET HIS UNTIMELY END
OUTSIDE THIS THEATRE
16 DEC 1897

THE ADELPHI THEATRE CO. LTD

Right William Terriss
© The Mander & Mitchenson Theatre
Collection

WILLIAM TERRISS, ACTOR.
Obit Dec. 16, 1897; Ætat. 46.

Right Eric Presland as Sir Gideon Petrie in *Shrivings* by Peter Schaffer

Left Malcolm Stewart
© Stephanie de Leng

Above Sarah Lockett,
Meridian TV presenter
© Meridian Television

Right Undated card
sent to Sarah Lockett
from Jeremy Dyer

Saturday 3rd April 11:44p

Dear Pocket,

So our citation reasons at easter. Christmas was 1/4 of a year ago. I wonder what you look like now darling. Have you changed? I see that American Tonight is on for an hour on Sunday. I wonder if you'll presume 16? I still have to video it as I'm going out... reading Vaclav, aunts, cousins, gran, sisters etc. (as well as my parents of course). But then I've already seen them today whose house we go to. Think I'm staying in in Kent. Good old parents of course...

My parents are SO supportive of the pocket Lockett. Publit this way, I'm 29 1/2 and I've never done a decent day's work in my life! etc. They don't care, as long as I (church our the odd Masters degree etc. Mother can be..) proud of my wonderful achievements and my "top rate" University of Warwick course.

Now that I'm back in Kent for a while

"Why do you think I suddenly disappeared in September... And stopped seeing my beloved Sarah on telly... and have to rely on stalking you during holidays...?"

My parents suggested I become a teacher, so I had to go to Coventry. All long as they charge up money etc I don't mind.

I would have been happy staying in real doing a bit of freelance writing etc on economics.

Maybe I appreciate at 1/2 you more because I only see you every now and then? I don't know.

Now you know some more about me. Actually I'm plying on your conscience neil.

"How could such a nice boy like Jeremy ever be a Stalker? surely you must be mixing him up with someone else?"

Anyway Darling Sarah, we have a couple of weeks geography.

By the way, I have (since coming home this afternoon) discovered that the video is set to record your shows after christmas...

WAS SWITCHED OFF

by my father. Oh well, never mind. Actually there was one edition of Meridian Tonight recorded which I watched earlier. From my novel... in my Lockett Watch File

Feb January (Monday) 1999   5:35 - 6:35 pm

This is the only one on the tape before my dad switched off the tape. Video.

There was a story about anti-twa...

and at the end you and Geoff said you had colds.

and did anyone know a cure. I expect your colds gone by now!!!

Anyway now I'm back I have lots of ideas for discover wishes.

I do miss your telly bump Jackie. Boo hoo. You will have to wait again a few times.

Okay, lets have a strategy meeting. How is our stalking experience going?

What do we want out of Easter?

1. Re-establish our relationship
2. Locate "Operation Locket watch – Easter"
3. Send some letters, presents etc
4. watch Sarah on MTM.
5. other

Another idea I had was to give you an opportunity to get rid of that 'stalking'. This is your chance to get rid of your "annoying stalker" or to show you "don't mind" me writing to you etc.

So, if you (Sarah Locket) wear your blue Jacket with the spiv down the front on Meridian Tonight on Friday 11 April – I (Jeremy) will stop all Contact with you...forever. If you dont wear ye I will continue to write...forever.

Hmmm, what is this mean? Is Jeremy serious, what shall I do, wear the Jacket and retract him completely/stopping turning him into an "ex-stalker" ?? ?.? Yet want the Jacket and have him continue stalking me. Wear the Jacket and Risk being controlled

by a seriously nice north Jacket and appear to be distancing Risk to Sarah and wear the Jacket and..

Sarah Might keep writing-making/waste of time

Sarah thinking →

This is the essence of clever Stalking/Sarah. Think of it like a chess game. In chess this is called ZugZwang (forcing your opponent into making a bad move).

It's not that I'm forcing you to make a bad move (as there can never be bad moves for darling) or that I'm even forcing you to make a decision.

All I am doing is giving you an opportunity to decide things for yourself. Your views are valid and to be respected, as are mine.

Okay, that's the end of our strategy meeting.

I'm watching Jerry Springer (on good old Meridian). They're discussing silicone implants. There are women with giant boobys. see picture →

while we're on the subject of womans breasts. How about wearing the Jacket which shows off your Knockers! Sorry. Just being crude (casual) I think it was a purple/red/pink Jacket I can't remember. Or maybe it was blue. I left the tape in Coventry so I dont know.

By the way I got the "Sarah stamp" (in the envelope) from your web site www.meridian.stalker.tv.co.uk etc etc. Hope you like being turned into a stamp.

That's enough for one letter

Take care of yourself

Lots of love from

Jerry springer/sessinger/sessinger/sessinger/sessinger/stalker

Above left Jill Dando's house and site of fatal shooting in Fulham, London
© Richard Gallagher

Above right DI Hamish Brown

Left Diana Lamplugh – founder of the Suzy Lamplugh Trust

Dakota Building, the same building outside which, ten years later, Mark Chapman would murder John Lennon.

Shaffer re-wrote *Shrivings* under its present title and, unusually for a playwrite, published this version before it was performed. It remained on the shelf for some time, then a small fringe company in Birmingham picked it up.

The late seventies and early eighties saw a huge explosion in fringe theatre. All over the place, out of work actors banded together, hired rooms and set about performing 'two or three-handers' for their admiring friends. Needless to say, some of these companies were better than others and some went on to gain considerable success in the established theatre. The Pub Theatre Company, despite its uninspiring name, was one of the better ones and had won a Double Fringe First at the Edinburgh Festival in 1976. Shaffer is an important playwright. In 1977, with his latest success *Equus* still relatively fresh on West End lips, he might have been thought too important to be premiered by the Pub Theatre Company – but, to the great delight of its director, Eric Presland, that's what happened.

Shrivings was a feather in their cap and a great success. Eric himself took the role of Sir Gideon, the flawed sage. He was enjoying the experience considerably – until Susan turned up.

Pub theatre isn't exactly the height of celebrity but a certain amount of reciprocal 'luvviness' goes on between cast and audience in the bar after the show. Some members of the public are apt to gush – it happens even after unmitigated disasters. An actor can modestly brush off the praise or can sit there and soak it up. Either way, it results in a not-unpleasant combination of embarrassment and pride.

Susan was a gusher.

The performance that night had actually been saved from near disaster in the third act. In this, the last scene in the play, the actors all appear nearly naked. The script has them covering their modesty with a minimum of clothing: one wears a bath robe, one a towel, one is wrapped in a sheet . . . On this particular occasion the young actor playing the part of Mark allowed his robe to slip. With some courage and great presence of mind, the other three actors all removed their covering and continued to play the scene completely naked – just as though it had been intended that way. In fact it worked very well and they kept it in for the rest of the run.

Nudity on stage wasn't unheard of in 1977, but it was not quite as commonplace as it is today. The company were performing in a small space, close to their audience. The house was packed – it was the penultimate night at that particular venue and the show was doing well. When the curtain came down, Eric looked forward to relaxing with a drink. For professional reasons he didn't usually encourage strangers into conversation after the show. The self-congratulatory indulgence which often resulted was as pointless as vanity publishing. He was always polite and would exchange pleasantries, but experience had taught him that making friends with your audience was not a terribly good idea if you wanted to stay objective about your talents.

Susan made a bee-line for him.

His first impressions were that she might have been a particularly intense mature student. She was in her late twenties but, from the way she talked, she appeared very naive and had a freshman's enthusiasm and lack of cynicism. She had long, wiry black hair and a thin, sharp face. Eric remembers a very faint Australian accent but time has passed and he isn't sure.

She cornered him and told him what a wonderful person she considered Sir Gideon to be. She talked about the ideas the character had put forward as if they came from a real person. She hardly seemed aware that what she had just seen was a play and the person she was speaking to was an actor. Eric soon got the measure of her and realised he was dealing with a person whose reality was not quite the same as other people's. After some time he managed to extract himself from the conversation. He thought no more about the strange woman – until the next night, when she was in the audience again.

This wasn't a worrying sign by any means. Her obvious appreciation of the play, even if it was a little off-beam, meant she was likely to want to see it again and this was her last chance to do so in Moseley. The cast were having a week off before going on to Dudley and elsewhere. After the performance Eric managed to escape her clutches. The cast were going for a meal together and none of them stayed in the bar for very long.

It was a small audience in Dudley – only about twelve people. She was there again and this time she sat in the front row. Eric noticed her almost immediately and as a result gave a dreadful performance. He didn't quite know what disturbed him about Susan. She wasn't totally mad for she did seem to comprehend that he wasn't the person she wanted to know. She treated him as though he was the medium through which she could communicate with Sir Gideon.

It was impossible to avoid her afterwards. She approached him and, in a very cautious little voice began, 'Hello. Can I talk to you?' He tried to give her a polite excuse but she insisted: 'I've *got* to talk to you.'

He tried to be blunt and said, 'We must clear this up.' She brushed his objections aside, saying firmly, 'It's really important I speak to you.'

Eric was expecting another eulogy in praise of the man he'd just played. Instead he was given a long and involved story about Susan's boyfriend. Apparently, he wanted her to move in with him, but he was sharing with other people in some sort of student household and she wasn't sure if it would be a good idea. She wasn't even sure if she really loved him. She needed Eric (or perhaps Sir Gideon) to tell her what she should do.

Being polite to strangers is one thing but organising their home life and advising on their love affairs is quite another. Eric told her he couldn't possibly voice an opinion. 'I'm sorry I really don't think I can deal with you,' he said. 'I don't want to give you the wrong advice and have you blame me for it afterwards. You must make your own decision.'

Little warning bells were ringing in his head but he didn't know how to wriggle out of Susan's clutches. He didn't feel able to ask her why on earth she considered him to be a suitable person to advise her. He was trapped by conventional politeness: don't confront somebody about their odd behaviour, just pretend things are normal.

On the next night Eric was half expecting her to be there and he was right – she was. He somehow managed to ignore her presence and salvage something of the performance he had given before Susan had arrived on the scene. He knew she would be waiting for him afterwards but this time he had a very good excuse: the set had to be dismantled and the whole company were going to be busy until long after closing time. She came up to him and, in the same cautious little voice, she asked if she could talk to him. 'No,' he said confidently. 'I'm very sorry but it isn't going to be possible.' He still didn't want to offend this strange woman but she was unnerving him and he would have rather she disappeared.

'On the Friday night when we opened at the next venue she was there again. By this point I was getting freaked. For the first time, I told the other actors about her. It was a bit of relief to share it with other people but I still couldn't put my finger on what was so disturbing about her. We are much more aware of stalking now than we were twenty-five years ago. The idea that anybody could have that sort of problem was not at all common knowledge. That night at the end I fled. I said, "I'm going. I'm not going to stay around for drinks. I'm going" and I dived out.'[1]

Eric's number (which was also the contact number for the company) was printed in the programme. The phone calls started early the following morning. It was about eight o'clock on the one day he was able to have a lie-in after a week of late nights. He was furious.

She opened with the line which was becoming her catch-phrase: 'I've got to talk to you.' Eric was tempted to put the phone down but, again, a conventional avoidance of confrontation got in the way and stopped him. He listened for some time as Susan told him he was the only one who could help her.

She was talking to a highly irate man whom she knew nothing whatsoever about, but that didn't seem to matter. Eric was, to her, the kindly, available, wise person she'd seen on stage. Sir Gideon would always advise, Sir Gideon would know what to do. In the play, she'd seen Sir Gideon at his most vulnerable and had been with him through a huge crisis in his life. She and Sir Gideon understood each other.

'You really helped me to sort things out when we had the conversation before,' she said. Eric was tempted to tell her this was absolute rubbish – he hadn't done anything – but he held back.

As the conversation went on, he became more forceful. He told her whatever game it was she was playing, she had to stop it right there. Susan was clever enough to keep him on the phone.

'She was in one of those mind-game situations. She would draw you in, like a kid saying "Why?" – "Why? What's wrong, I only want to talk to you . . ." And she'd push and push and push. Eventually, after a conversation going round and round in circles for about ten or fifteen minutes, I got angry and blew it. I put the phone down.'[2]

Eric's temper had warned Susan off – at least temporarily. She didn't appear at the last show in Walsall and there was a substantial break before the next performance. Eric had to go to Edinburgh for a few days to sort out a venue for the Festival. When he arrived back in Birmingham the company went straight into rehearsals for their next play. For a while he was free of Susan and he forgot about her.

Then the phone calls started in earnest. Sometimes there would be a nervous voice saying 'hello', after which she would ring off. Sometimes she assumed a pathetic, cringing tone which Eric describes as her 'don't hurt me' voice.

'Like when you get a dog who's been hit badly and it rolls over, looking at you as if to say "don't hit me again". It was like that. She would start with "I only want to talk to you" and then she'd go on at length.'[3]

Susan still didn't distinguish between the real man she was harassing and the fictional character he'd played. Through Eric, she told Sir Gideon she'd decided to devote her life to peace and he was the only person who could show her how.

Eric's reply was blunt and practical: 'Try joining CND [Campaign for Nuclear Disarmament].'

She was very weak, she told him. She needed somebody to inspire her. He didn't understand how much she needed him.

The situation had gone past the point where Eric worried about giving offence. He often put the phone down on her. She didn't seem to be put off by this at all. In the next few days she rang at all hours of the day and night, pouring her heart out and ignoring Eric's protests.

He assumed she wanted a relationship with him. He thought back to the first time she'd made herself known and wondered if the nudity at the end of the play had sparked all this off. The next time she rang he attempted to make himself absolutely clear: he didn't fancy her and he wasn't interested in any sort of relationship with her. For the first time she became angry.

'What's that got to do with it?' she said. 'What makes you think this is about sex? How could you think this was about sex?'

Susan's stalking of Sir Gideon Petrie through the unfortunate Mr Presland ended as suddenly as it had begun.

After weeks of peculiar phone calls, each beginning with that small, pleading 'I've got to talk to you', Eric was very worried indeed. He had no idea if Susan knew his address. He was beginning to suspect she might tire of being rebuffed on the phone and try something more desperate. She presumably knew when he would be out of the house – it was easy enough to check when the performances were – she could attempt to break in.

He wasn't sure what she wanted and was curious to know how she would react to his role in the next play: a classic dirty old man, a total seventies' stereotype of a homosexual. Who could fancy that? he thought. He was almost looking forward to giving her a shock by killing off Sir Gideon Petrie in this way.

There was gap before Susan rang again and it was Eric who got the shock, albeit a pleasant one.

'I'm ringing to say goodbye,' she said.

His voice was hurried and breathless: 'Goodbye,' he said. He made an attempt to sound as though this was a normal exchange and failed miserably. 'Well – Good luck!'

She rang off.

More than twenty-five years later, Eric says: 'In some ways it was rather flattering. He was a lovely character this man, Sir Gideon. He was funny and twinkly; he had huge energy and bags of charm. Shaffer puts all that over very well.

'I suspect I did encourage her flattery in the very early stages. I probably blossomed with the reverence with which she treated me. When you're being asked your opinion of life, God, the universe, of course you respond to it. It was only when it came to giving specific advice, answering questions like "What do I do in this situation"' that I couldn't cope.'[4]

He never again heard from Susan: a woman who fell for the idealism of a man who didn't exist.

Though Eric Presland is an actor, he is not a famous person. He is one of many, many ordinary people who have suffered at the hands of stalkers. It would seem, however, that the vast majority of stalkers are male and their victims female. The research being done at Leicester University has concluded one in five women in Britain today have experienced abusive stalking behaviour. A similar study is being done with men: of 210 males who were interviewed, 5.2 per cent had been stalked (a quarter of these by other men).

The full extent of the problem remains open to speculation: stalking, the often undefined ingredient in every sort of crime from domestic disputes to murder, frequently goes unreported. Though more information is available today than in the past, it is still possible for stalking not to be recognised for what it is, even by the victim. 'I thought I was being paranoid', is a phrase heard over and over again.

Stalkers enter into a life like a virus; they remain there, seemingly immune to any attempts to banish them. As most reported cases involve 'prior sexual intimates', it seems reasonable to assume that at some point, careful handling and the right combination of firmness and distancing could help to protect the victim from the worst excesses of their behaviour. Unfortunately, it isn't as simple as that.

The problem is: how does one predict the future? How do you know the handsome bloke who you've fallen for isn't just being – naturally enough – a bit jealous when he gets upset about your meeting old friends for dinner? When he says he never wants you to leave him, isn't that just his way of saying how much he feels for you? So what if every time he drinks too much he tends to get a bit angry – don't a lot of men do that? Being possessive isn't the worst sin – is it? When you've just finished a relationship and your partner doesn't want to accept it, surely his gifts and his tearful phone calls are only to be expected? After the time you have shared together is it fair to insist he should leave and not contact you ever again? On the other hand, how long should you give him to get over it? At what point is his pain self-indulgent; a refusal to accept reality? Will he transfer that pain into anger and then to revenge?

And if it's difficult to see the origins of stalking behaviour in a lover, it's even more problematic when dealing with a casual acquaintance. There's the person you see at the bus stop every day. He obviously fancies you and sometimes contrives to sit next to you. Is he dangerous? His conversation is interesting enough but if you are at all friendly to him, is he going to take it the wrong way and assume you're giving him permission to go further? Will he start to follow you home and loiter outside the house?

What are the warning signs? Where should the line be drawn?

Jean's husband, Philip (not his real name), was very possessive from the start. He didn't like her friends (male or female) to phone her. She was eighteen when she met him and she wasn't at all sure of what to expect from a relationship. As, bit by bit, she lost contact with her old acquaintances, she persuaded herself this is what being in love was all about: living for each other. She wasn't wholly convinced. It was clear her husband had a big problem with anybody who came anywhere near her.

Jean met Philip on the club-circuit. They were both singers though Jean was doing rather better at it than Philip who was still only semi-professional. They were introduced by the man who had got Jean started in the first place. Even before they met, she was already sorry for him. She was a collector of lame ducks and when she was told about Philip's fianceé leaving him after going off with another man she was already halfway along the way to going out with him.

He established the relationship very quickly – too quickly. Philip had almost nothing to his name. He had a job during the day which paid barely enough to exist on and he was singing at night. He didn't have a car, he didn't have many clothes. Had it not been for Jean becoming pregnant she might never have married him. When she found out about the baby, she saw little alternative. In those days that's what you did.

As soon as they were married Philip changed and all the niceness went. Jean already knew he could be jealous and possessive but she assumed it was because he lacked confidence. She felt sure he would settle down once she'd proved her commitment to him. It became worse – much worse. There was a very strong feeling, which she still remembers: a feeling of something closing behind her.

Jean earned far more than Philip but he insisted on dealing with all their finances. He had a strange attitude towards money in general. He didn't like it to be openly discussed or dealt with. She had to leave it for him so he could pick it up discreetly – as though it was embarrassing or shameful. He was domineering and selfish. He spent most evenings out of the house but when he was in he expected Jean to keep the baby quiet and well away from him. Throughout their marriage, he never bothered with his children. From enjoying a hectic social round, Jean found her life outside the home had whittled down to work and a game of whist once a week with an old lady she knew.

The couple had terrible rows over Jean's stage-wear. If the cleavage was too revealing Philip would complain loudly. He was a drinker. When the key went in the door, she never knew what was coming in. Whisky affected him the worst. His tempers were terrible.

He'd break things, smashing his fist into them. They were always things which belonged to her and he usually managed to choose items which were irreplaceable. Jean still didn't protest: she'd lived in that sort of environment as a child and it wasn't strange to her. She had been frightened of her father and her mother had resembled a mouse.

Philip's moods couldn't always be predicted. Sometimes he would come home and behave perfectly normally, then suddenly, from nowhere, his anger would come crashing in. 'If you ever try to leave, I'll be round every corner. You'll never get away. You'll never have a relationship with anyone else.'

Jean believed him. On one occasion he held her up against the back door with a knife to her throat. The attack was utterly unexpected. They hadn't had a row, everything had been normal – as normal as it ever was. She had been washing up and Philip had come up to her and started talking. He proceeded to work himself up, letting his imagination goad him into a frenzy. 'If you ever try to leave me,' he said, 'if you ever try to take those children . . .' All the time he had the knife pressed into her. She asked him what the hell the matter was? She had just been washing up, she said. Where had all this come from?

Fear kept her there for nine years. During that time there was the constant threat in her mind: 'If you ever try to leave me . . .'

It was only later, when she established a friendship with some other women, that Jean realised she needn't put up with Philip's abuse. Her friends were incredulous about how much she'd already let him get away with. She attempted to leave him, escaping to her mother's, the only place she could think of.

Philip hounded her. A neighbour intervened and assured Jean that while she knew what Philip had been like, she believed him when he said he was determined to change. That night Jean went back but soon realised she'd made a mistake. Philip was exactly as he'd been before. Jean put up with him for another two years before realising she couldn't stay with Philip for the rest of her life.

She tried to do it in as fair a way as she could. She'd imagined horror scenarios: dragging her children out of bed in the middle of the night and it being in The *News of the World* the next morning. She wanted to part legally, in a civilised way.

Philip realised he'd had his last chance so he got back at Jean through the children. She was the partner who had absented herself from the marital home and so he used this fact to make sure he gained custody of them, displaying a fondness which had been markedly absent in his years of marriage. Jean found herself unable to see her two sons, who were aged four and nine at the time. When she came round to visit them, Philip would make sure they were out. She could see he was doing it deliberately and prepared to combat his revenge.

Her car was not an expensive one – 'an old banger' is the way she describes it – and yet it was then stolen. She had an intuition about the theft but nevertheless reported it to the police in a formal way, not mentioning her husband. About a fortnight later she found it herself, parked in the drive of the house where she'd grown up. It was locked and there was no sign of it having been broken into.

At this point Jean felt confident enough of her suspicions to mention them to the police. They brushed her story aside. She began to feel very alone. She remembered a film where a woman was being driven mad and nobody would believe her . . .

One night she and a group of women friends went out for the night to a club. When they came out, Jean found her windscreen had been smashed and there was a brick on the front seat of the car. Only her car had been damaged, none of the others had been touched.

Months after leaving Philip, Jean met another man. He'd clearly had nothing to do with her marital break-up but Philip immediately set about attempting to cite him as correspondent for the divorce. He also hired a private detective to follow her and report on her every move.

As well as being profoundly disturbed by this turn of events, Jean was also incensed. She had not left Philip for another man, she had left because of his unreasonable behaviour. It may have been too difficult for him to take, but she was determined that he wasn't going to get away with saying otherwise. The thought of him wallowing in his role as the supposed injured party sickened her.

A few years later she was to meet a former compère from one of the clubs they'd both worked in, a man who had known both Philip and Jean separately and later as a couple. After exchanging pleasantries he'd asked her about Philip. Jean explained the situation and didn't have to wait long before getting an honest opinion of her former husband. The compère told her he'd always thought Philip to be 'a bit twisted' and nobody had liked him. She later found out that Philip had attempted to recruit a gang of men to beat up her boyfriend. Luckily he hadn't managed it, but Jean was appalled that he'd actually asked them to do something so violent.

She was living at her mother's once again. Her mother hadn't had a phone before but Jean felt very vulnerable. She had one installed.

It constantly rang in the early hours of the morning. If she answered it, there would only be silence and the sure sense of somebody on the other end of the line, listening and waiting. Again she told the police. It happened so regularly that in the end they took some notice. They told her to let them know next time it happened and promised to go round to Philip's house immediately. When they did, he came to the door looking like he'd just been woken up, convincing them he had nothing to do with the nuisance calls. Jean wasn't so easily persuaded.

Philip's revenge continued unabated for six months. By the time he tired of it, Jean was exhausted. She felt angry and powerless in equal measure. She remembers the insidious way Philip manipulated her; she remembers wishing she had been stronger and wanting to do something violent towards him. She sees him as a coward and a bully but she's still not sure at what point she had it within her power to stop him.

What happened to her illustrates the difficulty victims have in defining what is being done to them. Several times during the recounting of her story, she stopped to say, 'What I'm describing isn't really stalking though, is it?' Gavin de Becker's excellent book *The Gift of Fear* deals with these problems. de Becker is uniquely qualified to advise on personal safety, having been a consultant on the subject to thousands of people from all walks of life. He describes the warning signs which can help a victim of stalking (and other types of emotional and physical abuse). He says we have trained ourselves out of using our natural instincts for survival, arguing that we prefer to ignore or reinterpret the very feelings which we should be listening to and acting upon. According to de Becker, we rarely should be left saying 'I could never have predicted this'. We *can* predict. We *do* know when things are heading for disaster.

Kate's story illustrates how the stalker can manipulate their victim's good nature to make them feel guilty for being firm and for saying the one little word the stalker can never understand: 'no'.

8. ALL'S FAIR IN LOVE AND WAR

We shall call her Kate. She is just over thirty and the impression you get on meeting her is of being in the presence of a stock Yorkshire character from any soap or sitcom. She is (and she herself is happy to admit it) what they used to call 'big and blowsy'. She laughs a lot, does a good line in ironic self-deprecation and says she's happiest 'tottering on a bar-stool with a glass in one hand and a fag in the other'.

This is not to say she isn't all the things her stereotyped TV equivalent is never allowed to be: she is certainly intelligent (she has a degree); she has a lasting Christian faith which has been thought through and which she often questions; she is perceptive about her own emotions and is able to sum other people up with decisive accuracy. She resents the label 'victim'.

'I'm a sensible person on the surface and I don't like what's underneath. Since all this happened, I seem to have turned inside out. There's all this insecure crap on top and the real me is in my head saying "don't you worry, girl. You'll be all right." '[1]

She is sensitive about being patronised when she's told she certainly doesn't come across as insecure, there's an edge to her curt reply. Then, almost as if to remind herself to keep calm, she strokes the synthetic purple fur on her cushion-cover. She's fully aware of how this action comes across and shows it with a weary smile. She has to be objective about herself; she reckons all single people have to be. She doesn't bother with boyfriends at the moment. She might change her mind – she hopes she will – but not just yet.

'For a long time, I didn't trust anyone not to be the same as he was. I had one or two offers, you know? I'd go down the pub and somebody would get talking – or even if a friend introduced me to a bloke – I would always think, "yeh, but you could turn out to be just like him". And so I never let myself go, not even for a minute or two. I was always just that

little bit frosty – you know? Even if I fancied them at first –
which I did sometimes – it just took three or four jumps in
my imagination and I'd got them down as a nutter. I wanted
to trust them, but I couldn't. It was even worse if they were
nice to me and came across as being decent blokes because
that's just how he was in the beginning.'[2]

'He' was just a bit older than Kate and we shall call him
Peter. Kate is not averse to the idea of going out with older
men, but points out that her last boyfriend was five years her
junior. When 'the Peter thing' started (she objects to the
phrase 'when they first met' because it sounds as if she was a
participant), she had just finished a long relationship. The
split-up had been amicable and she was 'on the look-out'. She
was working for a well-known office bureau and had enjoyed
her first three weeks in a job which, though temporary,
promised to become semi-permanent if both sides got on.

Her new colleagues sometimes used to have Friday lunch
in a convenient local pub. In fact it was directly across the
road from the office: '*too* convenient' she jokes. The centre of
Leeds was a just a short walk away and, at the end of the first
week, Kate did some midday shopping and called in for a
sandwich on the way back.

Inside, there were four or five people she had already met
and one or two from other departments who made her feel
welcome. One of these was a man called David. He was
pleasant enough, but he came across as being 'a bit full of
himself'. He left the pub before Kate did.

Her overall impression was that she was going to enjoy
working for the company and her new colleagues were a great
bunch. She had already become friends with a woman called
Allison who worked in the same department and the two of
them had promised each other a night on the town.

The following Friday, David was there again and this time
he was joined by his brother. Kate didn't particularly notice
him at first but Allison introduced them briefly. 'Peter' was
unemployed and, she was told, turned up every so often and
usually left the pub much later, usually on his own. The
inference was clear: Peter was a drinker and a bit of a sad
case. Kate thought this was a shame as he wasn't bad-looking.

'He turned up that once at the end of my second week and I don't think I really spoke to him or his brother. I was with Allison. They might have made a few jokes at our expense – just between themselves. You know what it's like – and it doesn't bother me at all. I like to have a good time and I was keen to make a good impression. I mean, I'm not going to go around claiming sexual harassment if someone comes up and says I've got a nice body or something like that.'[3]

Another week went by and the two men were there again.

'I think I bought a round of drinks and I remember they didn't have anything because they said I hadn't had one when it had been their round earlier on. I said we'd have to get some joined-up policy or something: some daft joke. I didn't make any big thing of it.

'In between times, of course, I saw David at work but I didn't see Peter at all. I don't think I would have remembered him if I'd met him in the street. I was enjoying the job, though I'm not sure I was ready to give up temping and make it permanent at that point. On Friday, I went to the pub at lunchtime and, sure enough, Peter was there as well. Mind you, so were most of the other people who were with us the other times. He offered me a drink almost as soon as I came in and I said I would. I only drink orange juice – at lunchtime anyway. I was hardly going to think one orange juice was going to give him any ideas. He bought my friend, Allison, one at the same time. It's not as if you're signing your life away, is it?'[4]

Peter spent much of that lunch hour ogling Kate from across the bar. Allison's round came up and she included Peter. The return drink was accepted, and when Allison placed it on the table in front of him, Peter raised it in salutation to Kate. She assumed he thought the pint was from both of them and mouthed a 'cheers' back across the din. She noticed that his eyes lingered on her face and she got a fleeting glow of satisfaction from it. A minute or two later she looked back: he was talking to his brother and, though he twice shot her glances of appreciation, she still thought this was nothing more than a bit of harmless flirting. She would have preferred it if he'd been blond and not quite so hirsute, but she wasn't averse to his looks and was flattered by his obvious interest.

'I found out later that he was forty-one but he looked a lot younger than that. He had a nice enough face and he was smart. He was a bit on the skinny side and he had that sort of chest-hair that came right up to his throat. I thought as long as he didn't have a hairy back, I could cope.'[5]

Even if he did fancy her and, to use her phrase, she 'wouldn't kick him out of bed', she was quick to explain she had no intentions of doing anything about Peter. Though the relationship she'd just finished had died a natural death, she was worried about starting another one 'on the rebound' and thought it best to give herself a break from men for a while.

Allison had noticed the looks Kate was getting and ribbed her about it. The two women laughed together. Both shot Peter surreptitious glances, giggling all the more when he caught them doing it.

David came up to Kate later that afternoon and left a piece of paper on her desk. It was his brother's phone number. He said Peter had asked him to pass it on, and would she give him a call? He attempted to hurry away, saying he'd leave it with her, but she called him back. She told him she wasn't up for dates and asked him to explain to his brother and say 'thank you'. David asked her to at least ring Peter and let him down gently. He didn't often make the effort to contact women and Kate must have had quite a big effect on him for him to have summoned up the courage. He was having a bit of a bad time at the moment and would appreciate a few encouraging words.

It seemed perfectly reasonable and Kate agreed. She decided to get it over with that evening. She didn't want to lead anyone on, but she saw no reason why she should upset him unnecessarily.

'I finished work and was coming out of the reception area. I saw Peter standing across the road and he looked like he was pissed. I assumed he'd stayed in the pub all afternoon and I didn't think he'd be in a condition to talk about things properly. I pretended I'd forgotten something and went back into the building. I left a different way. When I was crossing over the road to get my bus, I got a quick peak round the front of the office and he was still there. He *was* pissed, I was sure of it. I thought I'd had a lucky escape and best not phone him after all. I'd ask David to take a note to him instead.'[6]

She wrote the note as soon as she got home, taking some time to choose her words and making sure she said nothing which might be misinterpreted. She didn't want him to think the reason for her refusal was that she'd seen him drunk. She predicted the protests: 'Don't think I'm always like that.' Also, she didn't want to give him the impression she thought him unattractive. David had said his brother needed a confidence boost and she wasn't at all averse to admitting her initial appreciation of him.

If she had been totally honest, the picture which she now had of Peter as a lovelorn no-hoper who was shy of women, had put her off completely. She preferred men who 'had something about them'.

'I let him think I wasn't free. I didn't exactly lie, but I said there was another bloke who I had to consider – or something like that. I'm not that good with words, but I think I put it quite nicely. If I'd been him I wouldn't have been offended about what I said. I would have just thought "Oh well, that's the end of that then".'[7]

But it wasn't.

During the first part of the following week, Peter rang Kate at work. He told her he'd received her note and he understood where she was coming from. He asked her if she'd meet him in the pub at five o'clock. When Kate said she didn't think this was a good idea he took it to mean she was bothered about his brother seeing them together. He suggested another place where, he assured her, David never went. She told him she didn't care at all about David. He asked her what she wanted to do instead then? He now seemed to think the objection was to meeting in a pub, as against a restaurant or some other place.

'I said I didn't think it was a good idea us meeting because there was nothing for us to say to one another. I told him again what I'd said in the note: that I wasn't into meeting anybody at the moment. He said, "I won't let you down you know."

'I was still trying to be understanding. I really didn't want to upset him. I know it's stupid, but I said I'd meet him this once but he wasn't to read anything into it because he wasn't going to end up taking me home or anything. He said he had more respect for me than that.'[8]

Kate believed she was dealing with a shy man who evidently had a lot of old-fashioned values. She felt sorry for him and still believed she could let him down gently. Although she was reluctant to do it, they arranged to meet at the regular local. She considered taking Allison with her but when she asked her, Allison said Kate was asking for trouble and the best thing would be to 'blow him out'.

Peter was sitting on his own. He was cheerful enough and had an orange juice ready for her as she entered the building. When she sipped it she discovered it was, in fact, vodka and orange. She made a joke about it, asking him if he was trying to get her drunk. His reaction was 'creepy'.

He took her joke to be a serious comment. Sounding ridiculously pompous, he asked if she drank a lot. It was evidently an invitation to share her darkest secrets with him; it was intrusive and uncalled for. Kate laughed it off, saying he needn't worry on her account; she rarely had more than one glass of wine. Despite her protests Peter took the drink away and ordered her a glass of wine instead.

Kate had no idea how to take this. He might have thought he was being the old-fashioned gentleman; he evidently had no idea how offensive most women would find his attitude. He continued to offend, by assuring her, quite unnecessarily, that he wouldn't let her have too many because he didn't like females to make a fool of themselves. Old-fashioned gentleman was one thing, but Peter was practically Victorian.

He started to talk about the way 'some girls' get 'tarty' and said how glad he was she didn't drink. He thought it was good, too, that she knew how to dress. She pointed out she was dressed for work and, in any case, it wasn't anything to do with him if she wanted to drink – or dress – in any way she pleased. She describes Peter's response to this as 'weird'.

'He said I could cut that out. If we were going to get on, I didn't have to pretend to be a tart because he knew I wasn't one. He wanted to know why women always thought men went for "that type" and he kept going on about the fact that *he* didn't. In a way, I was stuck – because I'd already got talking about this whole thing that was sod all to do with him. Every time he started to lay the law down about what I should be like, I felt I just had to say – generally – that that wasn't the sort of thing he should say to strangers when he met them. I was a bit angry and I was a bit – well, I wanted to help him. If he was going to meet someone else he was hardly going the right way about getting anywhere with them. I suppose I should have just told him to sod off and left as soon as possible.'[9]

She stayed about an hour. Then, realising she was getting nowhere, she told him she was meeting somebody. Peter wanted to know who it was and became angry when she wouldn't tell him. She left. When she got outside she realised she was trembling. Peter had started to worry her.

He phoned her the next day at work. He apologised for being annoyed with her and suggested going out again. She refused, of course, but still tried to make light of the whole thing. She said she was generally quite busy and she didn't go out much after work. Maybe they would have a drink together one Friday lunchtime but she'd prefer to leave it at that.

'I'm not having that,' he said and he sounded genuinely angry.

Kate bridled and asked what he meant.

'You were all over me in the pub,' he told her. 'Then you think you can just ignore me. I'm not going to be messed about.'

Aware she was being listened to by others in the office, she resisted the strong temptation to defend herself. She put the phone down on him. It rang again. She didn't pick it up for a moment or two and was relieved when she did – it was somebody else.

She had a word with David. He once again excused his brother by saying he'd been through a hard time and needed understanding. He thanked Kate for meeting Peter and promised to have a word himself. She needn't worry if she saw Peter again because he wouldn't bother her. He was harmless.

Several weeks passed and it seemed David was right. There were no more phone calls and Peter didn't turn up at the pub on Fridays. On one occasion Kate thought she may have seen him outside work but she wonders now if she was being paranoid.

The subject became something of a joke between her and Allison and, inevitably, other people at work gradually got to find out about it. All of them treated it with understandable levity. Every time Kate's phone rang, the cry would go up: 'that'll be her boyfriend'.

Kate got a call at her flat. It had been taken by the answering machine. It was Peter.

He said he knew she'd been laughing at him behind his back and if she didn't want to go out with him all she had to do was say so. Then he asked if she'd give him another chance. He'd call again and they could arrange where to meet.

'My heart just sank. I just thought, why doesn't he just take *no* and go away? I did feel a bit guilty when he said that about laughing about him because it was true – I had.'[10]

He rang again about eleven o'clock that same evening. He launched straight into what he had to say, without any preliminaries, beginning by telling her he wasn't annoyed any more but they needed to 'sort this thing out'. She now considered him nothing more than a pathetic nuisance and he'd certainly lost all physical attraction as far as she was concerned. She told him there was nothing to sort out.

She presumed, correctly as it happened, it was his brother who'd found out about their treating Peter's advances as a joke. Reading between the lines, it seemed he'd told Peter in order to impress on him that he'd no chance of attracting Kate. Peter, however, had taken the information in a different way. In his mind, it seemed they had already been far closer than in reality. He saw Kate's conflicting reactions, not as a tactful way of telling him she wasn't interested, but as disloyalty. He again asked her to meet him and she flatly refused. She still hoped he would get the message, but his persistence and his assumptions really worried her.

She had another talk with David. This time, surprisingly, he seemed to have little time for her problems. He evidently believed Kate had led his brother on and even referred to her being 'all over him' in the pub: the phrase Peter himself had used. When she told David no such thing had happened, he clearly didn't believe her. His brother had told him about it, he said. Peter was very upset at the time.

David denied passing on Kate's home phone number – he didn't know it himself – but admitted his brother had, on the first occasion they'd met, asked for her last name. Kate realised, with some fear, that Peter must have looked her up in the directory.

As she recalls all this, Kate is almost apologetic. Few people would blame her for indignantly denying any responsibility for Peter's obsession but she has questioned this carefully. She describes each outrageous incident and almost always follows with some mitigating comment about her own behaviour. Her conscious mind tells her she is completely innocent but old habits run deep. Her friends have noticed this tendency to put herself down; they've often teased her about it. She blames her childhood and her relationship with her parents. Her up-bringing wasn't traumatic she says, but it was stamped with repeated warnings about 'getting above herself'. She usually assumes she is in the wrong, even when other people and the evidence of her own experience say she isn't. She wishes she were less sensitive.

She spent a sleepless night wondering if she had encouraged Peter's unwanted attention. She constantly brought her mind back to the time in the pub when she and Allison had been laughing at his appreciative glances. She wondered if this could have been misinterpreted.

No, she told herself, it must have been obvious she wasn't interested and she'd been absolutely up-front with him from the very first time he'd asked her out. This fleeting self-assurance was immediately undermined by other insecurities. Had she made a terrible mistake in agreeing to see him after the original letter? She knew there was no way she'd intended to make him think there was some hope, but she'd obviously given him that impression. She wondered over and over what it was she'd said – what had she done?

Again, Peter was waiting for her outside work. Briefly, she considered taking the other exit again but decided he'd no right to make her do that. By this route, she had to pass him on the way to the bus stop. Taking a deep breath, she headed straight for him, looking determinedly ahead of her. As she approached him, she quickened her step and passed without looking in his direction. She was angry with him for making her feel wretched about herself and hated feeling scared of him.

'I thought that if he treated all women like he had me, there was no bloody wonder he hadn't got anywhere with any of them.'[11]

Keeping up with her brisk pace, he followed her towards the bus stop. He spoke to her several times. He twice called 'Kate!' When she pointedly ignored him, he called her name in full. He did this a second time and followed it with her address. Kate felt her stomach turn. Of course, she'd already worked out that if he knew her phone number, it was more than likely he knew her address as well, since both were in the phone book, but his having memorised it was quite another thing. Also, by stating it in the way he did, he was sending her a message: 'I know where you live.'

He stood some feet away as she waited for the bus. She continued to pretend to ignore him. He spoke about her to various passers-by, sarcastically explaining to them that she was unable to speak to him.

'It's a shame when they get like that. What would you do? . . . Give her one – or ignore the fucking cow? . . . Hey! Kate! Can you speak yet? Have you seen me here?'

He went on in this vein. Kate fixed her gaze on a shop-front; she began counting the books in the window. She realised everybody knew she was the subject of this tirade but at the same time reckoned if she made any sort of protest, it would just seem as though she was more involved with him than she actually was.

'He wanted me to get annoyed and tell him to fuck off! I felt like doing this, but I just kept biting my tongue because

I didn't want it to look like he was my boyfriend and we'd had a row or something. This woman standing next to me was getting more and more disgusted because of his language. I was hoping she'd start arguing with him and take some of the pressure off me, but she didn't. It seemed like ages before the bus came, but I suppose it was about quarter of an hour. For a minute I thought he was going to get on with me. If he'd tried it, I really would have told the driver he was following me and not to let him on. I went over it in my mind: if the driver had said he wasn't going to help me, I would have got off the bus. Then, if Peter had got off at the same time, I would've had to get a taxi. As it turned out, I was all right. He just stayed where he was. He ran alongside the bus and banged on the window. It really scared me. I felt dead embarrassed all the way home but it wasn't my fault.'[12]

Kate was aware, even then, that she was being stalked. She'd read about stalking in the press and had seen a film which, at the time, she'd dismissed as over-the-top. She had thought the victim on the TV screen was a fool and was totally convinced no such thing could ever happen to a woman with any sense. She was now regretting what she'd thought. She realised there was very little she could do to dissuade this man. If he wanted to follow her and cause a scene at the bus stop, he was quite able to do it. She anticipated an escalation of events: flowers or other gifts arriving, more phone calls.

She didn't see him for a few days. When she next encountered him, Peter was drunk. He rushed out of the pub and yelled across the road at her. She ignored him and hurried away. She didn't go to her usual bus stop but instead walked along to the next one. She felt a huge sense of relief when the bus came along and Peter was not on it. All the time she'd been waiting she'd subconsciously been expecting him to be. She had a growing sense of paranoia. Or as she put it: 'If there's any blame to be handed out, I'm going to say "yes, please. I'll have that!" – Even if it's me that should be giving it to somebody else.'[13]

To her relief she heard and saw nothing of him for about six weeks. She indulged in the luxury of feeling relieved and considering she'd had a lucky escape.

She didn't go to her usual lunchtime pub during this time. She had told Allison what was going on and the two of them had deserted their local in favour of one a few streets away. Other colleagues had remarked on this but they'd bought the excuse that Allison had given up smoking (which was true) and the new pub had a 'no-smoking' bar. Now, feeling everything was back to normal, they decided to risk a drink back in the original place.

It was the birthday of another colleague and they planned an extended lunch. They took precautions. Allison went in first and checked that Peter wasn't there.

The barman passed a casual remark about Kate having given her boyfriend the push. He said, innocently enough, if she was still free, he'd be willing to take her on. Angrily, she asked him what he meant. He said the 'boyfriend' (who from his description she took to be Peter) had been in the pub quite a few times. He usually stayed half the afternoon and left when he was quite drunk. He'd often said he was waiting for his girlfriend. The 'girlfriend' had apparently given him the push but he'd said he was determined to make it up with her. He'd been in some weeks ago and had rushed out when she had emerged from the office building across the road . . .

Kate was now very worried indeed. She thought long and hard about what she should do. If she antagonised Peter in any way, he might become violent. In any case it seemed unlikely from what she'd heard that he would desist. On the other hand, she couldn't let his behaviour go unchallenged. She doubted his brother would be sympathetic, though he did seem to be her best bet. In the end she decided to give this course of action a try. She reserved another option, which was growing in the back of her mind.

As she'd feared, David was not going to listen to her. Chillingly, it transpired that Peter had kept him abreast of an utterly fictitious affair which he'd claimed he'd been having with Kate. It had, according to what she gleaned from David's conversation, been a tempestuous one. David freely confessed he'd advised his brother to give up it up, but not for the reasons Kate had hoped. He'd decided Kate was what he called a 'prick-teaser' and he thought his brother was better off without her. He had, he told her, not said much about her alleged behaviour to the people at work, because he considered himself to be above that kind of gossip. He reckoned Kate would 'soon start messing around with the wrong kind of bloke and get taught a lesson'.

When she came away, Kate was reeling. It seemed the brother was almost as delusional as her pursuer. She needed to talk to somebody. She and Allison met up that evening. On their way to town, as they chatted, Peter faded in Kate's mind into being something ludicrous and irrelevant. It was only later when they were sitting down in an Indian restaurant that her anger surfaced again.

'He had no right to have said those things about me and his brother was as bad as he was, for believing him. Allison said I should take it up with David's superior at work but I didn't want to cause any trouble there because I was getting on quite well and there was every chance the job would continue for months, if not years. Temps don't have the same employment protection as permanent staff which is one of the drawbacks, although it's compensated for in lots of other ways. I told her what I really needed was just to get it all off my chest and have a bloody good moan about it. She was more worried than that and kept on at me about doing something about it officially. I might have put that idea in her mind myself because it was me that mentioned stalkers. She asked me did I reckon he was one and I said "yes, I was pretty sure he was." '[14]

Kate had decided on her reserve plan of action. She outlined it to Allison who was doubtful about it at first but, after a drink or two, thought it was a great idea. Kate proposed to enlist the help of her sister's husband, Gary. He was bigger and broader than Peter, had no compunction about using his fists if it was in the right cause and was very protective of his friends. She felt sure a visit from Gary would dissuade Peter from bothering her further and provide her with a much-needed feeling of satisfaction. She was aware what she planned was 'dodgy' but she considered it appropriate after the stress she'd already been put through. In any case, there wasn't much else she could do about it. She thought (wrongly as it happened, since this was after the 1997 law) the police wouldn't do anything to help her.

The trouble was, she had no idea where Peter lived. She could hardly ask David to arrange for him to be in the pub, then get Gary to give him a beating. Putting that difficulty aside, she plucked up enough courage to ask Gary that same evening. He deduced, quite correctly, that she'd had too much to drink and told her he'd do what she wanted if she could come to him sober and ask the same thing. She said, she certainly could – and would do.

Peter's presence in the pub at lunchtime and near the office after work was a frequent if not regular occurrence. They could easily avoid him in the pub, all they had to do was walk in and walk straight out again, but five o'clock was a different matter. He had found out how she managed to give him the slip by using the side exit and was positioning himself where he could see both doors. As a result she stayed late on several evenings. She was getting extremely nervous at home. She lived alone and was more or less certain he'd turn up at her door one day soon.

In fact, unknown to her, he'd been turning up for quite a long time.

Kate started getting silent phone calls. She knew it was Peter and, taking advice from a programme she'd seen, answered each and every one by blowing a whistle down the phone. She had a chain fitted to her door and was disturbed to find she tensed every time she heard footsteps on the walkway outside her flat. Peter was getting to her and yet he'd done virtually nothing she could pin-point as being beyond the pale. Most people, she felt sure, would dismiss the whole thing as the mildly unreasonable behaviour of a would-be boyfriend who'd been given the brush-off. In common with other victims before her, Kate was approaching the stage where she almost wished he would do something major in order to give her the excuse of going to the police.

After the sixth or seventh silent phone call, Kate blew her whistle, swore down the phone and was about to put the receiver down when:

'. . . I don't know, something told me he was still on the line. I didn't want to put the phone back against my ear because I thought – stupid but I did – that he'd know I was listening. On the other hand, I was curious. I know I should have just slammed the phone down but the whole thing had become like a game and I was playing it as well as him. I was frightened, yes, I was angry, bloody right I was, but I was playing the game too. I put the phone on the table in front of me and just sort of looked at it for ages. Then I heard him saying "Are you there? Kate? Are you there?" And I cut him off.'[15]

Later that night the doorbell went. For a moment, Kate went confidently to answer it but her normal reaction to the familiar sound lasted only for a split second. The surge of anxiety which supplanted it was bigger than she'd felt about anything. A flickering series of images went through her head: the woman alone, the man outside. She tried to pull herself together, arguing that her fear stemmed from an overactive imagination fed on a diet of thrillers and horror films. The idea that she was now a part of one and was playing the victim seemed nothing short of ridiculous.

Still – she wasn't expecting anyone and it was after nine at night. Feeling rather foolish, she crept towards the door on all fours, hoping to sneak up to the spy-hole and see who was there. There was a window but it had net curtains over it and, as long as she kept low down, it would be impossible to see her. She got there and eased herself up. Even then, she wondered if the person outside would be able to see her eye, blocking the light from the hallway. She resolved to experiment later to find out.

There didn't appear to be anybody there, which meant it was either some innocent caller who'd given up or, and here Kate freely admits the influence of Hollywood, that he was hiding at the side, waiting to pounce on her as she checked the walkway. She opened the door a few inches, keeping it on the chain and called 'hello'. There was no response.

Then she noticed a box on the floor at her feet. It was one of the standard white packages with red and black lettering which the Post Office sell. It was small, maybe about six inches square. She opened the door a little wider but carefully, very carefully. She snatched the parcel and took it inside, slamming the door behind her. Her heart was thumping. It felt like she had just undergone some huge ordeal but all she'd done was open her front door. She cursed the man who was turning her into this nervous wreck and again wondered how much of it was due to her own sense of the dramatic. She assumed the parcel had arrived by some official carrier and had been left by them when they couldn't get an immediate response. It would make sense, since busy people seldom want to stand around on doorsteps for too long. The label was typed with her name and address and the lid was held down with adhesive tape. The box had been used before. She opened it.

'It nearly made me sick. I just opened the lid and the smell hit me full in the face. I knew straight away who'd sent it.'[16]

'It' was a piece of excrement. There was nothing else in the box and the thing was still warm.

'It was childish in a way. You do that sort of thing when you're a kid don't you? Fall out with your friend and send them a parcel of shit. Somehow I couldn't see it like that though. Apart from him doing what he'd done, it made me feel so insecure in my own house. I didn't sleep all night. I even thought of ringing somebody up and asking them to come and stay with me but I was determined not to let that wanker get the better of me.'

She looks back on the incident with ironic humour. 'Other people get unwanted flowers and things like that. I get a turd. Trust me to pick a stalker who doesn't bother with the chat up bit.'[17]

She took the parcel into work next day and, full of righteous indignation, marched into David's office and slammed it down on his desk. She doesn't remember his reaction, she was too upset. She told him his brother had left this thing on her doorstep and he could give it him back, preferably full in the face. She stormed out.

David didn't contact her about the incident. In fact, she rarely saw him again during the course of her working day. If he was deliberately avoiding her he was soon to be saved the trouble. Kate received a call from the agency. Her job at that company had been terminated. It was nothing to do with the quality of her work, they assured her, it had just come to an end. Kate was furious. She felt positive David, Peter or both of them were behind this. She went into David's part of the building the very next day and 'let fly'.

'I was really blazing. I said I hoped he was satisfied because I'd really liked this job and that I wouldn't touch his f'ing brother with a barge pole. I said I was going to get the police in on it and – I don't remember – I was just really, really, blazing. It was a right scene. Amy, who works next to him tried to get me to calm down but I was going to have my say. Then I just burst into tears and ran. David came up to me later. I couldn't believe he'd have the cheek but he said the end of my job was nothing to do with him or his brother. For some reason I didn't believe him. He said his brother had told him about the phone calls and the 'visits'. I asked him what visits? – I thought he'd only been round once. I could see he looked a bit uncomfortable and then he said Peter had been coming round to my place and watching my flat loads and loads of times. I was freaked out, I can tell you.'[18]

According to his brother, Peter had parked his car in the car park and spent evening after evening listening to the radio and watching the light in Kate's flat. He'd told his brother it made him feel close to her. It was from the car he'd made the silent phone calls. One of Kate's telephone connections is by the kitchen window and several times he'd been lucky and seen her in silhouette, picking up the receiver. David had thought all this was mad behaviour and had told his brother to get a life. Kate was by now quite determined to get the police involved. David said, in what she described as a cold sort of voice, 'I wouldn't do that if I were you. He's quite harmless. He just wants you to go out with him again.' She protested once again that she'd never been out with him in the first place. David didn't believe her. Apart from accepting that the parcel of excrement was 'way over the top' (his brother had 'probably been drunk' when he delivered it), he really seemed to believe she had nothing to complain about.

'It wasn't all the time, like you read about, and he wasn't doing very much. It was almost like he was playing at being a real stalker and he wasn't doing it very well. Part of me hoped it would just fizzle out – obviously – and another part of me was thinking: No, he's gone way too far already and I have to make him see he can't do this sort of thing to people just because they don't happen to fancy him.'[19]

She contacted the bureau and was again assured that no complaint against her had been received by them. There was another job to go to next week in a different part of town. At least she would be rid of Peter's presence after work. That evening she said a temporary goodbye to Allison who said they must stay in touch. Kate then went round to her sister's place and, sober as promised, asked Gary to come round to hers for a few evenings and, when Peter appeared, sort him out. Gary couldn't that week because he was going away (he was a lorry driver) but said he'd be glad to the week after, especially when he heard about Peter's presence outside Kate's flat.

She decided to spend the coming weekend in Blackpool. Some people she knew were going, among them an ex-boyfriend who had become a platonic friend. It promised to be a weekend of drink and wild times: just what she needed. She said her goodbyes at work, not an unusual occurrence in her line of employment, and left at five. On the way out she noticed Peter looking across the road at her. She yelled some obscenities at him. He responded by waving at her as though she had said something pleasant. Determined not to let him get to her, she hailed a taxi and went home to pack.

She threw some things into a suitcase and rang a regular firm for a cab to take her to her friend's house. She took the precaution of asking them to ring the doorbell three times. She made up an excuse: that her flatmate was also expecting a caller and didn't want to be disturbed unnecessarily because she was studying. The excuse sounded clumsy and long-winded. Kate realised that she was, even in this, feeling guilty again.

She hadn't told her friends anything about Peter and had been musing on whether she should do. In the end, she decided she would. Feeling like it was going to be a fun weekend, but also one for getting some things off her chest, she sat down and waited.

The bell rang, but only once. Panic rushed up to take over her brain but she deliberately calmed herself down. It wasn't at all certain or even likely it would be Peter. He had only rung the bell before on one occasion and that had been much later in the evening. There was a long pause and then it went once again. She waited to see if there was a third ring and, sure enough, it came. This time it was a double ring: not the signal she'd asked for but maybe enough. She went to the door and, without opening it, called 'Who is it?'

'Taxi!' said a voice. Even then she wasn't sure. What if Peter knew she'd rung for a taxi? What if it was him pretending to be somebody else? She told herself not to be so stupid, but even so answered the door with the chain on. It was safe.

As the taxi pulled out of the car-park, Kate turned round to see another car following them at some short distance. Peter was in the driving seat. She told the taxi driver they were being followed by a 'creep who was bothering her'. Seeming to quite enjoy the challenge, the driver accelerated and, just managing to get through the lights before red, left Peter some way behind. He took a circuitous route round the block and then joined the main road. Peter had vanished and, with considerable relief, Kate settled down to forget her recent problems and enjoy her holiday. The driver was curious about what had happened and was keen to give her his own thoughts on nuisances who followed women around.

Blackpool was a good idea. She was able to talk to her old friends about her worries and they all agreed with her: it would be best to let Gary give the man a fright. He wouldn't be so keen to follow her if he knew somebody was looking out for her. Once again, the entire episode quickly became unreal. It was only at night that it surfaced again to plague her imagination.

She went through every scenario and considered just about every terrifying outcome: she imagined Peter with a knife, Peter prosecuting her for setting her brother-in-law on him – and worse. She changed her mind over and over again. She thought of going to the police again. They would at least take the harassment seriously now it had become so obvious and she might be able to persuade them to have an officer on hand next time he appeared.

The new job was all right, but was nowhere near as good as the one she'd left. She still had a sneaking suspicion Peter had been behind her losing it. (She never found out this definitely wasn't the case, but now she thinks it wasn't.) At least she had no worries about his being there after work. She was, however, careful about leaving the flat in the morning just in case he'd decided to follow her. She was also concerned about him breaking in while she was away from home. She had a word with a neighbour who promised to keep an eye on things.

The phone calls continued sporadically. They were mostly silent and occurred only once or twice in the evening. On one occasion she received one when other people were with her. Her ex-boyfriend snatched the receiver and told the caller in no uncertain terms to 'go away'.

Gary was still an option. Kate's sister rang and said he'd been in contact from France where he was working and had said he was still willing to sort 'the bastard' out.

When he arrived back, Gary phoned and told her the next time she saw Peter's car she was to ring him. He would be there in minutes and he assured her the problem would soon be over.

'I told him I didn't want him to go getting violent or anything. I just wanted the bastard warned off. He said that's exactly what he was going to do, but he had that sort of voice on him. I wouldn't like to have been in Peter's shoes. Our Gary's a big lad.'

It wasn't long after her return from Blackpool that she found a reason to call her new 'bouncer' (as she christened Gary): she had another silent phone call. She reached for the whistle which by now felt pretty stupid as it didn't seem to deter Peter in the slightest. Then she stopped, listened for a while and put the phone gently on the table. She crept over to the kitchen and, without putting on the light, peered out.

She couldn't really see the cars parked outside because it was too dark, but she felt sure she could make out the shape of Peter's among the few which were there. She went back into the living room and dialled Gary's number on her mobile. Without any preliminaries, he answered her call with the words 'I'll be right over'.

'Peter had finished his little routine. I put the phone back on the rest and sat there on the sofa. I was really worried but I was, like, excited as well. After a little bit I went into the kitchen and checked out the car park again. He was still there. If he was going to do his usual thing, he'd wait for an hour or two and then he'd ring again. He usually waited for exact hours and half hours before he called: it was always exactly on or just after. I'd worked out that he probably listened to radio programmes and did his bit of heavy-breathing just after each one had finished. I wondered why he didn't bring his tea and make a picnic of it.'[20]

After a short wait there was the distinctive roar of another car engine being driven too fast. Gary had arrived.

Feeling braver now she had her protector on the scene, Kate pulled the net curtain aside to watch. Gary's car screeched to a halt in the middle of the drive. He jumped out and, first looking up towards her window and giving a brief wave, he looked around the car park. Kate ventured out onto the balcony and indicated the car she could now clearly see Peter sitting in. Gary ran over to it and banged on the driver's window.

Peter had locked the door and was attempting to drive away but Gary's vehicle was blocking his exit. Gary thumped on the window again as Peter backed off the other way, towards the wall. He drove threateningly towards Gary's car, and for a moment or two Kate thought he was going to smash into it. He didn't – mainly because it wouldn't have solved his problem and would have just served to give Gary more of an excuse to use violence. Eventually, he wound down his window an inch or two. Gary was standing 'like an LA cop' with his hands on the car roof and his gaze lowered to Peter. Kate listened as the following conversation took place:

Gary: 'What's your problem, mate?'

Peter: 'My problem?'

Gary: 'I'm going to give you a fair warning, right? Either you fuck off now and don't come back – ever – or I fucking brain you and you leave here in an ambulance. Right?'

He kicked the side of the car viciously and repeated 'Right?' Kate couldn't hear what Peter's reply was; Gary said afterwards he'd made some comment about it being a free country. After a few more kicks, Gary got into his car and cleared the way for Peter to make his escape. Gary parked and came upstairs 'like a pest-control man who'd just done a good job on the rat problem.' He told Kate he didn't think she'd be having any more stalking problems but, if she did, she only had to call him. If he was away, he would arrange for a mate to be on hand.

When he phoned again, Peter was unrepentant and threatening.

'You shouldn't have done that,' he said.

Kate lost her temper. She repeated what Gary had told her and made it clear she was more than willing to take him up on his offer of protection. Peter wanted to know who Gary was. When told it was none of his business he retreated into a whining attempt to win Kate's sympathy. He hadn't meant to frighten her and he was sorry he had. It was only because 'their relationship' was very important to him. He'd never felt like this about anyone before. He knew he'd messed things up but if only she'd give him another chance . . .

She told him to fuck off.

Pizzas which she hadn't ordered were delivered to her door – four or five times. They came from different places and Kate rang round every takeaway in the district to warn them not to take any notice of orders with her address.

Her worst experience arrived on the doormat one morning in a padded envelope. She picked it up with the other post and, as was her habit, checked the post-code to see where it had come from. It was stamped and post-marked Liverpool but, when she later inspected it more closely, she found the postage was well out-of date. The parcel had, in fact, been delivered by hand. The address was written mainly in capital letters with the odd lower-case letter mixed in. She knew before she opened it that it was going to be something unpleasant.

Inside was the remains of a dead bird. It was matted with blood and might well have been found on the road-side – Kate hoped so. There was nothing else in the envelope – just a few pathetic-looking feathers. She was revolted.

She checked the car-park but Peter's car was not there. Gary's intervention had done some good – he'd frightened Peter away from direct stalking.

A letter arrived – a piece of paper covered in frenetic scribble; the ballpoint had gone through in several places. It was illegible. She went to the police. To her surprise, they were sympathetic and very concerned. The officer told her to contact them the very next time anything happened. Meanwhile they took a note of the only address she had for Peter, care of his brother, and assured her they'd have a word with him. They also informed her about her rights under the law which she'd previously been unaware of. She felt much better and settled down to wait for Peter to hang himself with his own rope.

'I was almost looking forward to the next thing he did after that. I knew it wouldn't be long and all he had to do was carry on and I'd have him. He wasn't phoning me at that point and, in a way, it was better that he'd started doing things that I could take to the police. I should have shown them the dead bird but I'd binned it.

'They told me they'd got Peter's address off David and they'd been round to talk to him. He'd given them the usual line about it being me who'd started all this and they'd said they weren't interested – it had to stop. He'd had one official warning and they seemed to think that might be enough. He just changed his tactics.'[21]

Kate had had several different assignments since the trouble with Peter started. She was about to begin work as a cover for someone on leave, only for a week but she quite liked that. When the bureau asked her to contact them on the Monday, she assumed they were going to change the arrangement and send her on a more lucrative mission. She was surprised at the call for they very rarely bothered unless there was something major to discuss, but the supervisor pretended it was nothing very important. Kate gave in to instant anxiety, fighting it with stern rebukes to herself – it might be something good that had happened. The positive side of her nature didn't win and she spent the weekend wracked with nervous apprehension.

On the Monday, she knew she wasn't going to be able to wait until five. She told her new employers she had a long-standing arrangement to look after a friend's child that lunchtime. It was hardly worth the elaborate lie, they were quite happy to let her go at whatever time she wanted.

'It was a complete wind-up. The girl at the bureau is really nice. She didn't know me well, but well enough to know I'm to be trusted. She was trying really hard to put on this teacher-who's-found-the-fags-in-your-bag look. Actually, I think she's younger than me so she was on a loser from the start. She said they'd had a serious complaint about me and they wanted to know my side of it before they decided how to proceed. I knew I hadn't done anything and I was quite sure where the complaint had come from. I just asked her outright if it was him. She "wasn't allowed to tell me". I told her if it *was* him she could take it from me it was a pack of lies and I had the police on his case. She backed down then. She saw I meant what I was saying and she must have known how angry I was. It turned out they'd had a phone call saying I was round at his house every night and I'd been ringing him with obscene calls. I put things through his letter-box and I'd been sending unwanted items to him, including takeaway meals. I was gobsmacked. He'd had the nerve to accuse me of just about everything he'd been doing himself. Either he was suicidal, or mad, or both. I calmed myself down and asked if she was willing to make a statement to the police. She was a bit iffy about it at first but, as I said to her, if any of what he'd said was true I was hardly likely to want the police to know about it, was I? She said she'd get it typed up that afternoon and I could either collect it or she'd post it to me. I said I'd call round for it as soon as I'd finished work, I wanted the cops to have it as soon as I could possibly get it to them.'[22]

The call to the bureau got Peter his second official warning. Kate was advised to have an exclusion order taken out against him.

'If I'd let myself go, I could easily have become a jibbering wreck but I found a kind of strength in me I didn't even know I had. A lot of it was anger and I knew I had to be careful because that sort of thing can destroy you just as easily as going the other way. I really, really, tried to feel sorry for Peter and I'm not sure I managed it. I haven't done even yet, but a lot of it is knowing that none of this was making him happy. He could have done whatever his sick little mind dreamed up and he wouldn't ever have been satisfied. If there is such a thing as Hell, he was in it right from the start.'[23]

Kate never heard from Peter after that. For months afterwards, she lived in nervous apprehension of his next move but none came. She learned some two years later that he had been killed in an accident. He had been hit by a motorcyclist who had lost control on a busy main road. She also found that he had 'made a nuisance of himself' with two other women. The one he was following at the time of his death had been about to take him to court after repeated violations of a restraining order she'd taken out against him.

9. WILD JUSTICE

Imagine you are accused of something which you didn't do. Be it a big thing or a minor misdemeanour, it is natural to feel aggrieved. Still, you feel fairly confident everyone who knows you – really knows you – won't believe a word of it. Even so, at the very least, unfounded allegations are hurtful and they're often damaging.

Let's suppose the accusation relates to something you allegedly did at work. You are in a position of trust: a senior lecturer at a university. It is your word against your accuser's and that accuser is one of your students. All you have in your defence is your previous good character and the faith your friends have in you. If you are to keep your position, there are numerous colleagues and superiors whom you must also convince of your innocence.

Furthermore, let's suppose you're accused of a misdemeanour which the most morally stalwart amongst us are capable of – an unwanted proposition. The incident was supposed to have taken place during a one-to-one interview in your office between you and the student, a respectable, middle-aged, married woman.

It's not true of course. This person is not attractive to you in the slightest. You are undergoing enough emotional problems in your private life without her problematic imaginings. You are dealing with the aftermath of a divorce and the frequent emotional advances of a close friend which you could well do without. Nevertheless, the accusations persist. Now the student says you're looking at her in an inappropriate way. You're doing it in class – in front of everybody.

Is it a matter which is worth making anything of? The student is, perhaps, a bit of an odd-ball. If you loudly protested your innocence, any number of people would rush to your support. This woman's interpretation of what, at the very most, was an innocent glance or two in her direction is probably born of her own sexual frustration. If she's honest she would admit she's attracted to you, she guesses her desires are not reciprocated and so she chooses to express herself in this odd way.

The reason? – What? – To give herself a cheap thrill? To have a brush with the possibility of physical desire? To objectify her own 'unpleasant' longings, subconsciously obeying some forgotten (perhaps religious) indoctrination?

Whatever her motivations, it's a scenario straight out of Kafka. Once such an accusation is made, it cannot be fully eradicated until it is proven to be unfounded. Even then, if the accuser persists with her allegations, they will still be there, shadowing your career, until she is discredited in some way.

The temptation is to leave the matter alone, but if it is not dealt with the problem will grow bigger and her case against you will seem stronger. So what then? Protesting your innocence is futile. This woman sees proof of your guilt in everything you do. You 'protest too much', she says, 'there's no smoke without fire.'

Now you feel your every move is being analysed by your colleagues. People are gossiping in the corridors, over a pint and on the bus. We've all done it – played the amateur psychologist, given in to tempting snippets of scandal: 'I saw the way he looked at her when she came in this morning. Did you notice? He was trying to appear normal. If he hadn't done anything he wouldn't have to make all that effort.'

You tell yourself this is pure paranoia; everybody appears to support your innocence, but it seems impossible to act normally. You find you are looking furtive, guilty and awkward every time you catch the eye of anyone who might misinterpret your intentions.

Your accuser sits in the middle of all this, triumphant. She has proved, to her own satisfaction if no one else's, that you are a liar and a charlatan. Your honesty cannot be relied upon and your morals are highly suspect. When you meet her you get nervous. You know she has noted the sweat on your forehead. You begin to doubt your own sense of logic. Black is being proven to be white and what you know to be true no longer looks as obvious as it did before.

Nothing you say or do will shake this person's relentless persecution. She wants what she claims is justice – she wants you to suffer.

Robert Fine's story illustrates the slow, crushing grip of power which the stalker can have over their victim's life. Stalking tips the scales totally, it gives absolute control to the perpetrator and robs the unfortunate victim of self-confidence, respect and rational thought. If they are to retain any semblance of calm and reason, they are now having to make exaggerated efforts to achieve normality. Like Alice in Looking Glass Land, they are going to have to run twice as fast in order to stay still.

Dr Fine is a Reader in Sociology at the University of Warwick in Coventry. He is a likeable, outgoing person. It seems incredible anyone would want to do him damage. It's obvious he has a highly-developed sense of social responsibility and conscience. On meeting him, you get the impression it wouldn't be too difficult to become his friend. In fact, maybe it's this very affability which was to blame for the strange (and entirely unsolicited) relationship one of his students chose to inflict upon him.

The student in question, whom Robert chooses to call 'Mrs M', was a woman in her middle years, married with three grown-up daughters.

'In her appearance she seems to aspire to old-fashioned respectability: she is fairly tall, of average weight, tries to dress smartly, and has dyed her hair red. She used to be recognisable by her rather striking royal blue coat.'[1]

He is careful not to judge her, reluctant to speculate on her psychological motives and genuinely willing to seek explanations, if not excuses, for her behaviour. After all, he is a sociologist:

'I'm always loath to psychoanalyse her too much. I have a lot more views than I would express publicly. I just say what happened. I don't actually know a lot about her of course. I've never been in her house. I've never seen the family, except in court. I've only ever talked to her about me. There's always a limit to the information the victim would have.

'I got the impression there were certain things about my personality which deeply "got up her nose". I'm not a particularly grave teacher – in fact I'm quite light-hearted and open. I represented something very different from what she knew. I didn't really care about the formalities and had a very relaxed way of working. I let students talk, we'd discuss things together. I think that whole way of teaching was something she found very threatening.'[2]

Robert has managed to distance himself from his experience. The passage of time, an analytical mind, sheer necessity, all play their part. If he's bitter, he doesn't express it; if he's wary of a recurrence, he doesn't let it influence what he does.

His troubles began in the autumn of 1993.

Mrs M was not in the top range of academic achievement but she had certain abilities. The course she'd chosen, a degree in sociology at Warwick, was difficult and demanding. She had, entirely through her own efforts, successfully secured the place and had passed A-level sociology in order to do it.

There was a rage boiling away just under the surface of Mrs M's conservative respectability. In this she was not unique. Many, many people can justify similar emotions in themselves. The world is not fair and we're sent into it with unequal amounts of status, talents, luck. Mrs M had had to fight hard for what came so easily to others, others who didn't even appreciate what they had.

The class had been set an assignment on Karl Marx. One of Mrs M's fellow-students had not prepared properly and as a result Mrs M had to give a reluctant solo presentation. Robert noticed her disproportionate anger at having to do this:

'I saw in it a quality of unforgiving self-righteousness which I associated with an earlier, less reflexive age . . .'[3]

It wasn't a particularly portentous incident. In itself it was fairly typical of dozens of other irritations between students. Nevertheless, Robert decided to discuss any concerns Mrs M might have – but later, when she'd had a chance to cool her temper.

She came to his office at the beginning of the following week and he gave her a mild ticking-off. She shouldn't concern herself with the failings of others, he told her, she would have her work cut-out to complete the course without those sorts of distractions.

There was no real reason to suppose the incident would be repeated. He fully expected this to be the end of the matter.

It wasn't.

'On Wednesday evening at 8.30, at the end of another late-finishing seminar, Mrs M asked to see me alone in my office. Resisting the siren calls of whisky and TV football, I agreed. Once inside, she passed me a folded sheet of paper on which was typed a message. It took me some time to grasp its meaning but I got there in the end: cryptically but definitively it contained the charge that I had sexually propositioned her during that previous encounter in my office.'[4]

She claimed she had 'a perfect memory for detail' and asked Robert to admit the offence and apologise for it. She threatened him with the loss of his job, claiming her only intention was to protect other students.

This claim is interesting. In making it, she's invoking the support of society as a whole and she's taking it upon herself to do this unpleasant job as a matter of principle. By giving herself these higher motives, she adds veracity to her claim. Such self-sacrifice would surely not be appropriate if there was any doubt about whether the incident had actually happened. Like a hypochondriac who is willing to pay for a private specialist, she's making an absolute commitment to her beliefs. Or so she believes.

Robert trusts in rational argument. With hindsight he would have had less faith in its power. He assumed Mrs M to be sincere and tried to put it to her that, though he'd no doubt she believed the incident to have taken place, she was mistaken. He suggested they put the problem behind them and get back to work.

This reasoned approach was not going to get him anywhere where Mrs M was concerned.

His lectures finished at seven. This left just enough time for a short break before seminars began some five minutes later. In these few minutes Mrs M regularly took her chance to make her accusation again, loudly and entirely publicly.

As time went on her complaints grew more elaborate and somewhat bizarre. She was now saying Robert was giving her headaches. She suggested he visited her bedroom in a paranormal way. Robert recalls 'quite vivid stories' in which the stress caused by his unwanted attentions was impinging on her subconscious. On top of all this, she alleged that he continued to harass her.

Robert could have gone to the university bosses; he was advised to do so by a colleague and this advice was to prove sound. At first he held off, thinking the problems could be sorted out in a less formal way.

'I'm a child of '68!' he laughs. He means he likes to avoid involving authority figures wherever possible.

Things got steadily worse.

Mrs M sent a questionnaire to the homes of other students:

Did you notice Dr Fine look at Mrs M for longer periods than normal?
Did you see Dr Fine stand behind Mrs M at all during seminars?
Did you see Dr Fine sit next to her at all?
If you sat near Mrs M did you notice Dr Fine looking more than usual in that direction?
Did you observe anything between them at all?
Did you believe that they had 'something going on?'[5]

She would sit there in class, Banquo-like, silently demanding justice. When she wasn't doing that, she was playing psychological games which may have looked innocuous to an outsider but carried an easily detectable message for those in the know. Take, for instance, the occasion that she handed a note down the class, from person to person until it reached Robert (to whom it was addressed). It proved to be about nothing in particular but she'd demonstrated to everyone that she was in communication with her tutor about something private which she wasn't necessarily going to keep hidden.

There were other incidents. During the summer of '94, she took it upon herself to attend every one of Robert's classes, including the ones which were reserved solely for full-time students. She tried to insist on a supposed 'right' to tape-record the lectures. This demand (which, along with other similar ones, could be read as provocation by stealth), became a typical trait. She always maintained her requests were harmless and that they were justified within accepted rules or laws. She made it clear she would fight tenaciously for what she saw as an important principle.

Her behaviour was, at this stage, still difficult to pin down as being threatening but the accumulation of various incidents were beginning to take their toll of Robert's self-assurance. She was, in effect, on the slip-road to the full-scale stalking of him.

'I think from her point of view,' Robert says, 'she wanted me to confront the truth. That was the original driving force. Then it became revenge – because the lack of acknowledgement was so upsetting as far as she was concerned that it had to be punished.

'I always felt it had nothing to do with *me*, which was quite comforting in a way. Normally when someone accuses you of something there's something there. You've done something that you know led to the accusation. There's a relationship between the accuser and the accused: you recognise the common ground. In this instance I always felt that, on some basic level, the accusations against me had nothing to do with me. It just happened to be me she'd picked on. It could have been anybody else.'[6]

Though previously having resisted the urge to put his own position in front of a higher authority, Robert did go some way to protecting himself against further maligning. He dictated a letter to a colleague, Helen Davis, the lecturer responsible for part-time students. He didn't send it, instead he asked the departmental secretary to file it away. It was an insurance which he hoped he wouldn't have to call upon. He was looking towards the end of term, believing it would also be the end of 'this unhappy acquaintance'.

Mrs M did not have his qualms about calling in the services of officialdom. She'd already involved Helen Davis and voiced her complaints. She'd also gone to the head of Robert's department, Jim Beckford.

The time came to retaliate. Robert finally sent the letter. It detailed his position and refuted all the accusations which had been levelled at him.

In June 1994 Mrs M made a formal complaint of sexual harassment, reiterating her allegations in a hefty document of nearly thirty pages.

An Investigating Committee was established to decide whether there was a case to answer. This was my first step into that world of 'committees' and 'courts' that were to become a major part of my life for the next three years.
She said in her statement:
. . . a distinct sexual advance was made.
. . . (Robert was) thinking of sex.
. . . (He) wanted sex there and then.[7]

According to Robert's perception of the document, there was in it a strange preoccupation with his eyes:

. . . how they glanced, stared, penetrated, pierced, suggested, undressed, propositioned and terrified . . .
'his constant fixed stares unnerved me and gave me an uneasy feeling';
'he fixed on me with a hard stare which almost seemed to pierce into me. It made me feel shaky and nervous';
'he was looking discreetly at the back of me – looking me up and down . . . he took into view the whole of the front of me';
'he got right up to me; his head and face fractionally off my bust and then he looked up at me; and deeply into my eyes';
'he had invade my personal space . . . it had sexual significance';
'he was looking at me hard . . . he looked at my legs';
'he looked at me really examining every detail . . . I felt naked . . . He moved his eyes to my bust again.'[8]

He saw her phraseology as reminiscent of that used in old-fashioned romances. True, her descriptions of their encounters would certainly not look out of place in a bodice-ripper, but she casts herself as something other than the demure heroine. She is still the moral crusader, sure of the principle she defends and resolute despite the emotional personal-cost of her crusade:

> I edged up to him but he reacted quickly – dropped his eyes looking at my bust again and thumped his hands hard down on the table as if trying to stop himself from touching me. This frightened me and I remained riveted to the spot. He said that I should not go to his room again but would not explain why. Eventually, I said 'Now let's get this straight you don't want me to come to your room again in case you say something we both know you've said but you may wish to deny later? Is that right?' 'Yes,' he said with a laugh. He said, 'Can't you treat it as a misunderstanding?' 'Sorry,' I said, 'Can't do that.'[9]

Because she was so sure of Robert's guilt and saw evidence of it in his every movement, she assumed her colleagues noticed exactly what she noticed and drew the same interpretation from it. In fact, Robert found other students offering him their support against Mrs M. Unknown to him, two of them had written to the committee enclosing a letter Mrs M had sent to them. They entirely refuted Mrs M's version of things as she had written them. Mrs M's letter stated that an 'incident' had occurred which they must have witnessed. Robert had supposedly 'looked at her' but quickly looked away when she turned to meet his gaze, the implication was that by doing this he was displaying his guilt. The tone of the letter was clearly paranoid. Mrs M, ever sure of her probity, was hanging herself with her own rope.

Her complaint was declared to be unfounded. She was duly cautioned not to repeat her allegations. It was mid-July 1994 – eight months after the original accusation.

Robert went to France for his summer holidays believing the whole sorry episode to be at an end. He returned to a new term with the vestiges of his old enthusiasm and an optimistic attitude towards his vocation.

It was then that the stalking began in earnest.

* * *

The word 'torment' is related to the Latin verb *torquere* which means 'to twist'. The image is one of persistence, an accumulation of effect. The malicious stalker knows full well how to turn the screw, how to build, bit by bit, on the insecurities of the victim until minimum effort is needed for maximum effect. A glance across a supermarket, a sighting in the street, a silent telephone call: anything can be the straw which breaks the camel's back. When your nerves are shot to pieces it doesn't take very much to see sinister intent in almost anything. The sheer persistence of another person who has declared their hatred for you will begin to wear you down in the end.

Mrs M, often aided by her family, became a past master at these tactics.

It began slowly. At first no one noticed – except Robert's neighbour, who had several times seen a strange woman hanging around outside his house.

Robert himself first became aware of it in September 1994. Had it not been for the previous trouble, what happened could have been put down to almost any motivation. He noticed Mrs M's car parked outside his house. Her husband, whom he'd had no previous contact with, was in the driving seat. Robert was about to walk his dog. The couple watched him. They were still there some time later when he arrived back. They did nothing: merely sat in the car and watched the house. What could be done? Ignore them? They might take this as carte blanche to continue. Or challenge them? This, as Robert would subsequently find out, was not a very effective course.

That first time Robert tried, in effect, to do both these things. He didn't make any direct response to their behaviour but instead reported it to the Chair of the Investigating Committee, Chris Duke. The letter was handed on to the university's deputy registrar, who asked Mrs M to see him about the incident.

Mrs M was not impressed. Firm in her moral superiority, she stated her public right to go wherever she liked (as long as she wasn't trespassing); she could also park her car wherever she liked (as long as it wasn't causing an obstruction). Besides which, she pointed out, she'd not been driving the car at the time Robert had seen her and therefore was not responsible for its location. The university had no right to tell her what she could and could not do outside its environs. She had checked these rights with the police and was sure of them. Pre-1997, Mrs M did indeed have every right to spend her life on Robert's doorstep. There was little if anything he could do about it.

The letter was written in a style which could have been read as facetious. It seemed she was making fun of Robert's attempts to protect himself legally. Reading between the lines, it was saying, 'Very well, if you want to play that game, I'll show you how far it will get you.' She suggested any objection Robert could possibly have to her presence outside his house must be motivated by guilt. She demanded that any future correspondence on the subject should be sent directly to her solicitor.

She said she had a special relationship with the police. The death of a relative of hers had led to her getting to know some officers. They'd even attended the funeral. Here again, a threat lurked beneath the actual words on the paper: 'I'm well-in with powerful people and can call on them at any time.'

To his dismay, Robert's hopes of the business coming to an end with the summer were not to be. During the autumn term, every week, Mrs M waited outside the room where he took his seminars. Her behaviour was always challenging and she knew exactly how far she could take it. She neither spoke to Robert, nor did she threaten him. She was well aware she had no need to do either. Watching and waiting were enough – for now.

On one typical occasion she stood outside his office window for over an hour, just gazing up – nothing more. She sometimes turned up in the evenings with her husband in tow. For reasons best known to themselves, they used their visit to examine the staff photographs on the notice board. She waited for lectures to finish and made sure Robert was aware of her presence when he passed.

Both she and her husband spent more and more time outside Robert's house. He remembers one time which was representative of many: he found her, despite the cold weather, waiting in the driveway. He asked her to leave. She went back to the car where her husband was waiting. They drove past the house, turned round and drove past again – slowly, ominously.

That autumn also saw a number of attacks on Robert's car. He stopped short of accusing Mrs M of these; it couldn't be proved she'd had anything to do with them, but the circumstantial evidence suggested her as a likely suspect. After Robert had alerted the security guard to the possibility of her involvement, Mrs M was seen examining the vehicle in the university car park. Furthermore, the attacks always happened on days when Mrs M had been in the building (apart from one occasion when the wing mirror was damaged while the car was parked in Robert's driveway).

Eventually the car was stolen. Robert went with a friend to Mrs M's house, expecting to find it parked there. It wasn't, but that did little to allay his suspicions.

This was the first time Robert had seen the place where his stalker lived. Mrs M's house stood out from her neighbours' because of the number of security devices it had. Mr and Mrs M felt their own privacy was something to protect and they were at pains to deter unwelcome visitors.

The car was reported as having been seen in Leamington, driven by an offender who was already known to the local police. It was found a week later and further expensive damage had been done to it, but it seemed Robert's suspicions had been ill-founded. He wasn't entirely persuaded and pressed the point: 'Would the police ask the person who had been spotted in the car if anyone had put him up to the theft?' He heard nothing back until some time later when he was told there'd been a mistake: the known car-thief was not guilty and the police were still in the dark. Such crimes are virtually impossible to clear up unless there is concrete evidence. The police did nothing. The car had been found, there was nothing else they *could* do.

Nor was there much they could do when someone entered Robert's house one evening while he was out. Nothing had been taken and there was no obvious sign of forced entry. However, all the radiators had been turned off and a hot water tap was on, draining the tank. It appeared to be yet another calling-card. Someone was telling him that they could come and go as they pleased and there was absolutely nowhere he could hide.

The legal situation was depressing. The incident was deemed to be a civil trespass and, as nothing had been stolen, it was not a police concern. It was after the break-in that Robert took to going to bed with a stick beside him for protection against other unwelcome visits.

Mrs M continued her hateful vigil outside Robert's house. Her customs were not absolutely predictable but were mostly variations on the same theme. She would watch until she was sure her presence had been acknowledged; then she would stroll up and down (to emphasise her right to do so in the face of Robert's objections); then she would slowly walk away.

Robert's office at the university was vandalised. What he describes as 'murky liquid' was poured into the waste-paper basket; papers were thrown about the place – and one, last, perturbingly-ludicrous gesture – a roll of toilet paper had been unrolled, rolled up again and placed on the desk.

Mrs M had been the silent and threatening presence across the street; now at a point where Robert was beginning to fear both for his property and his own safety, she came closer.

It was Sunday morning. Still not properly awake, Robert stumbled across the lounge and opened the curtains to be confronted by Mrs M's face. She did several tours of the house and carried on her watch while Robert had his breakfast. Irritated and, despite himself, no longer able to disguise the fact, Robert tried to dismiss her with a wave of his hand. She waved back and returned his look with one of triumph. She knew how difficult it was to rile these quiet, reasonable types. Robert had consistently fought against her goading. Now, at last, she was getting inside his head and she knew it.

Later that morning, unable to get her out of his mind, Robert went out to see if Mrs M was still there. Sure enough, she drew up in her car and wound the window down. Mrs M must stop this he said, she was stalking him (it was the first time he'd used the word); she needed help and if she didn't get it she would find herself in trouble with the law.

At that time this, of course, wasn't true. She might well have been a likely suspect for the several illegal incidents which had taken place, but they were unproven and were sure to remain so. The actual harassment which Robert was suffering from was not illegal and Mrs M was happy to remind him of this fact. She said she had been to his house a thousand times and intended to come a thousand more. She added with some sense of the dramatic that she would destroy him as he had destroyed her. It was, Robert recalls, chilling.

The next time Mr and Mrs M turned up that day, Robert was with his friend, Alan. Buoyed by having a witness and the moral support of another person, Robert decided he would again challenge his tormentors. The two men went after the stalkers; they'd got some few hundred yards before it became apparent Mrs M realised she was being pursued. When she did, she turned round to reveal a video camera. Maybe she had carried it with her many times, sure in the knowledge that Robert would one day give her something worth filming. On the other hand, maybe, as she'd chosen that day for increased activity, she was confident of the result of this goading and had come prepared to record it.

There was an altercation between the two couples. Mr M turned nasty. He reiterated the threats his wife had made while she continued to film. She was grinning in a strange, almost gleeful way and answered Robert's warnings with a sarcastic 'I'm so scared! I'm so scared!'

Mr M's part in all this (and later their daughters' as well) is worth considering. We can typecast him easily enough: the sort of man we see in cheap documentaries; the 'neighbour from hell'; the aggressive champion of tabloid values; the thug whose allegiance is to an unquestioned belief or person. You can meet him almost anywhere where his simplistic demands conflict with reality. He is spoiling for a fight and doesn't care who knows it. He may need a little persuasion but once he's decided upon his enemy, he is tenacious.

Was Mr M such a person? Did he really believe everything his wife had told him? Had he ever tried to dissuade her from this course of action? Robert is not happy with speculation but he went as far as to say he was convinced of Mr M's loyalty to his wife.

'I don't know if "love" is quite the word for it. I think he absolutely shared her world view. Anything she felt, he would echo, but with the added threat of violence. He was, if you like, the muscle. There was no sense at any point of his being anything other then an exaggerated version of her productions. It was quite scary in a way. Her daughters were like that too. I didn't often see them but when I did, for example at the court case, they manifestly shared all the levels of hatred and accusation they had learnt from their mum.

'I think he *was* spoiling for a fight but I don't think these two things are incompatible. He did believe her. He *really* believed her. He believed everything she said. And he was afraid of her as well. She had a lot of power over him: emotional power. God knows what lay behind all this but she sort of pushed him. She very much dominated him. He was a rather backward guy. I think he was a bit of a loner. Very unprepossessing.'[10]

Six months after this behaviour had begun, there was still no let-up. Robert's friend, Jessica Tipping, recalls how Mrs M approached the two of them while they were walking Robert's dog on the common:

'Mrs M came very close to us, partially encircled us, walked through the trees behind us and then left. Her approach had a strange combination of intent and denial; she walked straight towards us but having reached us refused any acknowledgement of us.'[11]

Both Mr and Mrs M then followed them back to the house and loitered outside. Robert called the police, who arrived too late and could do nothing to help.

Robert's office was vandalised again, the same 'murky liquid' was left in the wastepaper basket, a toilet roll was again left on his desk, rolled and unrolled in the same way as before. Perhaps more seriously, his computer went missing. He was thankful it had no hard-drive and therefore the thief couldn't use it to access private information.

In the spring of 1995 the university took formal action to prevent Mrs M harassing him. A disciplinary committee was set up and a hearing set for 17 March. Mrs M, aided by her lawyer, once again maintained her right to intimidate Robert.

She reiterated her original charge and claimed, disingenuously, that the stalking was more in Robert's imagination than in reality. Despite her scornful repudiation of Robert's grievances, she was found guilty and suspended. She responded to the decision by appealing to the Lord Chancellor, Lord McKay, and even writing to the Queen, calling on her for protection as 'a loyal subject'.

Meanwhile in April 1995, Robert instigated legal proceedings against Mrs M. He consulted a lawyer who began the tedious process of bringing a civil action.

The stalking continued unabated. There was a gradual increase in the, now familiar, behaviour but occasionally Mrs M would lose her malevolent equilibrium and give in to verbal abuse. Robert's house was marked by her presence, as was the local common. He had now come to expect her unwelcome company anywhere in the immediate vicinity of his home. He had but one haven – which was about to be invaded.

Robert had long enjoyed an early-morning swim at his local leisure centre. In the late spring of '95, Mrs M began to encroach on this pleasure. He was forced to put up with being tailed on his way there and (Mrs M having waited outside for him), on the way home. At first this was all she did. It wasn't long before she increased the effect.

On leaving the pool, Robert saw her standing near Fudge, his dog. Fudge was sick for some hours afterwards. Aware of her capacity to be litigious, Robert was wary enough to acknowledge he may have connected his dog's illness to Mrs M out of paranoia.

She waited for some two months before progressing from waiting outside the leisure centre to coming inside. Robert marvels at how quickly he got used to her presence in the water with him. At first it actually made him feel nauseated but, as one does, he adapted to it and they settled into a routine.

. . . she followed me from my home or waited at the pool; she then came into the water with me, swam near me for a while and watched me swim from the Jacuzzi; she got out when I got out and thanks to quick changing was waiting for me outside the pool by the time I left; she would then hide behind a little copse opposite the leisure centre, emerge from the shadows of the trees as I passed and follow me closely as I walked home. Once near my home she would quickly overtake me and double back, coming close to my face and muttering insults. Then she would walk up and down either directly outside my house or on the common while I took breakfast and sometimes disappear into the woods at the rear of the common only to reappear some minutes later. . . . Occasionally she would be accompanied by one of her daughters or her husband.'[12]

Robert tried to have Mrs M banned from using the pool. The usual thing happened. Mrs M was not breaking any law with her presence; she was doing nothing which contravened the rules. Even if she was, the management could not be expected to keep her at bay, nor did they have the resources to do it. Finally they decreed the situation was a personal matter between two customers and therefore was not their responsibility.

To add insult to injury, Mrs M countered Robert's complaints with one of her own. His attitude towards her, she maintained, encouraged other customers to 'stare at her'. She accused him of having made an assault. This referred to an incident where Robert had, in front of another customer, accused her of stalking him. He had turned from her and was walking away when she had rushed at him and collided into his back. Later she was seen taking a photograph of the customer who had witnessed the incident.

There was the odd day when nothing happened, but usually Robert could expect Mrs M to be present outside his house, in the pool, at the university. Most disconcerting was her habit of gazing in through the window while he was conducting lectures.

She would follow him in her car through the town, on his way to work. She sometimes kerb-crawled him. She turned up, either alone or with her faithful cohort, in all the various places where Robert went: on the common, outside the shops, in the bar of the Arts Centre. Robert tried to put some of these meetings down to coincidence but, with the best will in the world, it stretched credulity to say that of all of them.

Where the offences were criminal, her involvement could not be proved. Robert's car disappeared again. Once again he drove round to Mrs M's in the vain hope of seeing it in her drive and thereby having something concrete to charge her with. She saw his approach from the window. Some time afterwards, her solicitor wrote to Robert accusing him of making 'unfounded allegations' against Mrs M and threatening legal action should these 'libelous accusations' persist.

Robert's health was being affected. His life was being ruled by his stalker. The frustration of being an innocent victim, continually at the mercy of a groundless, concerted, relentless stream of malice, without any redress or protection, was wearing him down. Mrs M's presumable intention was to make him suffer and this she was doing extremely effectively. When his suffering manifested itself in rare and understandable bursts of anger, he records the satisfied smiles and gloating expressions which answered him.

Without any concrete evidence and with each incident being, in itself, relatively trivial, the law sat firmly on the fence. Robert acknowledges the efforts of one diligent policeman who tried vainly to trap Mrs M in the act of doing something illegal. His concern about the case was by no means typical and, anyway, he eventually had to give up his efforts.

On the rare occasions when Robert's complaints were taken further, the proposed course of action was futile and sometimes insulting. For instance, he was himself served with an official paper enjoining him to keep the peace, the logic being that Mrs M could then possibly be seen to be inciting him to break this undertaking. Needless to say, the ruse did not work.

Mrs M, who was a great respecter of the law when it was serving her ends, cared little for it when it wasn't. Robert's legal campaign seemed to be working: he succeeded in bringing an action against her which resulted in a High Court hearing. Despite giving a legal undertaking to stop her stalking him, she was back at her post the very next day. When challenged, she denied ever having made any such promise.

She also occasionally spread her activities to include Robert's neighbours and friends. Several people attest to the uneasy feelings, the sense of threat they experienced from Mrs M's strange behaviour. She photographed them, argued with them or was seen, standing some way off, quietly observing them.

Robert went on holiday. Fantasy images of Mrs M pursued him to the Alps where at least he had the satisfaction of imagining the ghostly presence falling down a crevasse. Back at home, the real woman had not let the fact he wasn't there stop her. With her usual victim absent, she focussed on Robert's neighbour and began by photographing his house.

Like Robert, his neighbour was told there could be no police intervention as no law had been transgressed. His garage was broken into; valuable fishing tackle was taken – as much as a few thousand pounds' worth. Mr and Mrs M were not questioned about this. Nothing could be proved against them.

The Lord Chancellor had reached his conclusions in response to Mrs M's appeal. He upheld the gist of her argument: that the theft of the car, and the vandalising of Robert's office, could not be connected to her without sufficient proof. This, he ruled, invalidated the university's hearing. Although he stopped short of reversing their decision, he ordered that Mrs M be given 'relief': i.e. the case against her would be as though it had never been heard. She demanded reinstatement and, by way of compensation, that her fees should be waived. (After much deliberation, she withdrew this condition.) The Lord Chancellor's department also ordered she be readmitted.

Colleagues at the university backed Robert's position by refusing to teach her. Eventually, Mrs M won the day but she was left in no doubt as to the general attitude towards her. She was able to explain this away as a conspiracy between Robert and his cronies. The original hearing had, she said, been prejudged. In her view, she'd once again fought a just fight. Despite overwhelming odds, she'd emerged with her integrity intact.

However, she still had charges to answer. She sacked her counsel and proceeded, in a series of self-righteous missives, to represent her position herself. At this point her main objection to the case against her was its location. Robert had purposefully chosen to go before the Royal Courts of Justice in London. It was a deliberate attempt to make life difficult for Mrs M and it's certain this point had not eluded her. She was unsuccessful in her attempts to have the case transferred.

The stalking of Robert Fine had now been a fact of his life for two years. He had considered virtually every approach in order to rid himself of Mrs M. He had put many of these approaches into practise. Like an avenging Fury, she would not relinquish her vendetta. Robert records his heavy despondency. His fiftieth birthday, in November '95, was marred by the increasing depression he felt. It was the damp, cold, dark time of year when the nights grow longer and the imagination easily sees threatening things in the darkness outside. Robert's nightmarish vision came in the form of a respectable middle-aged woman with dyed hair and a smart, blue coat. She wasn't a likely devil but it was imperative she be put to flight.

Extracts from Robert's diaries of 1996 (when the stalking was into its second year) make monotonous reading. The locations of the stalking show the map of Robert's day: from the house to the pool, from the pool to the house, at the university during teaching hours; in the corridor afterwards, in the pub in the evening – or in Robert's garden – or outside on the street – and so to bed.[13]

The court case ground along. Robert's solicitor asked that he go to a psychotherapist in order to establish the emotional damage that had been done to him. He prevaricated at first but acquiesced in the end. The experience went some way to unburdening him but the therapist was patronising and audacious. He suggested Robert was subconsciously holding onto Mrs M's presence in his life. If he could rid himself of the need to be stalked, she would withdraw.

Legally, these consultations were not much use. No concrete proof of psychological damage was achieved.

Robert put forward a proposition which could have ended the whole dismal affair with no great loss of face on Mrs M's part. If she would stand by the terms of the injunction, i.e. if she would desist from her campaign and stay away from him, he would waive his claim for damages. Mrs M was having none of it. She totally rejected the offer. To her, there was still a bizarre principle at stake.

She notified the university of her intention to re-register in September of 1996. It was suggested Robert take a year's sabbatical in the Bahamas; a proposal he reluctantly turned down. Robert's colleagues still refused to teach her. The tutor whose classes she would be joining took his objections to his union. He cited health and safety as the reasons for his reluctance. With the Lord Chancellor's ruling dictating its course of action, the university had no choice but to admit Mrs M, which they did on the 29th of that month. With no member of staff to teach her, she suggested she should sit the examination without attending the classes. The situation was quickly reaching a stalemate position.

The forthcoming hearing in the High Court promised some sort of resolution. This hearing took place in November 1996; three years had passed since Robert had unwittingly upset this woman.

The Royal Courts of Justice stand at the end of London's Strand, just before it becomes Fleet Street. It's an imposing edifice, familiar to viewers of television news bulletins. Robert was surprised to discover how much press attention he had attracted. He found himself amid a gang of eager pressmen and women, all clamouring for a statement. What had started as a minor misunderstanding between a lecturer and his student was about to make the national news.

Mrs M had not desisted in her stalking. She had been outside Robert's house before he left Coventry and made efforts to 'invade his space' inside the court. Her actions showed her absolute conviction that she would be able to use these proceedings to vindicate herself. She wanted licence to further 'punish' Robert.

She used attack as a form of defence. On her instructions, her barrister contended Robert had been the aggressor all along. He had persistently sought to provoke Mrs M; he had assaulted her; he had displayed an unreasonable attitude to her innocent presence. Robert's council countered these allegations with the testimony of Robert's colleagues and friends, which the defence sought to invalidate on the grounds of their partiality.

More significantly for British law, the defence tried to focus on individual incidents, putting forward alternative, innocent explanations for each one. The admissibility of accumulated events would become an important part of the legislation against stalking. Robert's assertion that 'There was not one incident, one frame. One frame would have been nothing; it was the accumulation of frames that made the film' established a precedent.

Mrs M, having already been in the witness box, requested she be cross-examined again in order to clarify her defence. This request was agreed to. For her, it was to prove to be an extremely unwise course of action.

She confidently stated that she had indeed walked outside Robert's house (in breach of her legal undertaking). She had done so purely because she had been forbidden to do it. She was the only citizen in the country who had been told she couldn't use that particular footpath and she felt it necessary to demonstrate her opposition to this unfair ruling. She had not agreed to the undertaking; she had sacked the barrister who had persuaded her to sign it. In any case, she disregarded it because the court hadn't stamped it: it was therefore not valid. She had, in fact, retracted her word and now stood by that retraction.

She again tried to paint Robert as the aggressive party, recounting his visit to her house after the theft of his car. The judge, Anthony Thompson, asked her what had been so threatening about Robert's presence in a vehicle outside her house (he had been driven there by his former partner, Pat Volk). She declared he'd been there 'to provoke trouble', to 'intimidate her'. Was it, the judge wanted to know, intimidating to be outside a person's house in a parked vehicle? 'Yes,' came the reply. 'The way they did it.'

Robert describes her double-standards as 'almost agonising'.[14]

The case went against Mrs M. She was ordered not to go within 200 yards of Robert's house. Robert was awarded £5,000 damages and costs. It was the first occasion in British law where damages had been won in a stalking case.

It wasn't, however, the end of Mrs M's stalking activity.

'Despite all the court cases, she would be outside my house as usual,' Robert says. 'It actually stopped when I got married: I got married to one of the other lecturers here at the university. Actually, it stopped a little bit before that – when I moved to where I live now. During the removal she and her husband stayed parked outside my house for the whole two days. She tried to follow us to where we were going; we managed to give her the slip at the petrol station. Since then I've never seen her. Something happened, something clicked in her mind – she couldn't carry on. Maybe it was the fact of moving but I'm sure she could have found me.'[15]

Robert has rationalised his ordeal. He speaks of it in a thoughtful, objective way and, despite contrary feelings which he admits to having had at the time, he has always been aware he did nothing to provoke this sustained attack. He was simply the means by which a disappointed and frustrated individual could get back at a society with which she saw herself as being at war.

10. I'LL BE WATCHING YOU

When I began my research on this book, one of the names which came up almost immediately and kept reappearing with insistent regularity, was that of Tracey Morgan.

She is the victim of a stalker who has plagued her life for eight years. Her work on behalf of other victims and her campaign to change the law has gained her the respect and admiration of professionals, media people and the public. Whenever there's a story relating to the law against harassment, she is called upon to voice her strong opinions on how Britain could tighten its legal system to prevent people going through the misery she herself has suffered.

She is evidently a woman of strong character, yet she's also self-effacing, shy and, after some years in the public spotlight, can still come across as rather timid. She's had to fight against these personal traits in order to survive. Her life has been altered beyond recognition by her experiences. She has changed more than she ever thought possible. Though she looks towards the positive aspects of these changes, it's also true that her stalker came close to ruining her life. Perhaps the worst aspect of Tracey's ordeal is that it's still going on. Her stalker has not given up and, despite several prison sentences and the myriad precautions she takes every day of her life, he shows no sign of releasing her.

It all began in 1992. In those days, Tracey Sant (as she then was) was a diffident young woman, married for three years and thinking about starting a family. She worked as a civilian administration officer at HMS *Collingwood*, a naval base in Hampshire.

She felt sorry for Petty Officer Anthony Burstow. He was always alone and seemed to be permanently depressed. He was married himself, though his wife was working in Hong Kong. Tracey was the only female he had any contact with (the only female in the branch). He didn't have any friends in the area. She saw nothing wrong in giving him a shoulder to cry on.

So, at lunchtimes, she would invite him along when she went into town. They would have a cup of tea and a chat. She and her husband, Andrew, took him out on a couple of occasions. Burstow's depression was worrying her since at times he seemed almost suicidal. She thought her friendship was helping him but Tracey Sant was fast becoming Burstow's hobby.

The silent phone calls started, then she received unsigned mail. Burstow began following her. He was always there: watching, waiting. His friendly charade had vanished and it was terrifyingly clear to Tracey that she had attracted a malevolent man who was intent on doing her harm. In Burstow's mind, they had been on the brink of a relationship of sorts and she had rejected him. It wasn't true, but regardless of this fact, his behaviour was unwarranted and hateful.

In those days, before protecting herself became a matter of everyday routine, Tracey was apt to leave her handbag lying around at work. Burstow rifled through it and had a copy made of her door key.

Tracey was puzzled at first when she realised she'd had no mail for some time. Then some arrived at weekends, but whenever she was absent from the house there was nothing. Next, Andrew told her he'd left a message for her on the answering machine, and yet when she arrived home no new messages were showing. She assumed the machine was broken but, when she rewound it, sure enough, the message was there.

The most unnerving thing was when she went to take her contraceptive pill one night and found the last three in the packet were missing. She thought she was going mad. Was she overdosing? Was she taking them in her sleep? She tried to make sense of what was happening but couldn't. 'I think,' she said, 'if only then I'd been more aware. I knew my intuition was telling me but I wasn't listening to it.'

It soon became intolerable. She was worried about her safety and felt completely helpless. She was, she said, unnerved: very, very fearful. She thought, these things only happened in films; in normal life people just didn't behave like this. In the end she went to her bosses and made a formal complaint.

It was to be the first of many battles with authority and in the majority of them Tracey was to find herself alone and disregarded. If she'd doubted the validity of her fear of Burstow, she was soon to find out that the Navy had never given it any credence whatsoever. They believed her to be an emotionally insecure female and patronisingly advised her 'just be mature about it'.

'I was going in daily saying "He's followed me here – this or that's happening" and I remember distinctly standing in the doorway of the officer's room, saying "I think he could have bugged the house". I was just laughed out of the office. But I was right – he *was* bugging my house.

'I had two things going against me: I was female and I was a civilian. I was an administrative officer in the Civil Service. I wasn't taken seriously. If I'd been in the Navy it would probably have been a different matter. I was this silly female who was getting over-emotional about things. I'd say "Things have happened at home and I don't know how to explain it but he's followed me again." And I was just patted on the head and told not to be paranoid.'[1]

The Navy kept insisting they were 'dealing with it'. They carried on 'dealing with it' and meanwhile nothing was done to check Burstow's behaviour. Eventually, Tracey made it clear she intended to get the police involved unless she had some satisfactory action from them. Her employers were not keen on the idea at all. To use Tracey's words, they 'didn't want me to muddy the waters'. She somehow managed to preserve her faith in authority and waited. Meanwhile she was living a nightmare.

'The victim just completely loses control of their life. I don't know – stepping outside the door – if I'm going to die today. When I step off the kerb sometimes I think, is a car going to come at me from nowhere? When I pick up the phone is there going to be somebody on the other end? The post comes through the door, is there going to be anything there? And that's my life now: that's how I have to live.'[2]

Tracey Morgan has spirit. She knew she was going to either have to cope with Burstow's grip on her life or be forced to admit he'd won.

Eventually, Burstow received a Captain's Warning and was moved to a different base (though it was only three miles away). It wasn't enough to stop him stalking. He sent Tracey a variety of strange packages: headache pills, sanitary towels. His presence in her life was constant and terrifying. Tracey still tried to have faith in her bosses, she trusted the matter was being dealt with and, as her employer, the Navy was looking after her. She was, however, on the brink of a breakdown which she only avoided because of the help of a 'wonderful counsellor'.

Eventually it became obvious that the Navy were unable to deal with the problem and they at last called in the police. Burstow was taken to Gosport police station for interview.

Detective Sergeant Linda Dawson of the Hampshire Police described in a documentary for Yorkshire Television how Burstow came over as 'bright and articulate; it was only when you actually talked to him about Tracey and you saw the pattern of behaviour towards Tracey, that you realised there was something very wrong.'[3]

It transpired Burstow had his own, private version of Tracey Sant: the woman who'd been almost about to have an affair with him, one who had touched him and accepted his physical responses before rejecting him.

Burstow became a regular in court. With her trust in the legal system ever-diminishing, Tracey watched in dismay as each appearance ended in his being bound over 'to keep the peace and be of good behaviour'. In other words, he was ticked off like a naughty child and told to be a good boy in future. He was being given a clear message that the law was powerless to stop him.

His employers, on the other hand, could no longer ignore his activities. He was sacked from the Navy 'due to continuing confrontation with (the) service over (his) attitude to Mrs Sant.' His wife divorced him.

He blamed Tracey for this and, consequently, his communications became ever-more worrying. A card with the inscription: 'You are always on my mind'; quotations from the Bible and from Blake; a letter which began, 'Unfortunately for all concerned, the final chapter has yet to be written'.

Tracey was a prisoner in her own home. In the evenings she would keep all her curtains shut and put every light on in the house. 'So if he had a gun,' she said, 'he wouldn't know which room I was in; he wouldn't know which to aim at.'

Understandably, her husband, Andrew, was breaking under the strain of being unable to protect her whilst at the same time being at no small risk himself. He once tackled Burstow physically, grappling him to the ground and yelling at him to stay away from their home, to stay away from Tracey and to keep out of their lives. Burstow, who huddled up for protection, replied he would give it 'some consideration'.

In August 1993, after the Sants had suffered some nine months of Burstow's ugly persecution, the police decided to cover their house with surveillance cameras. It wasn't long before Burstow was recorded on them, lurking about outside. The cameras proved their real value when they showed a clear image of Burstow pouring oil over Tracey's car. It wasn't much, but it was tangible and an undeniable charge could be brought against him. He was arrested for criminal damage.

During the time he was in custody being questioned, Burstow may have had an attack of remorse or, more likely, he intended to crow about his power over the young couple. He asked to speak to Detective Sergeant Dawson in private – off the record. She agreed. What he had to say was horrifying. He had, he told her, been thinking about killing Andrew Sant.

The police had known it before, but now there was no doubt at all that they were dealing with an extremely dangerous individual.

No charge relating to this conversation could be brought against him. There was no evidence and he would certainly have denied it having taken place. Consequently, he was sentenced for the attack on Tracey's car and sent to prison for three months. His stalking activity didn't stop.

While Burstow was remanded in custody, awaiting trial, Tracey should have been able to consider herself safe from his malice. It wasn't to be: hateful items arrived with each post.

One of these was Burstow's 'Final Term "Mindgame" crossword.' He was now confident enough in his effect to know his victim would actually take the trouble to solve the clues and find out what lay behind them. The answers proved the extent to which he had penetrated Tracey Sant's privacy. Her national insurance number was there, her vehicle registration numbers – and Andrew's. There were details about her family and references to Burstow's stalking of her. One clue calls Burstow 'the hunter' – Tracey is referred to as 'the prey'.[4]

A letter he sent had three crudely-drawn coffins at the bottom. They were labelled, two with an A and the other with a T. Burstow wanted Tracey and her husband dead and he didn't care if it cost him his own life to achieve it.

When he was sentenced for damaging Tracey's car the only psychiatric assessment which the courts have ever asked for was done on Burstow. The result, surprisingly, was that he wasn't considered to be suffering from either a mental illness or a personality disorder. The experts said it was a case of someone 'who needed to wash the woman out of his hair'.

Today, Tracey is philosophical: 'They didn't know what they were dealing with,' she says. She hasn't always been so matter-of-fact; and back in 1993 she was outraged. The way the British legal system ignored and patronised her was to become the spur which eventually goaded her into fighting back. She told Yorkshire Television in 1999: 'For people to just dismiss it and say I've just got to pull myself together and ignore what he's doing. How dare they? They want to come and live in my house for a week and see what it feels like really.'[5]

The beleaguered couple had the promise of six months of peace while Burstow served his sentence. They weren't so rash as to suppose his prison term would reform him in any way, since they realised they and their property would only be safe while he was physically prevented from approaching them. Snatching the precious time available to them, they left for a much-needed holiday in South Africa.

'Strange adapting to a life where you didn't have to watch behind you. It was a bizarre experience. We had a lot of tension to get rid of – but we had a nice time. We came back, the police came round – the detective who'd handled the case originally. He told us Burstow had been released on appeal the very day after we left.'[6]

The detective had not been told at the time of the release and consequently he'd no idea where Burstow was. It was arranged that Tracey should have a police escort to work the following day. Wherever Tracey was, they could be certain Burstow wouldn't be far away.

'And the detective left. I went to have a bath and clean my teeth. I got wet feet at the sink. There was water coming out of the cupboard underbasin. Andy came up to look then went downstairs to check the kitchen and found the same. The water pipe had been loosened. As I came downstairs Andy went to the lounge window and pulled the curtain back – the pane was missing. Burstow had burgled the house. Our wedding videos had gone, photographs, jewellery, our video machine, personal things . . .'[7]

Burstow protested he knew nothing about the break-in, but it was easy enough to prove him a liar. An audio-cassette was found in his car; on it was recorded the soundtrack of the Sants' wedding video. It was enough evidence for the police to search his home, where they found the missing items along with Tracey's underwear, photographs of her (also stolen from the house) and – most worrying – a written account of Burstow's intentions. This last, scribbled in several prison notebooks as well as on loose paper, referred to Tracey's forthcoming birthday as 'judgment day'.

'I appear to have sorted out how judgment day will be enacted. I'd rather it be an evening – A at home, T away for a few hours. Sort out A and enjoy some time alone waiting T's return. And then . . .'[8]

He told the police 'judgment day' was not a definite plan. 'There was a lot of times I was very annoyed about things and I would come up with stupid ideas of things to send to wind her up further and that was one of them. If I'd got out of here (out of prison) and if I'd stayed out November, December, I might have got round to doing something with that to muck around with her brain, that was all – as I've done ever since this all started.'

'You agree that's what you're doing?' the interviewing officer asks.

'That's what it's all about,' Burstow agrees.

'You're mucking yourself up and you're mucking . . .'

Burstow interrupts quickly , 'I don't give a shit about myself.'[9]

What had been vindictive scare-tactics had developed into mania. It now had the added danger of having become a crusade – Burstow admitted as much to his probation officer. He blamed Tracey for destroying his marriage, his career, his home and his life, now nothing mattered to him other than achieving his desired aim – to destroy her in return. He wasn't going to stop until he had.

The law was helpless. Burstow's harassment of Tracey Sant was not illegal in itself. He always denied everything and so continued to avoid serious charges because of lack of concrete evidence. Even in March 1994, when he was questioned about an attempt made from inside prison to pay £3,500 to have Andrew Sant murdered, there was not sufficient proof to bring him to court.

All that could be done was to convict him on the minor counts which could be successfully prosecuted. He was jailed for burglary. Even with her stalker behind bars, Tracey's life and that of her husband, were in serious danger. All she could do was wait and see what his next move against her was going to be.

The evidence of his intentions continued to turn up. In his cell he had a number of computer discs which contained, amongst other things, poems whose meaning was unequivocal:

FATAL ATTRACTION
The Message
Do not get involved with the woman you feel
passionately about . . . but if you do, KILL HER![10]

The couple moved house while Burstow was in prison in July 1994. It was an extreme step to take. Thinking back to the time when she first extended the hand of friendship to this 'sad case', this 'loner', Tracey must have marvelled at how on earth things had got this far. The helplessness she felt began to metamorphose into constructive anger – and that anger was soon to motivate her into becoming a very different person to the demure civil servant Burstow had first met.

Her 'safe house' proved to be useless. Ten days after they moved they started to receive suspect mail. Burstow was still in prison at this point. Later they found he even had a ground-plan of each room. He was promptly arrested again. He kept notes of his planned activities and, at this stage, they included sending spiders, slugs and snails. The most bizarre and frightening discovery was a huge collection of medical equipment including swabs, needles and a blood transfusion kit.

Having had documents taken away and used in evidence against him, Burstow had taken the precaution of writing in code. The police found a log of the various times he had broken into the Sants' house, a record of what he'd taken and – to their utter dismay – evidence that he'd placed bugs in Tracey's office, in her sofa and actually in her bed. She was horrified to find that he had been privy to just about everything which had gone on in her life: her conversations with her husband, friends and family, even her sleep had been tapped. Somewhere close to her house, Burstow had been there in his car, listening in.

Andrew Sant was buckling under the strain. Through no fault of his own, he was unable to defend his wife against this constant danger. Tracey was gradually becoming a stranger: the enormous effort she had to expend in order to stay sane in her everyday life was pulling her away from him.

'When I got married I was a quiet person and my husband got his own way most of the time,' Tracey says. She laughs as she remembers less significant scuffles: 'Certainly he got his own way with regards to sport.

'Part of the reason the marriage failed was not only the pressure, it was also the fact that I'd changed personality completely. Andrew was fed up of my depression – I was often on a down – and he couldn't cope with the sleeping pills, the Prozac . . . He couldn't cope with all the looking after me, but also he couldn't cope when I began to have a mind and opinion of my own. For instance he often played rugby – I started to voice my objections when it seemed another whole weekend was going to revolve around sport. Before I would have just kept quiet for fear of making him unhappy.

'I don't think it would have headed that way but for Burstow. I think I would probably still be little Tracey who's so shy, quiet – carrying on. We were just about to start a family as well. That might have been another factor. Andy couldn't cope. It didn't help that he didn't believe in counselling, but I became a fighter and he didn't like that. He didn't like *me* any more.'[11]

She moved back to her parents' house. Here, the support she needed was available from more than one person and some of the emotional pressure eased. However, it was a retrograde step to a protective environment she had long since thought she didn't need any more. It was as though Burstow was pushing her into a corner from which she was never going to be able to emerge.

'I'm still in the room I grew up in. I'm still at home with my parents. People say: "Just move on and forget it!" – I think, I'd *love* to have a place of my own, I'd *love* to have my own home. Then I have to consider: would I be able to live on my own? There'd be security: I'd have to spend the first few thousand on security – and would I actually be able to live there? Maybe I wouldn't be able to cycle to work – I'd love to have the choice, it's too risky though. All these things start coming in and I think: no, can't move on.'[12]

Tracey was undergoing psychiatric treatment and an attempt was made to charge Burstow with Actual Bodily Harm (psychiatric injury). It was a long-shot: no such charge had been successfully prosecuted before and this was to fail: it was dropped. He was convicted of breaking into Tracey's home but, as he'd already spent time in custody on remand, he was free to go. It was to be a turning point in Tracey's attitude towards his aggression.

'I was lucky,' she remembers. 'I had police officers on the case from day one that wanted to help me. When the case collapsed in February 95, they were the ones who said to me

"Will you go public? We need to highlight the loophole in the legal system. *We need a law* – because there's nothing; we can't protect you any more."

'I had nothing left really. I thought I've got nothing to lose – only my life. I had to get this stopped. We needed to highlight what was going on; the legal system has completely failed me.

'You lose control but speaking out gave me a voice – it gave me a bit of control back. That's why I say now – I'm privileged. I'm privileged because I'm a victim with a voice; I'm privileged because I'm able to do what I do; I have the contacts I have and I'm working with the people I do. We just kept chipping away and that's how we got there. We want to change things and we want to change things for the better. We want a rebalance. People seem to listen.'[13]

In order to take centre-stage on this issue, Tracey had to totally alter her personality. When asked if she would ever, in her wildest dreams, have envisaged herself as a spokesperson for any cause, she replied with feeling:

'God no! I've always lacked confidence personally. I was very, very shy. When I was five I had a disfiguring illness which affected me greatly. I've always had the feeling that I don't have confidence. Where this is concerned, I'm there on my soap box, but if you started asking me about something else I would be absolutely speechless. If I'm Tracey Morgan, campaigner, then that's OK, but if I'm me . . . It's weird – it's a strange situation. But I'm learning now that there's a new me. That's maybe the one positive thing that's come out of all this. It made me stronger.'[14]

The case hit the headlines. Burstow's harassment was graphically described in the national press and it provoked outrage. Even so, the government was reluctant to do anything to change the law; it would, they said 'present too many difficulties'. The objection centred around the possibility that Labour MP Janet Anderson's proposals were too stringent, and would inhibit the legitimate activities of investigative journalists and debt collectors. The situation might have seemed hopeless but there was nothing to do but to carry on. At least Tracey was now part of a growing movement which was fast gaining public and media support. There were still questions in her mind about the methods she had elected to use. She considered, for instance, the very real danger that, by publicising his activity, she was giving Burstow exactly what he wanted.

'He gets the notoriety. He's labelled in the media "Britain's most notorious stalker". That's what these people feed off. The power, but also the fear. He likes to write to the police officers with stupid ideas. His game now is to beat the legal system – it hasn't been his obsession with me for a long time. It was only initially me, as soon as he's told not to do something, he'll do it just to prove a point. And the way the legal system works allows him do it. He has the rights and the privileges – he manipulates them and gets away with it.'[15]

Tracey was becoming well-known. She was appearing on television, in newspapers and on the radio. Other cases were gradually coming to prominence – in 1996, Robert Fine brought the first successful British prosecution for harassment against his stalker (see Chapter Eight). Slowly the wheels where turning.

Meanwhile, living over a hundred miles away from where Burstow had first found her, Tracey and her family were still subject to his daily presence in their lives. She and her friends filmed him – evidence that he was breaking the court orders to stay away from her. He stole washing from the line; he put offensive literature through neighbours' letterboxes; he littered the garden with condoms, he also put notes under the windscreen wipers of nearby parked cars: 'Tracey Sant is a stupid little bitch and a lying slut.' He sent a note to her place of work which read, 'Lady, a few words of advice. Never ever start something unless you intend to see it through to the bitter end and finish it.'

His lengthier letters show a malevolent skill at work:

'Do you long for that new era,' reads one, 'when you can wake up in the morning and smile at the day it brings, be it work or rest, weekday or weekend, and not be concerned about the motives and plans of another? Sit at the breakfast table and discuss what lies ahead without fretting over the contents of the postbox or agonising over possible untoward news from your father's short walk for the daily paper?' The letter ends: 'This is totally personal. Nothing will change how much I hate you.'[16]

Another includes the line: 'One day, engaging mouth before brain will get you into serious trouble. Are you still enjoying our little game? Is it still funny or even hilarious?'[17]

And: 'Tracey, some visual reminders of your previous life. Enjoy the memories. They are all you have left.'[18] The 'reminders' were photos of the houses Andy and Tracey had lived in, her aerobics class, Fareham college where she had attended evening classes, her workplaces and places they had visited socially.

Tracey was now living in a state of high security. She was compelled to shred her rubbish, to walk the streets in a state of perpetual anticipation of danger and to deal with the constant fear she felt for her family as well as the gradual toll her problems were taking on their peace of mind. It was, in fact, a family at war against a man and the system.

1996 was an important year for Tracey Sant. In March, Burstow was back in court. He was charged with assaulting Tracey's mind. He pleaded guilty and was jailed for three years. It was the first time such a charge had been successfully taken to court. She had made legal history.

Then, in May, the Conservative government blocked Janet Anderson's Bill. The Home Secretary, Michael Howard, said they had done so on the grounds that it was too widely drawn and would criminalise many innocent activities. He maintained stalking was a particularly difficult thing to define; the government wanted to be sure it had got the legislation absolutely right. As soon as he was satisfied they had a definition that was workable enough for them to legislate, they would do so.

The discarded Bill proposed the bringing into force of an exclusion zone around the victim and would have required the stalker to have counselling. Persistent stalkers would have received a maximum sentence of five years.

Tracey publicly expressed her disappointment at this failure but said she took some comfort from the Home Secretary's intention to bring the bill in eventually, albeit in a slightly different form.

She didn't have long to wait. At the beginning of July a 'comprehensive response' to the problem was announced.

The government's plans suggested, amongst other things, a civil measure to allow the victims to take out an injunction against their stalker. Breaching that injunction would be a criminal offence carrying a sentence of up to five years in prison. David Maclean, a junior Home Office Minister, said 'Stalking is a menace to society and a terrible scourge to the lives of victims. Stalkers can subject victims to constant harassment at home, at work, in public places, to the extent that they can no longer go about their normal lives. Innocent people should not have to suffer such a terrifying ordeal. These proposals would give courts the power to punish stalkers for what they have done in the past and, with the civil measures, stop them from repeating their behaviour.'[19]

A new offence of causing fear for a person's safety *whether or not this was the intention of the person charged* (my italics) was also put forward. This too would carry a sentence of five years maximum, plus an unlimited fine, or possibly both. Finally, causing harassment, alarm or distress, whether or not this was the intention, would carry a sentence of six months in jail, a fine of £5,000, or both.

The new law was welcomed by Tracey (as well as the other individuals and organisations who had fought for it) but it was not to have an entirely smooth ride. In September Mr Howard warned that he couldn't guarantee to get the bill through the Commons during that session of Parliament.

He said 'Stalking is a dreadful menace. I have enormous sympathy for the victims of this kind of activity. I am very keen that we should have a law which makes it a criminal offence and gives people proper protection.' He then added, 'It is likely to be a short session of Parliament as the government has to hold a general election by May.'[20]

Stalking was prominent in the headlines, partly because of the Bill, partly because of Tracey's efforts and partly because of other brave victims, among them Perry Southall, a dentist's receptionist, dubbed 'a Pamela Anderson lookalike' who had been subjected to over two hundred incidents of harassment at the surgery where she worked. Clarence Morris, her stalker, was convicted on charges of assault. From being an ignored problem which, it was considered, was 'impossible to legislate against', stalking now seemed an issue that had to be dealt with – and urgently.

The Protection from Harassment Act finally came into force in June, 1997. It was one of the last laws to go through Parliament before the General Election which swept Tony Blair's 'New Labour' party to victory.

Tracey says, 'When the law came in it was a major relief, happiness seems the wrong word – but it was nice to think someone had listened. The major thing was that it was finally acknowledged that what victims were going through was unacceptable.

'I have been told that my case has been quite instrumental. A lot came out of the test prosecution for Grievous Bodily Harm (psychiatric injury) in March 1996. Two weeks after the case we launched the campaign for a specific stalking law, alongside ACC Wallis (Sussex Police) and the Suzy Lamplugh Trust. People were asking why, when the GBH was successful – we had to ask why a victim should become so psychologically damaged before a charge could be brought?

'The Protection from Harassment Act is an excellent law. It is very strong. It has the unique situation of being able to cross over into civil law. If there's a breach of a civil restraining order it's an arrestable offence which normally it wouldn't be. That's the key to protection for the victim. The Act is also unique in that it hinges on the effect upon the victim, rather than the intention of the offender. There were problems before because a stalker could claim what he was doing wasn't "intended" to cause alarm or distress. The new law stipulates that a "reasonable person" test should be used – if a reasonable person (eg: the investigating officer) believes that the actions are causing harassment/distress/fear etc . . . then proceedings can continue.

'However, there are two issues to think about. One: we need to do this properly and the judiciary and other interested people need to understand how to use the act. I've actually talked to victims who've said "My solicitor has told me I need to have two phone calls within a week for them to be able to do anything." *No.* It doesn't have to be within a week: if a reasonable person feels they would be harassed then it can be dealt with.

'Two: personality disorders need to be recognised ... When we met Dr Reid Meloy [editor: *The Psychology of Stalking*] he brought back the fact that every stalker in San Diego is assessed on arrest and treatment is part of their sentence. If they don't go for treatment, they stay locked up. That's what I want done in this country. Burstow has a diagnosable personality disorder. He, and others like him, are just going to go in and out of prison – there's no treatment.

'There's a difference between psychiatric problems and personality disorders. Personality disorders aren't deemed treatable by the English legal system; it's actually a case of they're being too hard to treat so let's not bother; but there are programmes going on in San Diego, America and Australia. They're actually working towards trying to tackle the problem which is what would be useful here.

'There are a variety of reasons behind the behaviour. One is rejection. It's the sadistic side – the vengeance if you like – of being rejected. Another is the undying love which, they believe, is going to be reciprocated one day – erotomania ...

'I want a network – a support line for victims and for potential victims of stalking – and their families – there is not just one victim; family, friends, neighbours can all be affected. There are people who might be being stalked but they're not sure and they're a bit too frightened to go to the police, especially when they're not taken seriously – which is still happening unfortunately. I want a network which will provide advice and education to all agencies dealing with the legal system and those within the legal system such as the Probation Service, the Prosecution Service. I'd like go and educate prison officers and see who they've got in there and what they're doing about it because they still don't understand about silent calls and mail from prison. To me, justice would be for it to stop, but at the moment justice means going through the torture of a court case and knowing he's going to come out again: knowing the problem hasn't actually been solved. The "problem" is his personality disorder. Until that's recognised, until that is dealt with, there is no solution.

'It may be too far developed for Burstow – it's been so long. Sometimes I think it would be easier if he came and attacked me or hit me, because I'd have a bruise to show – it would be easier. Because it's a mind game, because it's female, it's emotional, the authorities sometimes are chauvinistic about it. They don't take it seriously. I know everybody's different and every police officer's attitude's different, but I also know there's a hell of a lot of education that needs to happen. There are so many instances where people aren't taken seriously: "Oh come back when he's attacked you."

'Sometimes I've been told "Oh, you should be flattered. I wish I had a stalker!" I've said "Well, you can have mine – please!" People need to understand people's feelings better. I want to get to the situation where you have no right to dismiss that person with their fear or their complaint.'[21]

Burstow was released in July 1997. For a while it seemed Tracey was being left in peace. Then the arrival of an unsigned birthday card heralded a new onslaught of abuse. Someone wedged dog excrement up under the handle of her friend's car door – it was very carefully done so as not to be seen, just felt. Burstow frequently drove close behind Tracey. His own vehicle was a mobile stalking-base complete with a sleeping bag, first aid kit and change of clothes. He also kept with him the more worrying items: syringes and the blood transfusion kit. In the woods behind where Tracey lived, a hoard of documents was found. There was detailed information on Tracey, her family and even their finances. It transpired Burstow had been keeping a constant watch on them since the time of his release. The documents also made reference to the frightening 'Judgment Day'. This was the second time he'd used the phrase – the first 'Judgment Day' was Tracey's birthday in 1994 but Burstow had been in prison at the time so he'd been unable to do anything. Tracey comments: 'Nobody has bothered to find out when the latest "Judgment Day" might be – just have to wait and see, I guess.'[22]

Burstow was promptly re-arrested and convicted under the new law. He was given a sentence of sixteen weeks against which he immediately appealed. Tracey was subjected to a tortuous time in court. Because Burstow was appealing against sentence *and* conviction there had to be a full re-trial. In the end his sentence was upheld. She was given another, all too brief, respite.

Her life continues in this manner, only feeling a degree of security when Burstow is locked away. He literally alternates between prison and stalking. He shows no sign of stopping.

Although her life is restricted and she exists in conditions which most of us would find utterly intolerable, Tracey is philosophical.

'It feels I've got here by accident. A few years ago I wouldn't have said two words to anyone, let alone stand up in front of media and ministers and tell my story. I feel so passionately about the subject and people still being misunderstood and ignored that I have to do it. I've been told I come across well on TV and people say "Please carry on". I think I just can't do it. They tell me I'm saying just the right things and I think, right – I'll carry on then. It seems to have become most of my life.

'It's helped me immensely. Making a film was a big catalyst – if that's the right word – it's helped me to be a lot stronger. Giving my talks has helped too. Nobody can stand up and tell you that you're lying. They can't say "The legal system just doesn't do that" – well it does. It did to me. I tell myself they can't contradict me. This is how it is and they're going to listen because things aren't good enough. People are still being followed. People are still thinking about suicide because there's no other way out. They're desperate to be believed and they're *not* being believed.'[23]

One of Tracey's childhood friends, a garage technician called Tony Hurdle, was still one of the few men she trusted. He would accompany her out and look after her. The friendship blossomed into a relationship. They were together for four years but split in 1999, though they continued to be friends. It was in the last few months of 1999 that Tracey made another horrible discovery.

'We found out by accident as a result of the publicity for the Yorkshire Television documentary. Burstow's boss at that time called the TV company to verify that the man she had working for her was not Anthony Burstow because he looked very like him. Rachel Chadwick, the researcher, asked her about him and the lady said the man was called Tony Hurdle. Burstow had changed his name. Rachel called me immediately and I called the police.'[24]

It was, of course, a deliberate challenge to the law. As part of the restraining order, 'Anthony Burstow' was banned from holding any paperwork relating to any of Tracey's family or friends. With his new name, he could impersonate the real Tony Hurdle and acquire information with relative ease. He could also trespass into the 'banned area' which protected Tracey and show ID which wouldn't arouse any suspicions.

Even Tracey's extended family contacts were being affected. Her sister's boyfriend found his bank account had been tampered with: the address had been changed and other alterations made. Nobody has yet been held to account for doing this and the Crown Prosecution Service would not take action against Burstow as a result of his change of identity. There was a massive loophole in the new law . . .

And so it goes on. On meeting Tracey Morgan, you see a woman of poise and confidence. Her shyness is still evident but it's not difficult to imagine her addressing a crowded public meeting or holding her own with politicians and officials. She has found this strength within herself because she's had to – and she's paid an extremely high price for it.

'The barriers are up and I'm very aware of the people around me. I was sitting, waiting for a tube – there were some other people further up the platform and this man came by and asked if he recognised me. I said "Possibly . . ." He wanted to know if I was off the telly or in the newspapers or something. He went on asking questions until I told him that I was the one with the stalker. He started talking generally and I was thinking the whole time, "who are you? Why do you want to know these things?" He eventually left me alone – but it shows how difficult it is now to be natural with people.

'When Burstow's not doing anything people say it's good. It isn't – because I've lost control again. I don't know what he's doing but I know he's doing something and it'll come to light – something could happen today. It's like living on a knife edge all the time. You're willing something to happen – "Know where he is; get the court case done; have a bit of peace of mind for a few weeks – or months – or whatever."'[25]

Time was to prove that Burstow's vengeance would not be reserved solely for Tracey. His violent, obsessive retribution would be directed at any woman who had the temerity to refuse him. Amanda B (not her real name) began a relationship with Burstow believing his name to be Anthony Hurdle. In 1999 she happened to see the Yorkshire Television documentary about Tracey's nightmare and, to her absolute horror, recognised the man described as 'Britain's most notorious stalker' as her boyfriend.

When confronted, Burstow at first appeared to react reasonably. He said he was ashamed of his past and had only hounded Tracey because she'd had him sacked from the Navy. The whole incident was buried, he told her, and now all he wanted was for Amanda to give him a chance. If, on the other hand, she felt her discovery had changed things between them, he could hardly blame her and would get out of her life.

Unable to recognise the monster she'd seen on the television screen as the man she knew, Amanda eventually decided to let him stay. It was a terrible mistake and she realised it soon enough. She'd never noticed before but his jealousy, his need for control and his unreasonable behaviour, became obvious and incessant. In September 2000 she told him to go.

Then the stalking began: letters, telephone calls – Burstow prowling around her house, staring through the windows. It was obvious what she had seen on TV had been the truth, and he wasn't going to let her go. She endured his harassment for almost two months but it took a truly horrific attack to finally persuade the authorities that this man was a dangerous maniac.

Friday 24 November – Amanda's doorbell rang. She knew who it was, though when she looked through the spy-hole there was no one on the doorstep. She'd had enough; she was going to tell him exactly what she thought of him. Knowing he must be somewhere nearby, she opened the door.

She didn't have time to catch her breath. At once Burstow rushed into the house, forcing her back onto the staircase. He had his hand tight against her throat, nearly choking her, after which he propelled her into the kitchen. As he did so, he told her they were both about to die.

Amanda's eighteen-year-old son arrived home and tried to intervene but Burstow was raving, venomous. He whipped out a Stanley knife and, after threatening the boy, took hold of Amanda's arm. He held her wrist down on the draining board and dug in, almost severing her hand. Then he slashed his own wrists.

It bothered him that his victim was bleeding more than he was. He asked her why – why was she dying before him? Then: 'I'm going,' he said. The kitchen floor was awash with blood. Burstow, weakened now, slipped on it and fell, giving Amanda her only chance of escape. Somehow, with her hand half hanging off, she managed to get out of the room.

Paramedics arrived in time to save her life – and Burstow's. Had Amanda's son not arrived home when he did and been able to call the police, it's likely Burstow would have succeeded in killing both of them. His only grievance against her was that she'd tried to leave him.

Amazingly, 'Hurdle' pleaded guilty. He was jailed for a minimum of seven years. It will be the Home Secretary's decision whether or not to release him when the time comes. Meanwhile, Amanda has had to cope with unbelievable trauma, physical and psychological pain and a number of operations.

Tracey has been coming to terms with the last eight and a half years and the fact that this sickening attack could so easily have happened to her. 'It has taken a near death experience to prove he's dangerous,' she said. She continues to work for victims and to campaign for changes in the law. She welcomed proposals to set up a register of stalkers similar to that which keeps track of sex offenders. Her work, helped by the Suzy Lamplugh Trust, has resulted in the creation of the Network for Surviving Stalkers.

Their address is given in the back of this book.

11. THE FOOD OF LOVE

The world of classical music conjures up a sophisticated, intelligent image where audiences and performers alike enjoy cultured, sometimes esoteric pleasures. The baser, unpleasant everyday world is left outside and, for a few hours, our emotions are carried along by beautiful sound.

It's a world which has its stars and its stars have their admirers, but the devotees of a conductor or a violinist are usually those who genuinely appreciate the talents of the musician; they are unlikely to be cast in the same mould as, say, the fans of a pop icon or a film star where over half the attraction is sexual.

At the age of only twenty-three, Malcolm Stewart was the youngest member of the Liverpool Philharmonic Orchestra. He was also its lead violinist. Stewart's prodigious talent, coupled with Italianate good looks, suggested he was destined for a happy, rewarding career together with a fulfilling personal life.

So when an attractive twenty-seven-year-old woman appeared at the door of his dressing room one evening in 1984, Stewart, then six years into his career with the orchestra, was flattered, impressed by the visitor's bravado and not at all averse to accepting her offer of a drink.

The drink led, as such things do, to a brief and (Stewart thought) uncomplicated liaison. She came across as forward, but that seemed no bad thing. He had no reason to suppose Karen Cross expected any more from him than he was prepared to offer. Having recently come to the end of a long-term relationship, a flirtation was fine but serious commitment was not what he was looking for.

But it transpired Karen Cross had other ideas: ideas which were already becoming entrenched on that first meeting and which, as far as she was concerned, Stewart had unwittingly confirmed by agreeing to go out with her. Cross was going to become a severe blight on Stewart's life for the next fourteen years. Today he describes the experience as 'hell' and remembers a dangerous and vindictive woman whom he still has reason to fear.

At first Karen appeared as intelligent and perfectly normal. The time they spent together was, for Stewart, 'extra-marital activity' as he already had a girlfriend. When he finally decided to break with Cross, some two months later, her reaction was disturbing. It wasn't that she was upset, disappointed – angry even. It was as though she simply didn't comprehend what he meant. His words, he said, 'didn't register'.

In an interview in the *Daily Telegraph* with Cassandra Jardine, Stewart says, 'I assumed that, if I reasoned with her, she would sort herself out – but she didn't. It was a fix for her to come at me again and have some sort of communication.'[1]

She unearthed his girlfriend's name and attempted to find her. Not knowing what she looked like, she took a long-shot. Cross turned up at the Philharmonic Hall and approached the best-looking woman among those she'd seen Stewart talking with. She asked what she was called – it wasn't the right person. Stewart is sure that, had it been his girlfriend, Cross would have made a terrible scene. It was a worrying incident but he could scarcely have guessed what dreadful things lay ahead.

Cross's campaign of harassment escalated at an alarming rate. He admits he sometimes let her in when she came 'banging away' on his door. He was concerned for the peace of his neighbours and, in any case, knew she wouldn't give up. He had made vain attempts at hiding. He'd changed his telephone number six times and on each occasion she traced the new one. He saw her ability to discover his whereabouts and those of his contacts as unstoppable, and from then on, nothing and nobody seemed to be able to protect him.

Showing her total dedication to her deluded ideas, she moved house – to one which was just five minutes' drive from his home. She had no visible means of support but seemed always to have enough time and cash to devote all her energies to her stalking activity. Interestingly, she recalls this whole period as being a 'relationship' with Stewart who, she claims, asked her to marry him.

This 'relationship', though it existed only in Cross's fevered mind, was much more anguished for Stewart than it would have been had it ever been a reality. He conducted his other affairs with women in what amounted to a clandestine way, dodging Cross's car and making sure he never parked his own outside a girlfriend's house in case Cross found out where he was. He kept his stalker's behaviour to himself, not wanting to trouble others with his 'sadness'. His music became the only consoling thing in his life but even this was suffering. Cross's presence, more often than not in the front row, where he couldn't possibly avoid seeing her, was a constant reproach for the imaginary hurt he had done her.

Gradually, his attempted avoidance of her penetrated some way into her consciousness, enough to turn her longings into venom. Unable to stand by his side as 'a respectable wife and mother' she now adopted a different role in his life: that of a potential killer.

He described to the *Daily Telegraph* how, from her seat at the Philharmonic Hall, as he was about to start playing, she would make a 'murderous gesture', drawing her finger across her throat. 'Performance,' he goes on to say, 'at the best of times is like trying to walk the tightrope in a Force 8 gale. Yet I had to go on, night after night, terrified that at any minute she might knife me. There were times when all I wanted to do was run.'[2]

Although the police weren't unsympathetic, Stewart found a lack of understanding. He had difficulty finding continuity with 'your average bobby'. In any case, they didn't seem to think there was any real danger and there was nothing they could do until she actually broke the law.

'It was frustrating. You get all these blank looks. They think you're a nutter for talking about it anyway. Every time I spoke to them about it, it seemed I had to go to a different officer and start the whole story from scratch.'[3]

Stewart tried other means of ridding himself of this Virago. He tried her parents, her doctor and social services, but none of them could help him. (Her mother was initially extremely sympathetic but, when the matter eventually came to court, she backed her daughter absolutely.)

Cross's stalking grew ever more serious. It prevented Stewart from marrying a woman he became engaged to. He knew Cross would, at the very least, make a dreadful scene at the church but what finally persuaded him that marriage was too dangerous a step to take was when Cross followed him to his fiancée's house. Stewart knew his presence in another person's life put them in danger from his stalker's vengeance and, perhaps more chillingly, he predicted that any children they might have would become a target. He called the wedding off.

It seems his fears were not exaggerated. In July, 2000, Cross was walking past Southport Town Hall where a marriage was taking place. In the grip of some terrible rage, she ran amok and attacked the photographer, destroying his camera. The groom gave chase and, after counting to three, Cross began screaming loudly. The couple's big day was ruined and their photographs lost for ever. Stewart is convinced the attack had something to do with him. Could she have mistaken the bridegroom for the man she had fixated upon over a decade before?

He had had excrement, tampons and condoms pushed through his letterbox, he had received a 'tonnage' of letters (he ended up with over a thousand of them). The most sinister aspect was a weird religious fixation which dominated her letters and much of the verbal abuse she hurled at him. She went to St Andrew's Anglican Church in Bebington, 'though she was far from Christian', he says ruefully. She talked about 'fire and brimstone', 'the devil incarnate', she quoted the Bible as though she felt God was giving her his personal blessing to terrorise Stewart.

She always hand-delivered her letters; not one of them was ever posted. It was just another reminder to Stewart that he was accessible to her and his home was not a place he could hide. Nor was his work. She put notes in unsealed envelopes and handed them around the Philharmonic like flyers.

'She would say "can you give this to Malcolm Stewart?" Well, if you're given a letter and it's not sealed – eventually people are going to start looking at them, aren't they? People started distancing themselves from me. It was alienating me from everyone.'[4]

Her letters were sometimes conciliatory, sometimes aggressive. She had different moods and different characters appeared. Stewart read her threats only to attempt to stay ahead of her, to try and find out what she was going to do next. She was on a mission, a mission to make him pure; to unite her spirit with his. She took to standing near the Philharmonic car park and screaming this at him.

Cross smashed his windows, raided his bins and sent abusive letters about him to his colleagues. She followed him to Toulouse, where he leads another orchestra.

She accused him of raping her. She cleverly back-dated her claim to make it seem more credible. Stewart was called in for questioning. It was humiliating and, needless to say, completely fanciful. There followed weeks when he was left worried about his career as he saw everything he had ever worked for 'going down the tubes'. The charges against him were eventually dismissed, but 'mud sticks' and he was aware of the suspicions that surrounded him.

'The police called me in again. I kept getting messages to speak to this officer or that officer. This time it was a murder enquiry. There was a horrendous crime which was still unresolved. An eighty-year-old spinster had been battered to death and there were possibly some sexual overtones to it as well. I looked at the Day Sheet in the police station and it said 'because of scandalised life-style'. I always suspected it was Karen Cross – I can't substantiate that. But had it not been for her, they would never have come knocking on my door. I was taken to this Victorian prison where they house hardened criminals and I was fingerprinted. When I went to my solicitor, I could see that he was distancing himself from it. He said "don't say anything" and I could see "there's no smoke without fire". They give you plenty of time to sweat and worry.'[5]

Today, Stewart is still mindful of this woman's capacity for hatred. He has been approached by other writers and television presenters but is chary about speaking about it. It's virtually impossible, he told me, to encapsulate fourteen years of hell into an article. Above all, he doesn't want to give the slightest encouragement to her. She has claimed her attachment to him is in the past and even maintains it was all the other way round – that he was obsessed with her. He has nothing to fear, she has said.

One can sympathise with Stewart's sceptical attitude to this assurance for the emotional effects of his experience were profound and lasting. 'The contrast between my profession, which deals in the noblest of human aspirations, and the sordid mess of my private life was almost too much for me,' he told the *Daily Telegraph*. 'It caused me the most acute anxiety and depression. I couldn't sleep and I began to doubt my own sanity.'

He finally managed to get an injunction against Cross when she poured paint over his car. She ignored the ruling. Only when she sent him a written death threat were the police able to charge her. She was given a three-month suspended sentence and told she must never contact him again. He now looks back on fourteen years which should have been the exciting and enjoyable groundings of his professional life: fourteen years which were stolen from him.

12. TO HELL AND BACK

Sydney is a city which is synonymous with youth and beauty. It conjures up an image of sun, sea and clear skies. In England, we view it through the telescope of Australian soap opera where pouting, pretty teenagers compete for our sympathy as they go through their inconsequential love affairs. We put our feet up and enjoy pleasant speculation: 'Will they make it together? – Or will she opt for the bronzed, gym-toned hunk from the diner?' It's all safe and idealised. If tragedy befalls a character it's never real. The same, familiar good looks will soon be back on our screens in some other guise, or, just as likely, on the stage of our local theatre at panto time.

Gabriella Mazzali was offered the chance of living this dream. At twenty-five, she was young and attractive; a caring individual who, having studied nursing at Hampstead's Royal Free Hospital, had been given the opportunity to take a job at a private hospital in Sydney. She had always loved the sun and considered the move to be the fulfilment of her dreams. The job was everything she could have wanted: driving along the harbour in her air-conditioned Toyota, money in her pocket and the perfect, lovely flat. She was an outdoor type and loved being able to go camping, eating 'barbies' on the beach and generally enjoying what life had to offer. A snapshot shows her, the picture of wholesome good health, dressed in a bikini and standing next to her surfboard. She wouldn't have looked out of place in *Neighbours* or *Bay Watch*.

But the tragedy that was to befall her was to take her from happy beginnings to ongoing torment. It's two years since it happened and – probably for the rest of her life – she will live with the pain of what a crazed, violent stalker did to her. The healthy body in the photographs has been taken from her. She is back home in England and is severely disabled; in fact, it's a miracle she survived at all.

Gabriella has a quiet, determined voice which catches every so often, increasingly so when she recalls what happened to her. Sometimes it seems a struggle to articulate her thoughts. She mostly gives a plain, uncompromising statement of the facts; facts which are so appalling that professional interest seems irrelevant, intrusive and audacious.

She has her neighbour's dog with her 'Because it's a nice day and I thought why not?' The dog is small and cute but has an unfortunate habit of turning wild whenever it sees another dog on a lead. Gabriella extracts it from a fight, explaining that it came from a dogs' home and may have suffered some abuse prior to being rescued. 'We screw animals up and then wonder why they behave badly,' she says and protectively holds the animal to her. Her humanity is evident, as is her pain.

Gabriella met Stephen Rae at the Rocks, the area of Sydney which the first white settlers built upon. Up until the sixties it had been mainly working-class but it has changed its image since. It's now a popular tourist area, somewhat disregarded by the locals but increasingly popular with visitors.

It was St Patrick's Day 1996. Rae had been with some friends, but he'd lost them in the crowds. He asked if he could hitch up with Gabriella and her party.

Rae was not what you might call drop-dead gorgeous but he seemed attractive enough at their first meeting. He was from Crieff, Perthshire. Apart from impressing her by being able to speak Chinese, he had degrees in geology and a good job as a language teacher. He and Gabriella exchanged phone numbers. They went for a drink a week or so later and it wasn't long before they were seeing each other on a regular basis. Rae, being a fellow Brit, was a link with home. The pair spent their leisure time swimming, surfing and enjoying what Sydney had to offer.

But there was something he was holding back, something which worried Gabriella and that she couldn't quite put her finger on. At times – and increasingly – he seemed indifferent to the relationship. He couldn't, or wouldn't, discuss his feelings and was often possessive and moody. Gabriella came to realise she and Rae weren't going to work out as a relationship and she decided to break up with him. It's never an easy thing to say to your partner, and it soon became clear Rae wasn't going to be the understanding sort, who would smooth over the problem by appreciating the ultimate wisdom of Gabriella's decision. 'He didn't handle it too well,' she says understatedly.

When you have known someone for a year and a half, when you have seen them at their best and their worst, the bad times can be tempered by the good and threatening, worrying behaviour is disregarded. Friends don't see any lasting problem: 'Give him time and he'll get over it and be back to normal.' You believe them because it's impossible to accept that someone who has shared your life in such an intimate way could become a real danger to you. In Gabriella's case the signs were there that first time they broke up, but she didn't see them for what they were.

Prior to their split, the couple had booked a skiing trip. Gabriella asked Rae not to come. 'Please don't,' she said, 'we're not together any more.' It was irritating when he ignored her request and even more when he got very drunk and 'made an arse of himself' – irritating, but not as worrying as it should have been. Such clumsy attempts to win back a person who's rejected you are not seen as outrageous. The warning came in disguise and went unheeded.

A friend of Gabriella's came over from England. One morning, after Gabriella had gone off to work, her visitor was treated to Rae banging on the door, hurling accusations. 'It's all because of you we've broken up,' he yelled.

Don't be too hard on him, Gabriella thought, he's hurting and he'll get over it.

She still regrets she didn't see these incidents as concrete proof of imminent danger. 'Very naive I was: very naive. If I had known . . . If you want to break off a relationship, you just say "No. You're not to call me again. No, I do not want anything to do with you again." And that's the only way you can do it.'[1] She pauses briefly before her frustration comes rushing out in a brief torrent; what *could* she have done? There was no one to advise her.

'Sometimes these restriction orders can wind them up even more. Not all the time, but if they're mentally unbalanced like he obviously was, it can really wind them up. Sometimes it works, the threat means they know you mean business, but other times it just stirs them up.'

She stops herself going over it again, falling into silence. She focuses on those past events and, almost imperceptibly, she trembles.

Gabriella had to return to England to get her visa renewed. It was when she was on the verge of leaving that she met Rae again. He surprised her totally by asking her to marry him. She didn't give him an answer. He was drunk and her instincts were already telling her to keep away from this man. However, she was also conditioned to be kind to people and, somewhere inside, she felt sorry for him. She told him to ask her again when he was sober. Rae had managed to get to her. When she arrived back from her trip to England, she resumed seeing him. She now declares it was the stupidest thing she ever did.

He still wasn't willing to communicate or talk about things. Gabriella had assumed that, this second time round, knowing she wanted a monogamous, adult relationship where both partners were honest with each other, Rae would try his best to make it work. Instead he was more and more jealous and possessive. He hated anybody she befriended: 'That girl's horrible you hang around with', 'when are you going to have time for me?', 'who's that on the phone?' Worse than putting her friends down, he put Gabriella down. He was gradually attempting to chip away at her self-esteem.

If this was his intended goal, he didn't succeed. Gabriella was fighting back, aware now she'd made a mistake and looking for an excuse to end this miserable liaison. She cared enough about people generally, and Rae in particular, not to just dump him. Like other women in abusive, unhappy partnerships, she was waiting for the excuse to go; the one incident which she could reasonably say was totally unacceptable. The fact that her life was being made miserable by a series of nasty snipings didn't seem enough. Rae was aware of how she was feeling but this didn't stop him. The more disagreeable he became, the less chance the couple had of saving anything – even friendship – but he was not able to stop himself.

Towards Christmas, the lease on Rae's flat ran out. The idea of getting a flat together had been mentioned before, but only talked about; nothing had been agreed. Rae used this as a lame excuse to blame Gabriella for his homelessness. He moved in with her, rent-free.

Christmas came. As she was a nurse, Gabriella had to work over the holiday. Rae had the time off. She suggested he go away by himself on a surfing holiday and was thankful when he agreed. He had only been with her a short time, but the relief when he was gone was huge. He was away for a whole five days and for that short time she could breathe once more. It took this to make her realise what he was doing to her. She knew now beyond all doubt he was in no way what she was looking for and he was having a huge negative effect on her life. When Rae came back she summoned up her reserves of tact, courage and determination and told him to go.

'I said, "Look, while you've been away I've figured this flat's too small for the two of us and I request you find somewhere else to live." I wanted to help him out over the Christmas and New Year period. It wasn't that he had to move straight away; it was like – in your own time, but make it soon. He went out and came back drunk. I was encouraging him the whole time he was living with me, getting out the property pages and saying "Oh, look. Here's a possible flat for you." But he was taking no hints.'[2]

Gabriella eventually had to enlist the help of the landlord to force Rae off the premises.

'Apparently that's not a good thing to do either – to get another man – because then they think they've got their hooks into you, they've got you scared. He wrote this apology. That night I'd been out with my gay male friend – he hated him as well – he hated all my friends – that's a classic warning sign as well, because if he likes me he's going to like my friends. You know? My friends come with me, they're part of who I am.'[3]

She asked him to leave her alone: 'Please go away now. I don't want to talk to you right now. You're drunk. It's not appropriate I talk to you right now – we can't have a straight conversation.' He raked around the kitchen drawer where the knives were kept and then went and sat on the bath. Gabriella heard him gasp and cry out as if he'd stabbed himself, then there was silence. When she went to investigate, she found he was hoaxing.

Gabriella has since read Gavin de Becker's book *The Gift of Fear* and believes that, had she been able to interpret Rae's behaviour better, she would have been able to protect herself. De Becker tells us we have an instinctive, sometimes subconscious knowledge that we're in danger. If only we could trust it and act on it, we could drastically reduce the risk of harm.

A few days into January, 1998, there was an incident which should have served as a clear warning of what was to come.

Rae was refusing to let Gabriella out of her flat – he was drunk again and ended up by throwing wine over her. 'Here, have a drink,' he said. He then held a lighter beside her face.

Scared and not daring to admit to the awful fears that were pressing into her mind, she rang a friend, the gay man who she sometimes went out with. She told him 'Come and get me now!' Rae had stolen the keys to her company car, a brand-new Toyota, he was skidding up and down the road in it, swigging beer. As Gabriella's friend was coming up the corridor, Rae demanded to know where she was going. It was four in the morning but Gabriella was finally listening to her self-preservation instincts.

'I'm getting out of here,' she said.

Next morning she had to go to work. There were a lot of elderly people in the community to see and she went straight to the patients' homes, leaving going into the office until later in the morning. She was dismayed when she returned to her flat to find a tyre of her car had been let down.

After her friend had helped her change the tyre she went into the flat where Rae was crashed out, sleeping off his alcoholic binge of the previous night. Gabriella stole her flat keys back and left.

She got a call on her mobile phone. It was Rae and he wanted to meet her. She assumed he was going to be remorseful and apologetic – but he wasn't.

'He was laughing and he said "Ah, ha, ha! You'll never get me out of that flat." He was quite scary. I called my landlord straight away. I packed up some of his things and I said "Can you warn him off the property?" Well, that was that.'[4]

Rae went to live in a hostel – a simple, cheap place catering mainly for backpackers. Gabriella had her home back. She hoped she'd got rid of her ex-lover once and for all, though she was not at all certain of it. It didn't surprise her when the phone calls continued. Despite everything, she did feel sorry for him.

'You know, what with coming from a caring profession and everything. He didn't seem to have anybody. He played on that.'[5]

The phone calls became more of a nuisance. If Gabriella was on her land-line, Rae would call her up on the mobile and demand to know who she'd been talking to. She tried switching off her mobile but he'd still leave messages which were scaring her. She kept bumping into him when she went out in the evening or even during the day. She was still not at all sure she wasn't being paranoid about him. Sydney is a small city and people often frequent the same places, but Rae just kept on appearing wherever she went, it had to be more than just coincidence.

Rae befriended another male tenant in the flats where she lived. It was a clever ruse and clearly designed as a good excuse for hanging around. Gabriella asked her neighbour to please see him away from home if he had to see him at all. 'He's been told not to come near the property.'

At one time the landlord caught him hanging around. Rae lied, saying he'd come round to collect a washing machine from the shed 'Gabby said I could'. By now Gabriella was getting more seriously concerned about this persistent behaviour. She told her mother about it. Her mother was quite clear in her advice: 'Call the police. You've got to tell the police.'

Rae still had not done anything so bad that Gabriella felt she could follow this advice. She was still hoping against hope this was just a very juvenile way of letting go of their affair and that, given time, Rae would cool down and leave her alone.

'None of my friends were supporting me on it, saying "Watch out for him" or anything like that. This bizarre behaviour – turning up at my workplace with flowers and a card saying "Farewell" ... I remember saying to my colleagues, "If he turns up here again, call security straight away!" '[6]

When she eventually did call the police and told them of her concerns they asked her if she wanted to take a restriction order out. Looking back, she wishes she'd been referred to the Domestic Violence Unit where she might have been given some proper counselling on how Rae's behaviour was showing classic signs of danger and how to protect herself against it. The restriction order seemed like a huge overreaction to what she was desperately trying to see as a trying but containable situation.

The stalking persisted for a month: the following, the phone calls. Rae never declared any feelings of love for Gabriella, he just seemed to want to maintain contact with her. Sometimes he was angry and abusive, at other times he behaved as if he'd just popped round for a chat or he was calling to see how she was.

Several times she considered leaving her flat and disappearing somewhere where he wouldn't know her whereabouts. Then she would say to herself, 'Why the hell should I? Why should I have to move out of my lovely flat? He'll get over it soon enough.'

She thought he'd got over it when he announced he had a new girlfriend. Gabriella hoped he was at last going to get on with his life and leave her alone.

'It's just taken some time,' she said. 'It's taken some time.'[7]

On the night of 4 February 1998, nearly two years after meeting Rae, Gabriella had arranged to go out with a girlfriend. Rae phoned her. She was used to his calls by now. His new girlfriend had evidently not helped him put Gabriella aside. She told him she was going out and she hadn't time to talk. He was 'whingeing on' and she held the phone to her ear without paying much attention to what he was saying – she knew it all anyway.

He was demanding to know who she was dating; who was this man she was going out with? Maybe, she thought, if he felt less threatened he might leave me alone for the evening and give me a chance to relax. She wanted to forget about Stephen Rae and his emotional problems for a while. She summoned up enough patience to explain that the 'man' was in fact a female. It was a futile attempt. When she arrived at the bar where she was going to meet her friend, Rae had followed her. He insisted on talking to her. Still hoping to appeal to his better nature, still being nice, still being polite, she pointed out she was with her girlfriend and would talk to him another day. She was angry with him too. She resented him thinking she would give in to his demands and allow him her undivided attention right there and then.

He left, nursing her rejection and letting it grow. It turned into a monster inside him.

Gabriella arrived home later that night and instinctively checked to see if Rae's car was about. It wasn't and she was relieved. She had got into the habit of sleeping with her phones near to hand: her land-line and her mobile both primed with the numbers of the local police, her friend and two other male tenants in the block whom she'd warned of her concerns. The fear, she says, was signalling to her like a beacon and still she tried to dismiss it as paranoia.

It was almost midnight when the phone started ringing. It was Rae. Gabriella tried to placate him, repeating her promise to ring him another day. She had work in the morning; she was tired; she couldn't deal with this right now. The phone kept ringing and ringing. Eventually she picked up the receiver and replaced it immediately to cut him off. He rang again. She ignored him and went to bed.

Stephen Rae was already on his way to her flat. He had with him a two litre milk-carton – it was filled with petrol.

There are cases of terrible injury where the victim mercifully doesn't remember anything until they wake up in hospital. Gabriella was not so fortunate: she remembers every minute of the excruciating pain she went through that night.

She was woken by the ominous sound of the door being kicked in. She knew who it was even before she'd fully awoken. When she did wake up she was looking at Rae. He was standing there in her bedroom. He was speaking but she couldn't understand his words. When he raised the milk carton and spilt its contents over her she smelt the powerful odour.

Gabriella was seized by terror and a blind instinct for self-preservation. She knew she had to run, to get out of the flat. Wearing only her night clothes, she fled out of the front door and tried to rouse a neighbour. Another neighbour heard her cries and came running to her assistance. Gabriella was screaming 'He's got a lighter! He's got a lighter!'

Rae was there with them. He took hold of Gabriella and locked her in a bear-hug. The neighbour was desperately trying to get him off her but, before he could, Rae raised his right hand and clicked the lighter, turning Gabriella into a massive fireball.

She felt like she was melting. The pain was, she says, indescribable. Underneath it she heard a voice inside her head telling her to do something – anything. It was her own voice and she was praying: 'Dear God, do you want me dead or alive?'

There are some physical states where it is braver to go on living than to give in to one's fear of dying. With her health, her looks and her youth, disappearing in the furnace which surrounded her, Gabriella showed her resilience and her courage. She decided she was going to live.

She hurled herself down the stairwell hoping to smother the flames.

It didn't work and she lay there, curled like a baby. She was moaning now, still burning and only barely able to tell her horrified neighbour to pour water on her. He was in shock and, mechanically obeying her instructions, poured a small jug of water over her. 'I need more,' she said. He responded and, as the flames finally died, Stephen Rae stepped over her and walked away. It is reported that some time later he gave himself up to the police with the words, 'I've done a very bad crime.'

* * *

Gabriella Mazzali would not have survived this attack had it happened ten years earlier. Ninety three per cent of her body had third-degree burns. There were only a very few places where she had been spared the flames: her face, the soles of her feet, her palms, a small space on her abdomen which had been protected by her pants. There was not enough healthy skin left to graft onto the damaged areas. When she was told by an ambulance man how horrific her injuries were, she knew only too well that she'd escaped death by inches. Her fight back to some sort of life was going to be gruelling, painful and protracted.

Her body became infected by septicaemia and other complications which meant that the new, synthetic skin (a very recent innovation from America), which gave her hope of survival would simply fall away from her. Her family rallied round her bedside and somehow Gabriella fought her way back to some sort of health.

She was convinced there had been a reason for her survival and this belief kept her going through the agonising months which followed. From being that happy swimmer in the photograph she was now an invalid, forced to put on her clothes with the aid of a long stick because of her inability to bend lest her tight, thin skin should break. Doctors paid tribute to her determination and her will to live. There were times when it looked like she wasn't going to make it, but she has.

Now she lives in England again as the Australian sun would be too much for her but she doesn't hate the country. An evil person did this to her, she says, it wasn't Australia.

She wanted me to use her experience as a warning to other people. Gabriella can point to many incidents in her relationship with Stephen Rae where she knew, inside herself, that there was something desperately wrong. She was often scared by his behaviour but, like so many other stalking victims, she couldn't comprehend what her own mind was telling her. She is uncompromising in her advice.

'If you've got any doubts, any concerns in any way, be clear about what you want, be clear to former boyfriends. Tell them not to have contact with you. Don't let them down gently; if you're ending the relationship that's the end. It's important to talk to specialists: the police, the Suzy Lamplugh Trust . . . The police can refer you on to the Domestic Violence Unit, because stalking is domestic violence. Domestic Violence is a number one killer; a number one reason for murder. It's about gut feeling – knowing – trusting your instincts.'[8]

In December, 1999, at Parramatta District Court in Sydney, Stephen Rae who had pleaded guilty to causing grievous bodily harm with intent to murder Gabriella, was sentenced to serve a maximum of nineteen years and eight months' imprisonment with a minimum term of fourteen years, nine months. The judge, Angela Karpin, said, 'He extinguished forever the life she had as a successful and attractive young woman. She is doomed to be a prisoner of her injuries for the rest of her life.' Rae has now retracted his guilty plea, claiming he was pressurised into making it and his only intention that night was to kill himself. His father quotes him as saying there was a struggle, and the petrol went all over the place. 'It went on the carpet and Gabriella fell on it.'[9]

Gabriella is reluctant to make easy judgments on Rae's mental condition. When pressed she said, 'I'm not a psychologist but judging from his first reaction when I broke up the relationship, he was a time-bomb waiting to go off. If he'd stabbed me or shot me it would have been kinder, but burning me . . .' She trails off for a moment and then adds, 'I think it's fear of self – rejection of self.'[10]

It's a beautiful evening and she recommends an outdoor operatic event which is to take place in the grounds of the stately home we've been visiting. She is going on with her life. She has survived.

13. THE INVISIBLE THREAT

Imagine you are at a masked ball. This place exists only in your imagination; you have left all your worries behind in the real world. You feel bold enough to approach any of the thousands of guests who are milling around in the dimly lit, beautiful room. All of them are wearing splendid costumes – whatever sort of clothes *you* want them to; all of them are of the age, sex and build you've always found most attractive. All of them, including yourself, are holding masks to their faces.

Someone catches your attention. Although you can't see their face, your imagination fills in the details and you're sure this is your perfect partner. If you were to begin talking to them you would know they'd be happy to respond in whatever way you would wish them to. You reach out.

The conversation begins gently: they want to know your name. You give them a false one – better not give too much away at first. They give you a name and you have a suspicion it too is not the one they'd normally go by. It doesn't matter: this isn't real, nobody is going to accuse anybody of lying.

What does matter is what they are looking for in life: could it be someone just like you? They let slip more and more tantalising details about themselves and their secret desires. It seems you are absolute soul mates. You exaggerate some of your own achievements in order not to disappoint them – exaggerate just a little, not exactly lie. They might be doing the same of course but you don't care as long as the basics are real. When this game finishes and you meet this person in the day to day world you'll be prepared for a few minor disappointments. You'll cope – later. In any case, you don't want to be bothered too much about reality. Tonight might be all you have with this person and – for now – it's enough.

The exaggerations develop. You still have the mask up to your face. You're still safe. They won't know you're not quite the beautiful, wonderful creature you're now describing to them. You can even go as far as talking about your sexual desires. They need never find out that the last time you took a stranger into your bed was in 1982 after a drunken college party.

As you build up your fantasy image, so the stranger is building up theirs. It's like a drug and you need more of it. You have to encourage more details out of them. You're dimly aware that they're doing the same to you. Your inhibitions have now vanished completely. You are hoping so much that at least half of what they say just might be true. Something real might actually come of this meeting.

You don't even care too much when another stranger wanders up and begins to eavesdrop on your conversation. Occasionally he interjects. You discourage him but he stays nearby, listening.

Other people join the interloper and soon there's a crowd around you. You're oblivious to it. You have your mask; no one knows who you are.

Or do they? By now you are quite drunk and you're being indiscreet. You've already dropped into the conversation all sorts of details you didn't at first intend. This person you're talking to might live anywhere in the world: you hope he lives near you. You've mentioned a couple of pubs you drink in – pubs in the centre of town. If he knows them he might be local. He says he does know them. You tell him, casually, that you're interested in music: he is as well. You both seem to know a particular place where they play your type of stuff on Thursday nights. Perhaps he might like to meet you there sometime?

Soon you realise your mask is slipping away from your face. You've said so much about your life now it seems hardly worth keeping your identity secret. You're still hoping his mask will do the same but he's not moved it at all.

You become uncomfortable. There are too many people listening in. You want to go somewhere private; you want the stranger to be real now. As you press the point he backs away from you. The other people are getting closer. They're interrupting more and more. Suddenly you know they can all see you for what you are and not one of them has revealed themselves to you at all. You run out of the building. When you arrive home you worry about what you've said: how much of yourself you've given away. Will any of these people find you again?

We have the means to provide ourselves with just this experience. Millions of people enter that masked ball every night: I am, of course, talking about the Internet.

Stalkers who rely on their invisibility have found the perfect method of harassment and they can do it all at the touch of a button. These people are the nuisances who send unwanted emails or who hog the chat-rooms; they are the business people seeking revenge; they are also the downright dangerous predators who are looking for victims.

Stalking on the Internet, or 'cyberstalking' as it has become known, is growing like a cancer: as the Internet itself grows – so does the tumour. The good news is, we can protect ourselves reasonably easily. The bad news is, so can the stalkers.

Parry Aftab was the first 'Internet lawyer' before she was asked, as an interim measure, to take over a group who were then known as Cyberangels. Cyberangels, like their then parent group, the Guardian Angels, look after the welfare and safety of ordinary people with their volunteer force of workers. The Guardian Angels are familiar to us as being 'those people in the red berets you see on the underground' – patrolling the streets and tube networks on the lookout for muggers, thieves and vandals – a sort of volunteer police force. Cyberangels, (which in January 2001 became three major independent organisations, Cyberangels, wiredkids.org and cyberlawenforcement.com) works in much the same way, but on the Internet.

Parry intended this to be a temporary position until she was sent the details of a website which showed a young girl being raped. She was horrified; from that moment on she has devoted herself to making the Internet a safe place for its millions of users throughout the world.

Cyberstalking is becoming one of her big concerns. Research is still in its infancy (she hopes to get together with Internet Service Providers all over the English-speaking world and to do something about this). She is, however, already all too familiar with the profile of the Internet stalker. Like his 'real life' counterparts, he generally arrives in several recognisable guises.

The most common type, as is the case off-line, are those non-celebrity cases in which relationships have gone awry. Parry includes in this huge problem area the cases of unrequited love and other 'romantically connected' incidents. Obviously, there are crossovers into off-line abuse and off-line stalking but most cyberstalking stays on-line. A lot of it happens between people who are many, many miles apart and not unusually between a stalker and victim who don't know the first thing about each other. This is not to say we should think of it as less dangerous.

Parry: 'The cases so far where people have been killed as a result of cyberstalking or have been threatened with serious physical danger off-line are those which involve some sort of romantic connection – a jilted lover or past relationship or something like that.'[1]

When there is a relationship connection, of whatever sort, it might be assumed the victim knows who their stalker is. There are many who, though known to their target, somehow manage to stay 'invisible', a malicious presence whenever the victim goes into a chat-room or clicks 'send and receive' in the electronic mailbox.

A woman in Alabama, whom we'll call Mary (it's not her real name) was being stalked both on and off-line. The Internet stalking included threatening emails which described her day's events: where she went, at what time, with whom, details of her personal life and ex-husband. The stalker had taken over her Yahoo and Hotmail accounts and was able to send his victim messages from them. Mary contacted Faith, one of the Cyber Angels volunteers, who asked her some general questions. It transpired Mary had met a man (Bob) on the Internet during the time she was still married. She'd left her husband and, with her daughter, moved in with Bob and his own ten-year-old daughter.

The relationship soured and eventually Mary ended it. It was shortly after this she began receiving the harassing emails; they were then being sent to a new account she'd only just opened. It wasn't difficult to put two and two together: Bob had already expressed his anger at being thrown out. At the time he was living with his daughter in their car – he had plenty to fuel his malice.

But Mary wasn't convinced. She was sure Bob couldn't possibly be the person they were looking for. She told Faith he was helping to find the stalker and had reported the incidents to the police. Faith was determined she had the right man. She traced the threatening messages to a town some ten miles away from Mary's home. They were coming from an Internet café where Bob checked his mail. Still, Mary didn't want to believe her ex-partner could do this to her.

It seemed more and more obvious to Faith. The messages often referred to her relationship with Bob and usually told her she'd been wrong to end it and would have to pay if she didn't make amends. The stalker kept asking Mary to meet him by a particular lake. Despite good advice, Mary would turn up for these meetings but the stalker never showed. Later she would get an email telling her she'd been observed.

Things were getting out of hand. Mary continued to reply to the stalker's messages – another thing Faith had expressly advised against. Exasperated and not knowing how to help a client who wouldn't help herself, Faith warned she would have to drop the case if Mary continued to go her own way. She kept telling Mary to contact the local police, but Mary said they didn't believe her.

Then, apparently, Bob also started getting death threats. Someone was going to rape and kill his daughter and to kill him. He told Mary he'd reported this to the police. He even told her he'd talked to the FBI and they were on the case.

The story took an important turn when Faith traced the emails the stalker had sent and compared them to ones Mary was getting from Bob. They originated from exactly the same IP address and had usually been sent only a minute or two apart. Bob had known Mary's email account passwords, he'd known her personal history, he had a vendetta against her. He *had* to be the stalker and Mary *had* to believe it.

Bob had claimed (and the mysterious stalker verified it in the emails) he and his daughter had been kidnapped several times, but, conveniently they'd always been set free. He'd never been able to give a description of his attackers. Faith checked with the local police and the FBI. She wasn't surprised to learn Bob had never made any report to them.

Then one of the malicious emails was traced to Mary's own computer. Faith questioned her and found she'd taken pity on Bob and allowed him and his daughter to stay the night. The case was turning into a nightmare. The emails continued. Now they were saying the sender had video tapes of both Mary and her fourteen-year-old daughter having sex. They threatened to distribute them if she didn't 'right her wrongs against Bob'. They told her they'd kidnapped Bob's daughter and raped her.

Faith now had a record of over one hundred and fifty emails: all of them evidence against Bob. She asked for help from the local police who told her bluntly they 'didn't do Internet stuff'. Together with her co-volunteer, Richard, she even set up an appointment with the District Attorney who told her there wasn't any evidence the emails were coming from Bob.

Happily the case ended without a major off-line incident. Bob moved away and the emails mysteriously stopped. Mary had been through a horrendous experience and, but for the help and support she'd received from Faith, she might well have gone over the edge. She'd been on the point of suicide more than once. It had been an unusual case where the victim surely knew who her stalker was but preferred to believe in a mythical stranger. Not everybody wants to know the truth and not everybody is willing to be helped.

It might seem strange that people will actually read emails which they know are going to contain something unpleasant. Wayne Maxey of the San Diego Stalking Strike Force (one of only two special stalking police units in the United States) explained:

'Here in the Stalking Unit we have seen an increase of sorts in the area of cyberstalking, or at least cases of stalking where the computer and Internet are used to harass, threaten or research information concerning the victim. In some situations victims are afraid *not* to read the email, because there may be something that can at least let them know what's going to happen, or where activities may come from. One of our biggest cases of cyberstalking was a college student sending threatening emails (over one hundred during a year-long spree) to five different victims (also college students). The victims told me they were afraid to just delete the messages. In a couple of them the subject line was "Reply or you will die". Who wouldn't open it to find out what's going on? Our human curiosity takes over – who of us would throw away an envelope that arrived in the mail without opening it? Email has become such an accepted and integral part of our daily communication system that the same curiosity is influential. As of late, we have certainly seen hackers and other evil-doers use this to their advantage.

'Also, it has been my experience that most of these cases involve other activities – not just the cyber activities. In the previously mentioned case, our suspect not only sent threatening emails, he sent an anonymous letter with accompanying porno pictures (from the Internet, of course) to the victim's family, he surveyed the victims to some extent; tampered with their school lab experiments, causing bad grades; used a stolen credit card on the Internet to purchase information about them and attempted to purchase a weapon with it; posted the victim's phone number on the Internet – "for a good time, call" – that type of scenario. We advise organisations to take these situations seriously, because if their employee is involved in cyber crimes, they are also probably going to be involved in other destructive behaviours.'[2]

Parry's theories about relationships being the main source of Internet stalking are undoubtedly accurate. The first person in Britain to be convicted of cyberstalking was a Cambridge graduate, Nigel Harris. In March 1999, Harris, a computer programmer, was sentenced for stalking his ex-girlfriend, Claire. He'd met her three years earlier when they were students at Trinity. They had a two-year relationship which, the court heard, was 'stormy'. He used the Internet to harass her in a 'malicious and unrelenting' campaign for over five months. Some of the emails he sent daily were 'romantic' song lyrics, others were more hateful. He sent offensive emails to the children's charity where she worked. She received messages which included frightening references to the horror film *The Shining*, in which Jack Nicholson plays a deranged man who attacks his terrified family with an axe. Harris combined his Internet harassment with actual stalking, leaving his imitation of Nicholson's demented character on Claire's answering machine. It was after this particular incident that she involved the police. Harris was originally given a two year conditional discharge. The magistrates did, however, impose a restraining order preventing him indefinitely from making any contact with his former partner. Just five weeks later he'd turned up at her home in London's Waterloo, clutching a bottle of champagne. She'd taken the precaution of installing a video system and, when Harris rang her bell, she immediately called the police who arrested him as he tried to run away. He later protested that he was an 'entirely nice person'.

Types of cyberstalking vary, but there are patterns which become familiar to those who have to deal with it, for instance: business revenge. Stalking at work is generally increasing and it seems to follow that people will use the convenience and anonymity of cyberspace to carry out their private wars against those who reject them, compete against them or simply annoy them for whatever petty reason. Cases include unwanted emails clogging a mailbox (sometimes hundreds of them), pornographic or other offensive attachments, viruses being sent or threatening and abusive messages being left.

When used unwisely, chat rooms are a hot-bed of cyberstalking. Parry says, 'They (the stalkers) may not like the chat room you run; they may find you're too popular in a chat; they may just find you're a pain in the neck. There are discussion boards: we share a great deal of personal information about ourselves. You might go into a diabetes chat room and talk about the latest treatment you've been receiving for diabetes; you may talk about your child being a diabetic. They then have information about your child, and if they know where you live they can check the school. You have a particular problem which is peculiar to the UK: when children receive their email addresses at the local school, they receive it identified by that school – J Miller@bradfordjunior-school.uk.edu. Now the stalker knows that child's last name, part of the first name and the school. If you start pairing that with information already obtained, it allows someone to be in a serious position to either threaten the parent with serious harm to the child or threaten the child directly.'[3]

Celebrity stalking on-line is not quite the same as its real-life equivalent. On the Internet a 'celebrity' can be absolutely anybody who happens to be successful or popular in this strange new world. A cyber-celebrity can therefore be defined quite narrowly: the person who is popular in a particular chat room, the person who is best known on a particular website. Lonely people who live their social lives in front of a screen can easily be turned into 'green-eyed monsters'.

You don't have to be popular, you don't have to know your stalker, you don't have to have even made any sort of connection with him (or her). Another worrying category which Parry has had to deal with are those she calls 'hackers or hacker-wannabes'. They simply want to demonstrate their technical skills and prove they can use them to hurt people. Like the thug on the dark street, they loiter around waiting for a likely victim: it can be anybody and they need little or no provocation.

Parry: 'The victim's identity is totally irrelevant – the first person they find – and they can find them in a million ways. On-line stalking originates from a far greater range of perpetrators than off-line stalking. Off-line stalking requires that somebody gets up off their butt and actually goes out in bad weather, hides behind trees and bushes. On-line stalking is done from the comfort of your living room or your office. A lot more people are likely to cyberstalk than in real life because it's so easy. They believe they can't be caught. What would you do if you were invisible? A lot of people think the

Internet *means* invisibility – wrongly so – but they think so. People reach out to someone they don't like in their own work space, children reach out to fellow classmates. Someone who just annoys them can become their cyberstalking victim. There's even third-party cyberstalking: some people will actually put up a website offering you up for sex, or your child up for sex. The first case in the US was one of those.'[4]

Gary Dellapenta, a fifty-year-old former security guard, lived with his mother. In 1996, he fell in love with a religious woman who was just half his age. She asked him to leave her alone but he wouldn't listen. Nobody was going to tell *him* 'no'! In the end his love turned to hatred and he devised a horrible plan to avenge himself for having been rejected.

He logged on to the Internet but not as himself. He pretended to be a young woman who got her sexual kicks from violence and extremely masochistic rape fantasies. He was confident of replies and he wasn't wrong. When the responses began to come in, he gave them the young woman's address.

On at least six occasions she was woken in the middle of the night by men pounding on her door demanding sexual satisfaction. Her terror only served to encourage them. They believed her to be a willing 'victim' and genuinely took 'no' to mean 'yes'.

She was saved by the diligence and bravery of her own father. He found the offending web-site and indulged in the same subterfuge as his daughter's stalker. He posed as a sadistic man who wanted to sexually abuse young women and soon found Dellapenta. Stifling his repulsion he managed to persuade Dellapenta of his sadistic interest in his own daughter. The police had no idea how to respond to this crime and, in the end, involved the FBI. The investigators tracked down the message and were able to arrest Dellapenta who was sent to jail for six years.

How do we protect ourselves at this 'masked ball'? Do we have to remain secretive? The whole point of the Internet is to give us contact with strangers across the world and to allow us to access information which interests us and to share it with like-minded people who we may never meet in the flesh.

Are we to suppose we must always assume the worst? When we log on to a chat room for chess enthusiasts is it possible some predatory creature is listening in – someone who is collecting our innocent remarks and who will use them to harass us?

There are still lots of misconceptions about cyberspace. A recent newspaper article declared that every time we log on or send an email we leave behind information which can be used to track us in real life. This, Parry Aftab asserts, is 'absolute baloney'. In the UK we still generally use free Internet Service Providers (ISPs). Most web sites will not ask for your details but those of your ISP. If you're using, say Virgin or BT, it is their details which will go out, not your own. No matter how superior a stalker's hacking skills, they are extremely unlikely to be able to access the customer records of your ISP and find out where you live. Internet stalkers rely on people feeling secure enough to give the game away by small degrees. They rely on people using obvious passwords. Alarmingly many people use codes which can be cracked in minutes and with a minimum of information, such as their birthdate, their pet's name, their child's nickname. With very little research a few tries will result in success.

Parry also warns about having listed telephone numbers and addresses on-line. There are websites all over the world where, at the click of a few buttons, information appears about a person's whereabouts which is frighteningly detailed – even down to a map of the area where they live.

'There are directory pages – you have them and we have them here: we call them white pages or yellow pages – they're all the same and each country has their own. Now we're doing international ones. So you have a listed telephone number – in all likelihood, personal information about you is contained at those special sites. All somebody needs to do is press a button, and Map Quest or one of the others will give them a map to your home. If you have a profile which you put up on your ISP to let people find you and let people know that you're into Poker or Scrabble, that information is technically compiled along with other information. They can find out a lot about you.

'Use various search engines and search for your name in quotes: first and last name in quotes and your telephone number in quotes, your address in quotes, even your email address. See if somebody's put up a website and see where information about you may be stored on the Internet. You won't find everything but you will find a great deal. And ask for it to be removed. It's not always your right but they do generally remove it. We've now got the EU directive which gives a better protection in certain areas. It's still not enough. In the United States only children have protection, although we have better protection for the children on privacy than you do in Europe.'[5]

Wayne Maxey and Parry Aftab are just two of an army of experts in this new fight. The extent of the problem is still not known. Parry and her colleagues receive, at the outside, about six hundred and fifty cases a day in many languages and from all over the world. They have learned, by and large, that sixty per cent of these have connections to some type of relationship fall out; twenty per cent are abuse directed at, say, fat people who have logged on to a dieting chat room, or some similar target group; another ten per cent are children or teenagers 'ringing the doorbell and running away'. The remaining ten per cent is spread between people trying to prove their technical skills and those provoking arguments.

Where the cyberstalking involves someone a person knows or someone who seems to have information about where their victim lives, the advice is always to involve the police. It is important to keep calm and remember there is every possibility the stalker is bluffing.

Parry: 'The problem is, you don't know if they're capable of following through on the threats, because most of the time you have no idea where they are located at the time of the cyberstalking. Aside from the case where they're building a website and getting other people targeting you, which is an unusual situation, it's only Internet stalking. So if you've got a regular stalking and someone says "I'm going to kill you and I know where your children walk home after school and I know they pass this candy shop," to all intents and purposes you will see that as a credible risk of an off-line threat. Yet it could be that you've shared information about your children

243

coming home late from school and that they go past a candy shop every day. It could be the stalker doesn't know where you live at all.'[6]

Keep a record of any communications. You can move all the emails coming from that person to a special folder and never see them. You're preserving them for evidence and you don't have to change your email address. You don't have to read them and you won't be tempted to reply.

Don't reply. As with off-line stalking cases, there's always a chance the stalker will run out of steam if he gets no response whatsoever. If the seventeenth email receives a reply, he knows it takes that long to frighten you sufficiently enough to get his desired reaction.

Be careful what information you give out about yourself in chat rooms. Cyberspace can be great fun and a useful way of meeting like-minded people, but remember: it's so easy for someone to pose as someone quite different to who they actually are. If a chat room conversation results in a proposed meeting, remember the advice given about telephone chat lines and apply it. Meet in a public place; tell a friend where you're going and keep any details of the person you are meeting; take time to get to know the person before being alone with them and make sure they're aware beforehand that you may not wish to take the meeting further.

Keep passwords to yourself and don't make them obvious ones. Don't write them down and tell your children to keep them private, even from their friends (if the children need to know them in the first place).

Be careful not to provoke people on line. Don't go into a chat room and immediately start giving contrary opinions. Robust argument is healthy and good but there may be someone listening in who is just looking for a person to hate.

Parry is optimistic. She hopes there will be little need for her services in five years' time.

'I really hope there won't. I hope we will be creating wonderful resources for people on the Internet. We won't need to educate people about appropriate behaviour on-line.'[7]

The computer screen has become another weapon in the stalker's armoury. It's so dangerous because we feel relaxed when we log on. We're at home and we're safe – we have our mask over our face and nobody can find us. We must be aware that this feeling of security is the means by which they *do* find us. We must learn the rules and be on our guard. In time, safety will be an automatic consideration, as it is in other types of meeting places. Meanwhile we must remember that just as in the centre of London and New York, cyberspace has its brightly lit streets and its dark alleys; it has its interesting strangers and its thugs, its rogues and its killers.

14. YOU'LL NEVER GET AWAY FROM ME

At the same time as the protection from Harassment Act was going through Parliament, a worrying development was coming to light in British prisons. Victims of stalking whose cases were successfully prosecuted in court could be forgiven for thinking themselves safe for the duration of the offender's sentence. It was not so.

There are about seven hundred probation officers working inside prisons. From their information, it was discovered that many of the men who had been convicted of abusive crimes – men who had bullied, harassed and been violent towards women over a period of time, who'd been jailed for Grievous Bodily Harm or Attempted Murder – were continuing to harass their victims from behind bars.

The way they did it followed familiar patterns: they would send unwanted letters and make menacing phone calls. On occasion, when they found them out, the authorities would try to put a ban on an individual making calls, but with prisons like Wormwood Scrubs, which houses upwards of a thousand men, it was not always possible. To inmates, the phone card is a currency like cigarettes and cannabis. Individual prisoners might make two or three calls a day. It would have been unrealistic for the authorities to attempt to monitor a thousand-plus phone calls in any given day.

Harry Fletcher, the General Secretary of the Probation Officers' Association, says: 'Years ago, when a prisoner phoning out of prison was a rarity, we actually used to have people listening-in, recording what they said. Not any more; now there are so many. There are 66,000 prisoners. At the beginning of the nineties there were only 40,000. It's a massive increase and with it have come greater freedoms.'[1]

As inmates challenged, through the High Courts, the restrictions put upon them, they won rights. There are now phone boxes with phone cards on most prison landings and prisoners routinely queue up to make their calls. In the case of a small number of high-profile inmates, where the danger of their abusing the system is prevalent, an individual prison officer might listen in to the conversation and sometimes even record it, but for the vast majority this is simply impractical.

To someone who has been stalked, a phone call from the perpetrator, even one where no threats are uttered, is enough to bring all the misery of the ordeal crashing back into their life. That the stalker is able to continue from inside jail underlines the helplessness of the victim and gives the perpetrator a sense of power.

It seemed nothing could be done to stop them. When a complaint was made and precautions were taken to prevent a prisoner ringing a particular number or writing to a particular address, the offenders swapped victims. A letter from an unknown person or a phone call with coded menace behind innocuous pleasantries would have devastating effects and the perpetrators knew it. There were even cases where criminals who had been released would carry out attacks and assaults as a 'favour' to a friend they had left inside.

Harry Fletcher says: 'When we become aware of a scandal, do we go to ministers and try and deal with it softly-softly or do we go for a big bang? I knew it was worth a splash in a newspaper. Frankly, my experience is that if you go and talk softly-softly to ministers, nothing ever happens, but if you do it on a bigger scale, it does. So that's what I did.'[2]

Harry was out with friends, enjoying a Sunday meal at a restaurant in West Hampstead, when the story broke. The first editions had come out and most of them carried the report. Cases which had not previously been examined in the public arena were now causing outrage: like a man who had been sending his victim letters which he purported were for his lawyer, and had been completely uncensored. A woman who had suffered a terrible attack, in which her ex-husband cracked her head open on a radiator, stamped on her and bit her, was beaten up again by two men. She later found out they had been 'working' on her husband's instructions, passed on during their time in jail. The ex-husband served his sentence and was freed. He continued to stalk his former wife. The law caught up with him again after he drove his car into the wall of her house.[3]

Harry Fletcher's phone began to ring and it didn't stop. He had to abandon the meal and go home. He had been expecting the reaction and was prepared for it.

'The then minister was Joyce Quinn, and I got a call from her office: "Why didn't you come and tell us first?" and I just said "Why should we? We're not publicly accountable to the Government; it's a matter of public interest. Something's got to be done about it." '[4]

The government proposed the introduction of special swipe cards which would be doctored. If the prisoner attempted to telephone a forbidden number, it would be barred. The scheme was to be introduced in early 1998 at Full-Sutton Prison in North Yorkshire. Two years later Harry Fletcher is only aware of the cards being available in a handful of institutions.

'All this is about the same time as the Act came in in June '97. I would say the first time stalking became an issue, a serious issue, where ordinary people being stalked were being recognised, was in the mid-nineties. Before that, it was considered to be a problem for film stars in America.

'I think there are parallels with other crimes. As in the eighties, the degree of child abuse going on in children's homes was exposed by people like Bea Campbell. It was all denied – as hysteria. I think stalking is the child abuse phenomena of the nineties. It too was denied "Oh it can't be true – all these women being stalked in this way . . ." So as far as I can see, the government have introduced the phone bar in prisons with the more serious guys in them, people doing five years plus. But the rest . . .'[5]

The 'victim swapping' was still going on, even with prisoners who were being closely monitored. It seemed it was all too easy to get a mate to do your harassing for you. There was even more difficulty stopping inappropriate letters getting out. If the tone of the writing was apparently pleasant: 'My darling, I think of you every day . . .' who was to say whether it was genuine or not? The majority of these type of letters were escaping the attention of the prison authorities and there didn't seem to be any reasonable suggestions as to how they could be blocked. It's only possible to check about ten per cent of the letters posted from British prisons. Even then, many can get through because there is nothing obviously threatening in their content.

The victim-swapping continues today, as do the abusive phone calls. These are predatory, obsessive people who refuse to let a small thing like the law of the land stop them. Harry Fletcher considers that where there is a recognised problem, where the stalker can't (or won't) stop, and there's a known victim, consideration should be given to wiring up the victim's house.

'Electronic software – force the stalker to wear some kind of gadget so if he comes within four hundred metres of the specified area an alarm goes off. Tagging these people is a waste of time. All that does is confine the culprit to his house. Nobody knows what you're doing while you're in your house. You could be writing letters, you could be making phone calls . . .'[6]

He also agrees with a call made at the time by the Suzy Lamplugh Trust that stalking from within jail should affect the prisoner's release date. He is sceptical about cognitive behaviour courses which have proved effective in stopping some other types of abusive behaviour.

'I think the vast majority of people who stalk women who come to our attention are those who've known the person in some way. It's an illness and that's why I'm cautious if not sceptical of the degree to which the cognitive behaviour courses will work with people who are like that.'[7]

Stalkers are rarely required to confront their behaviour whilst inside prison. Prison is very much seen by society purely for its punitive purpose. Prisoners are considered to be criminals who are out of harm's way – at least for the duration of their sentence. It is thought the victim can achieve a degree of satisfaction in the knowledge that the person who harmed them is being punished for it. Clearly, this isn't the case. While the prison system is unable to offer effective therapy to the stalker and real protection to the people they prey on, a custodial sentence simply provides another opportunity to demonstrate the ease with which stalkers overcome any obstacle put in their way.

So what can be done by victims? I thoroughly recommend Gavin De Becker's *The Gift of Fear*; DCI Hamish Brown has also advised the police and the public on how to deal with stalking.

DCI Brown's background is that of a CID officer, almost exclusively in central London. He has dealt with all the horrific violence of the city: rape, murder . . . He notes them with professional detachment. Then came the case which was to put stalking firmly at the front of his work.

It happened during the time Brown worked in Staines and it had started some few months before he arrived. In September 1996, a seventeen-year-old McDonald's worker, a student at Brooklands College in Weybridge, found a letter left on her car windscreen. It was wrapped in cling film and had a picture of a punk where the stamp should have been. The note inside told her a person close to her needed her help. It warned her that failure to do anything might result in her death. 'You may have a very strong character . . . But my spirit for revenge will be hard to extinguish . . .'

Two more notes arrived the very next day. On one was written the details of the young woman's car. It told her that 'no power in the world will keep me away from you. Your time is almost up.'[8]

She had tried to believe the first communication to be a joke. Now she was persuaded to take the matter very seriously indeed. Her parents had already contacted the police, who had also been inclined to dismiss the incident as a sick prank.

They quickly changed their minds. The letters continued, sometimes declaring love, sometimes threatening death: 'Time is running out for the both of us. Neither you or I will be alive when this year is out. Our sacrifice will be a symbol to the world. You will become the most famous victim and I will be the most famous stalker in the world. This way I can't win or lose the game. It's the only way left.'[9] The stalker sent pornographic pictures of women accompanied by notes on what he would like to do to them. Hamish Brown and his officers proceeded to interview everyone connected with the victim.

She believed she was being followed everywhere she went. The stalker sent her a detailed and accurate diary of her life. Brown, who was now in charge of the investigation, elected to follow her as well. The stalker knew the police were on to him and responded with the words 'stupid bitch'.

But it worked. From their vantage point at Brooklands College, hidden inside a catering van, the police witnessed one of the victim's previous co-workers from McDonald's putting a note on her car. They pounced.

DCI Brown was able to ring the terrified young woman and tell her 'we've got him'. She was appalled when she found out who was responsible. He had been a friend of hers – one of the last people she would have suspected.

When the Home Office asked all police forces to think of a subject, research it and come up with some sort of product in response, Brown decided to look into the wider problem of stalking. His product would be an easy-to-follow guide for officers investigating stalking offences and it contains the following advice for victims.

15. ADVICE TO VICTIMS

- You don't have to be rich or famous for someone to follow you or spy on you or try to get more involved in your life than you want them to be.
- A total stranger or someone you know, or used to know, could very well be involved.
- If you think you are being stalked, report your concerns to the police, no matter how trivial the harassment may seem to you.
- The police must treat it seriously and will investigate your complaint.
- If you are in fear of immediate danger, call 999.

Help the police to help you
- By gathering evidence:
  - keep a record of what happened, where and when, every time you were followed, phoned, got post or email messages;
  - if possible, download onto disk and print out a hard copy of email messages, but do not delete the original – keep it for the police to examine;
  - if you have a mobile telephone, do not tamper with or dispose of it or its SIM-card without first consulting the Investigating Officer. It may contain valuable evidence;
  - the more details you have, the better: how the offender looked or sounded, what they were wearing, the make, number plate or colour of their car;
  - making notes in a diary is a good idea, as this may be used in any later court proceedings. Write information down as soon as possible when events are still fresh in your mind. Include details of dates and times of the incidents, and people who may have witnessed them;
  - find out if any of your neighbours etc, saw or heard what happened;

- keep letters and parcels as evidence: even if they contain frightening or upsetting messages, do not throw them away, keep them in a box so you don't have to handle them;
- if you recognise the handwriting, you can keep the letter or parcel as evidence without having to open and read the contents;
- tape record telephone conversations if you can, and keep the tape;
- make sure you keep any stored messages (including text messages) or telephone numbers that you have received on your mobile telephone and caller ID units;
- use 1471 on your phone and write down details of calls – even if you didn't answer them;
- try to get a photograph or video evidence of your stalker (especially if they are someone who has already been warned by the police not to come near you);
- tell your neighbours, friends and work colleagues about what is happening; and
- keep notes of anything they see and hear (for example if others answer your phone at work). They can act as independent witnesses, and tell you of anything they may see when you're not there.

How you can help yourself

- Take a mobile telephone when out and about.
- Carry a personal attack alarm and learn how to use it – but do not carry anything that is meant for use as a weapon.
- Think about improving your home's security – ask the police for advice.
- Try to alter your daily routines, ask friends to go with you whenever possible, and always try to let someone know what your plans are and if you have to change them while you're away from home or work.
- When out and about, if you feel insecure, look out for places such as 24-hour petrol stations and shops or police stations and other emergency services where you could go for help.

- If the stalking is at college or university, think about telling a tutor or head of department who might be able to put a stop to it. In-house support groups are available.
- At banks, building societies and other cash outlets you are asked for your mother's maiden name as a security password. This name is available to anyone researching public records. It is okay to use something else.

If you know or find out who your stalker is
- Remember not to confront your stalker or even engage them in conversation:
  - do not **under any circumstances**, agree to a meeting to talk about how you feel about them constantly bothering you;
  - do not respond in any way to calls, letters or conversations. If you ignore the phone nine times and pick it up on the tenth, you will send the message that persistence pays. Once they have your attention, they will be encouraged to carry on;
  - ask friends or your solicitor to contact them if you want to get a message to them.

Avoid unwanted phone calls
- If someone makes phone calls that are offensive, threatening or simply worryingly frequent:
  - just say 'hello' when you answer, do not give your name or number;
  - try to keep calm and not to show any emotion – many callers will give up if they don't think they're making any impression on you or your feelings;
  - use an answer machine to 'screen out' calls and only talk to people you want to. Caller ID units are another way of ensuring you know who is calling before you answer the telephone;
  - ask a friend to record the outgoing message on your answer machine, for example a man's voice might throw the caller off balance;
  - make sure your message doesn't make it clear you're

alone: 'We can't come to the phone right now' rather than 'I'm not at home';

- if the caller rings again, put the handset down on a table for a few minutes and walk away – the caller will think you are listening. After a few minutes replace the handset – you do not have to listen to what the caller has to say;
- dial 1471 and keep a note of the number that called, when and for how long;
- contact your telephone company – the operator will be able to tell you who to talk to;
- decide if you want to change to an ex-directory number.

Avoid being stalked on the Internet

- Always remember you are never totally anonymous on the Internet. Use your 'stranger – danger' instincts:
  - use an on-screen nickname that doesn't make it easy to guess your real identity (or even whether you are a man or a woman);
  - never give out your password, even to someone who claims to be from your Internet company;
  - do not give personal information, such as a photograph of yourself or details of telephone numbers and credit cards, to people you talk to in chat rooms or newsgroups;
  - be careful if you answer 'junk mail'; and
  - log off (leave the 'room') if you are uncomfortable with what is being said in chat channels.
- It is safer not to meet people you have chatted to on-line. If you do decide to meet them, take a friend and meet in a public place where you feel safe.

If you are stalked on the Internet

- If you get offensive or threatening emails or messages on screen:
  - do not delete the messages – save them onto a disk or print out the screen;
  - keep all paper and hard copies, together with any other evidence, and call the police;

- you can contact your Internet Service Provider, who may be able to block incoming email from specified addresses; or
- you can always change your email address.

Internet safety for children

- Schools and others monitoring children should be careful when giving out details of school trips, sports activities etc.
- Families might want to keep computers in a shared space, rather than a child's bedroom. This will make informal control of what they see on screen easier.
- Make sure children know the dangers the Internet can pose. Explain about:
  - not supplying personal details; and
  - not getting into conversations or arranging to meet people.
- And encourage your children to tell you about anything they've seen that worries them.

This section is taken from DI Hamish Brown's *Stalking and Other Forms of Harassment: An Investigator's Guide*, Metropolitan Police/Home Office 2000.

CONCLUSION

When I began writing, my file of newspaper clippings about stalkers and their victims grew rapidly and alarmingly. It bulges further every day. The stories range right across the board and involve every conceivable type of person:

– a mother who was stalked by the neighbour she helped clear of murder. She testified in court that she'd seen the accused in the garden of his home at the time of the killing. Afterwards he sent her hate mail, loitered outside her house, shone a torch through her windows and eventually forced her and her three terrified daughters to abandon their home.
– a dressmaker who was stalked by a London barrister she'd once had an affair with. Every day she was subjected to forty or more obscene calls. The man screamed abuse through her letterbox and shouted outside her windows. He told lies about her sex life, saying she could only enjoy threesomes, and threatened to 'wipe her out'.
– a seventeen year-old girl who was stalked by her own father. He followed her in the street, called her a 'slapper' and a 'slag'; he interrogated her about her mother's new relationship, pushed a tape-recorder in front of her to record what she was saying to her friends and threatened to kill himself unless she paid more attention to him.
– a female GP bombarded a (female) neighbour with malicious calls, punctured her car tyres and smeared holly berries over the vehicle. She left a message in wet cement by the garage door and, strangely, buried a packet of biscuits in the woman's garden.
– a victim who received threatening letters, some delivered, some left on her car, some in bushes near her home. She then began to get various horrible objects from headless dolls to chicken claws. Eventually she told a close friend about her ordeal. Seven years later she discovered he was the culprit.

Most dreadful of all is the story of a married woman in Leicestershire who had been stalked for seven or eight years. Her husband died and for some time she heard nothing from her stalker. Two years passed and she thought she had at last rid herself of him but he came back. He dug up her dead husband and left the remains on her doorstep with the message, 'What has he got that I haven't?'

These are all reasonably recent British cases. We used to think the crime was the sole problem of American film stars: it's now part of the domestic life of thousands of ordinary people across the world. In April 2000 in Japan a man stabbed his ex-girlfriend thirty-four times and left her to die. His arrest prompted legal experts to call for something to be done against stalking in a country which has 'lagged far behind in anti-stalking efforts'.

At the time of writing there is one important case which has been unsolved for some time. This well-known and as yet unresolved stalking crime is that of the murdered estate agent, Suzy Lamplugh.

Suzy was an attractive and vivacious twenty-five-year-old. She worked in Fulham in South West London where she arranged one day to meet a client whose name sounded both ridiculous and sinister: the now infamous 'Mr Kipper'.

On 28 July 1986, Suzy was seen driving away from her office at 12.40 p.m. Her car, a Ford Fiesta, was found abandoned about a mile away some hour and a quarter later. Suzy was never seen again.

Whether this was a stalking case is still not known. It seems somebody may have been watching Suzy for some time, loitering outside the office window where she sat unaware of the danger her good looks were placing her in.

In May 2000, the police investigation into Suzy's disappearance was re-opened after some people came forward with new evidence. As yet, nothing has been revealed as to the possibilities of a conviction.

Suzy's mother, Diana Lamplugh, is a diminutive woman with a kindly, wise face. She is elegant, firm and assured. She used to be a lecturer and trainer in health and fitness but you can more easily imagine her as the favourite primary school teacher whose gentle, sad displeasure would be more excruciating than the worst of punishments. She has a quiet, understated authority which is extremely powerful. After what happened to her daughter she saw that she had a choice: a choice to either give in to her feelings of despair or to use the experience to some positive end.

Mrs Lamplugh set up a trust in her daughter's name and now is the UK's leading expert in personal safety. At the launch of the Trust she said, 'Suzy was lively, attractive, especially appealing when she was excited. When she was trying to sell something she would be very attractive, but she still had no idea how a man might react to her. She was doing a job without regard for the fact of being female.'[1]

The Suzy Lamplugh Trust has embraced Tracey Morgan's initiative to form a helpline for victims of stalking. It was one of the major advisors when the Protection from Harassment Act was being discussed, and has helped the Network for Victims of Stalking through its early stages.

Mrs Lamplugh maintains stalking is more about control than it is about lust or some warped view of love.

'You're talking about a person who's using power – using it in order to create terrible disquiet. Stalking is something which is pushed. It really does not stop. It goes on, and on, and on.'[2]

As has been said, stalking is a crime which is perceived by the victim and great distress can be caused whether or not the perpetrator has malicious intent. In March 1998, the need for legislation was demonstrated only too clearly by a judge at Manchester Crown Court who heard the case of a thirty-two-year-old property developer and member of the Church of the Latterday Saints, whose amorous intentions towards a florist had resulted in two years of misery. She'd even found it necessary to sell her shop to get away from him.

The judge, Adrian Smith, is reported as saying, 'One looks to see if there is a violent act in this case but there is none. You cannot elevate a series of Easter eggs, cards and Valentines, which on the face of it are innocuous, to make this man guilty. It is not even alleged they are malicious.'[3]

In fact the man, who was acquitted of causing grievous bodily harm, had, according to his victim, not only kept up a stream of gifts and flowers, but was constantly 'in her shadow'. He watched her from outside her shop, occasionally sent 'dirty' letters as well as a good number of 'loving' ones, and left messages on her answerphone. The woman had been too scared to challenge him by returning his gifts: she had no idea how this man, who did not appear able to listen to reason, would react. The threat of violence was certainly there in her head, even if it was not intended. It's easy to speculate on the sense of personal invasion she must have felt: an unwanted admirer not accepting no for an answer is bad enough, but still assuming, two years later, that his supposed 'charms' will win out is exasperating, demeaning, frustrating and threatening.

The case brings back to mind the alarming pronouncements of crusty old judges who used to say a woman wearing lipstick was a deliberate and calculated invitation to rape. The lack of perception is mind-boggling. Diana Lamplugh says: 'It still shocks me that the judges have a total lack of understanding of real people. We have a long way to go, we've got to climb this hill. I think the younger ones are a bit brighter.'[4]

Maybe this is true, but it is not the age or sex of the judiciary which is changing, it is Society itself. The provisions of the Protection from Harassment Act should have helped the florist's case but, more than that, public awareness of the misery engendered by those who don't take 'no' for an answer is rapidly altering the way such incidents are dealt with. As we become more sophisticated, we must find ways of expressing our disapproval of the predatory ways of some male persons and the assumptions we make about some females.

Stalking is a social menace: the effect on the victim is the same whether the culprit is a barking mad stranger; a domineering ex-partner; a conceited Romeo or a lonely Juliet. The same statements occur again and again: 'I thought everybody would think I was being paranoid'; 'I don't feel I have any control over my life any more'; 'I feel depressed, suicidal'. Diana Lamplugh wants the victims to be listened to and respected far more than they are:

'You're a very embarrassing thing (as a victim). We've just had a review of our case which is just about to be reopened. The police have a completely different way of doing things now. They asked to go and see the window: my daughter's window, in the church. They wanted to see whether we had something to actually take the place of having a body because we probably won't find her. They didn't know whether they had to spend all their money on trying to find Suzy's body or trying to find the person who killed her. So we went up there and I said to the priest "Tell them how the congregation felt." In fact they'd wanted us to go away. People find it very difficult to accept victims because you're a great fear for them. You're there demonstrating that it could happen to them and this is a very nasty shock. Such things always happen to somebody else. You almost feel you ought to be confined to bed – or that people in this situation will either crumble up, have their blood sucked dry, or will actually go bananas.

'People should actually start to feel they are doing something and they're listened to, because after all, if you're a victim you should be listened to. This is where the police have done a remarkable job on us (the Lamplugh family). Taking us totally into consideration. Also, victims need to care for other people – to say, "Look, it's all right. How are *your* children?" I had to go and do the flowers so people would talk to me. It's our job.'[5]

Mrs Lamplugh has used positive visualisation techniques to come to terms with her loss. At first she did this more or less instinctively but has since become interested in what she describes as 'rapid eye movement'. It's a way of confronting the dark images which trouble our minds and coming to terms with them by a combination of mental process and physical eye movement.

'It's being researched at the moment. It's usually done by doctors. You concentrate on the image of the fear – the really nasty things that have happened, like seeing your child murdered. You don't actually talk to people about it, but you visualise it. You look at it and then you move your eye – you're told to look at the fear – and then to look forward. You talk about the way forward and what you can actually build out of it. It's very, very effective. It's about really physically healing the brain. You don't forget what's happened, but it becomes part of you rather than coming at you. It's amazingly quick too. I found I could actually take it through to being able to imagine holding my daughter's hand – when she was dead. You have to, otherwise it can torture you for the rest of your life.

'When you tell somebody about a problem, you inevitably change it. You'll either change it so you don't dump it on them or you'll change it so it's amazingly big – because that's the only way you'll get it through to somebody. As you change it, you lose your ability to actually look at it clearly yourself. I've had to face how my daughter might have died, might have been murdered. Our fears can produce something much worse than what had actually happened.'[6]*

Stalking is a form of rape: a desire for control and possession which goes against every ethic, every reason, every refinement which makes a human-being human. It is a primal instinct which seeks nothing other than its own fulfilment. It poses in various costumes: 'love', 'despair', 'sympathy', but it is ultimately a form of selfishness. The stalker seeks to punish his innocent victims for the emotional lack he feels in himself. Stalking leaves people at best suspicious and wary, and at worst horribly disfigured, emotionally or physically. The people who have walked through these pages – brave, understanding, caring individuals – made the mistake of trying to see the best in someone; of trying to comprehend the assaults and intrusions they experienced; of being tolerant where they would have been better advised to be firm and unapproachable.

So how should we react when a perfect stranger, or an ex-lover, or a person we had once been kind to suddenly

---

* This interview took place on 3 May 2000 shortly before newspaper reports about the reopening of the case. On 13 May it was announced that a key witness had come forward saying he had seen Suzy in her car some eighty minutes after the last known sighting. It seems the disappearance may have involved more than one person and forensic evidence may now be able to identify them. Some of the suspects are already serving sentences for violent crime. Recent attempts to find Suzie's remains have so far been unsuccessful.

presumes that degree of intimacy and ownership? What do you do when, at a party, a person 'invades your body space'? How is it best to say 'you're very nice but you're not my type'? Gabriella Mazzali advocates that you should say no, underline it three times in red ink – and get out. This policy is to be highly recommended, but sometimes even that is not going to work. If this is the case then it must be time to stop thinking you are paranoid, to stop considering the niceties of social convention; it is time to alert whoever you can and make it clear this person is not welcome in your company.

Most of the people who have talked to me about this subject have that message to give: trust your instincts and stick to them. Stalkers are manipulative, they know how kind you are and they abuse that kindness and use it against you. Harry Fletcher said that child abuse was a similar crime in that its victims were not listened to, were not believed. Child abuse has been going on for centuries, so has stalking. It is not a crime of the late twentieth century; it has existed as long as people have; it is a manifestation of the animal in all of us. Stalkers are often pitiable, sometimes harmless, sometimes murderous. Though we stare in disbelief at the results, many of us are at least able to understand the beginnings of obsession. Long ago, when we were finding out what our own bodies were for and how our emotions worked, many of us felt that same desperation. We must always have compassion. We must also make ourselves safe.

NOTES

CHAPTER ONE: LOVE LOCKED OUT
1. Emily Bronte, *Wuthering Heights*, Chapter 15, 1847
2. Epigram, Quentin Crisp 1931–1999
3. Interview with the author, December 1998
4. Email to author, April 2000
5. Letter to Stuart Taylor Jnr. of the *New York Times*
6. The *Independent*, 1996, quoting BBC1 documentary, *Inside Story: Stalking the Stalkers*, July 1996
7. Interview with the author, April 2000
8. Email to author, April 2000
9. L Sheridan, GM Davies, and JCW Boon, *The Course and Nature of Stalking: a Victim's Perspective*, University of Leicester, 2000
10. Email to author, April 2000
11. Doctor J. Reid Meloy, *The Psychology of Stalking: Clinical and Forensic Perspectives*, Academic Press, 1998
12. Article, *New York Times*, March 1996
13. *The Times*, October 1997
14. Sheridan, Davies & Boon, op cit.
15. Letter to the author, August 2000

CHAPTER TWO: A MAN WHO WASN'T THERE
1. Jack Jones, *Let Me Take You Down*, p. 126, Virgin Publishing Ltd, 1993
2. Ibid., p. 129
3. Ibid., 129
4. Ibid., p. 179
5. Ibid., p. 195
6. Ibid., p. 206
7. Ibid., p. 219
8. Ibid., p. 241
9. Ibid., p. 252
10. Ibid., p. 51
11. Mark David Chapman, date unspecified.

CHAPTER THREE: YOU MADE ME LOVE YOU

1. Letter to Jodie Foster, 1981
2. Tape recording, 1981
3. Ibid
4. Unsent letter found after Hinckley's arrest, 1981
5. News agency reports, May 2000.
6. Quote from A.J. 1982

CHAPTER FOUR: THE HERO OF MY OWN LIFE

1. The *Daily Telegraph*, December 1897.
2. George Rowell, *William Terriss and Richard Prince, Two Characters in an Adelphi Melodrama*, p. 62, Society for Theatre Research, 1987
3. The *Daily Telegraph*, op cit.
4. George Rowell, op cit., p. 62
5. The *Daily Telegraph*, op cit.
6. Ibid
7. George Rowell, op cit., p. 64
8. Seymour Hicks, *Between Ourselves*, p. 36, Casell & Co plc, 1930
9. Ibid., p. 38
10. Ibid., p. 39
11. Ibid., p. 44
12. George Rowell, op cit., p. 59
13. Ibid., p. 69
14. The *Daily Telegraph*, op cit.
15. Ibid. (Rowell has: 'Mad? Mad? You will hear of my madness. The whole world will ring with it.') – op cit, p. 69
16. The *Daily Telegraph*, op cit.
17. George Rowell, op cit. p. 73
18. Ibid., p. 70
19. The *Daily Telegraph*, op cit.
20. Ibid.
21. George Rowell op cit. p. 71
22. The *Daily Telegraph*, op cit.
23. Ibid.
24. Ibid.

CHAPTER FIVE: POISON IN JEST

1. Letter from Jeremy Dyer to Sarah Lockett, 27 May 1998
2. Interview with the author, April 2000
3. Letter from Jeremy Dyer to Sarah Lockett, 1 June 1998
4. Interview with the author, April 2000
5. Letter from Jeremy Dyer to Sarah Lockett, 4 June 1998
6. As above, 7 June 1998
7. Interview with the author, April 2000
8. Letter from Jeremy Dyer to Sarah Lockett, 9 August 1998
9. Undated postcard from Jeremy Dyer to Sarah Lockett
10. Letter from Jeremy Dyer to Sarah Lockett, 11 June 1998
11. As above, 20 July 1998
12. Letter from Jeremy Dyer to N.K. 22 July 1998
13. Letter from Jeremy Dyer to Sarah Lockett, 9 April 1999
14. As above, 9 August 1998
15. As above, 18 August 1998
16. As above, 23 August 1998
17. Ibid.
18. Letter from Jeremy Dyer to Sarah Lockett, 21 February 1999
19. As above, 4 December 1998
20. As above, 29 December 1998
21. As above, 16 January 1999
22. As above, 23 January 1999
23. As above, 21 February 1999
24. Ibid.
25. Letter from Jeremy Dyer to Sarah Lockett, 7 March 1999
26. As above, 8 March 1999
27. As above, 3 April 1999
28. As above, 5 April 1999
29. As above, 7 April 1999
30. As above, 9 April 1999
31. As above, 13 April 1999
32. As above, Started 18 April – Finished 23 April
33. As above, 3 May 1999
34. As above, 11 May 1999
35. As above, 17 May 1999
36. Letter from Jeremy Dyer to S.L.'s co-presenter, 2 June 1999

37. Letter from Jeremy Dyer to Sarah Lockett, 2 June 1999
38. As above, undated (sent June 1999)

CHAPTER SIX: NOT HIMSELF
1. *Daily Mirror*, 3 July 2001

CHAPTER SEVEN: WHO DO YOU THINK I AM?
1. Interview with the author, May 1999
2. As above
3. As above
4. As above

CHAPTER EIGHT: ALL'S FAIR IN LOVE AND WAR
1–23 All quotes in this chapter: Interview with the author, July 2000

CHAPTER NINE: WILD JUSTICE
1. Robert Fine: *Being Stalked, a Memoir*, pp. 4–5, Chatto & Windus, 1997
2. Interview with the author, January 2000
3. Robert Fine, op cit., p. 11
4. Ibid., pp. 11–12
5. Ibid., p. 13
6. Interview with the author, January 2000
7. Robert Fine, op cit., p. 16
8. Ibid., pp. 16–17
9. Ibid., p. 17–18
10. Interview with the author, January 2000
11. Robert Fine, op cit., p. 43
12. Ibid., p. 48
13. Ibid., p. 57–72
14. Ibid., p. 124
15. Interview with the author, January 2000

CHAPTER TEN: I'LL BE WATCHING YOU
1. Interview with the author, April 2000
2. As above
3. Yorkshire Television documentary, *I'll Be Watching You*, Producer/Director Glyn Middleton 1999. Reproduced courtesy of Granada Media Commercial Ventures

4. Ibid.
5. Interview with the author, April 2000
6. As above
7. As above
8. Yorkshire Television, op cit.
9. As above
10. As above
11. Interview with the author, April 2000
12. As above
13. As above
14. As above
15. As above
16. Yorkshire Television, op cit.
17. Ibid.
18. Ibid.
19. David MacClean, 9 July 1996
20. Michael Howard, 25 September 1996
21. Interview with the author, April 2000
22. As above
23. As above
24. As above
25. As above

CHAPTER ELEVEN: THE FOOD OF LOVE
1. Cassandra Jardine writing in the *Daily Telegraph*, 30 June 1998
2. Ibid.
3. Interview with the author, August 2000
4. As above
5. As above

CHAPTER TWELVE: TO HELL AND BACK
1–8. Interview with the author, May 2000
9. The *Observer*, 26 December 1999
10. Interview with the author, May 2000

CHAPTER THIRTEEN: THE INVISIBLE THREAT
1. Interview with the author, September 2000
2. Email to author, July 2000

3. Interview with the author, September 2000
4. As above
5. As Above
6. As Above
7. As Above

CHAPTER FOURTEEN: YOU'LL NEVER GET AWAY FROM ME

1. Interview with the author, March 2000
2. As Above
3. The *Observer*, 22 June, 1997
4. Interview with the author, March 2000
5. As above
6. As Above
7. As Above
8. Letter to victim, 1996
9. Letter to victim, 1996

CONCLUSION

1. Speech made at the launch of the *Suzy Lamplugh Trust*, 6 December 1986
2. Interview with the author, May 2000
3. The *Daily Telegraph*, March, 1998
4. Interview with the author, May 2000
5. As above
6. As above

WHERE TO GET HELP

VICTIM SUPPORT
PO Box 11431
London SW9 6ZH
This is the Victim Support national office but referrals should
be made through a local scheme where possible.

THE SUZY LAMPLUGH TRUST
14, East Sheen Avenue
London
SW14 8AS
www.suzylamplugh.org.uk

S.O.S. (NETWORK FOR SURVIVING STALKING)
PO Box 7836
Crowthorne
Berkshire
RG45 7YA
Telephone: 01344 773832
Fax: 01344 773446
www.nss.org.uk
Registered Charity Number: 1088762

www.cyberangels.org
For any concerns regarding the Internet.

www.cyberlawenforcement.com
This is a network of law enforcement officers who specialise
in cybercrime investigation. Parry Aftab, cyberspace lawyer
and noted Internet safey expert, and Richard Riley, law
enforcement officer and Internet crime specialist jointly head
this group.

www.wiredkids.org
This site handles all issues impacting on children online
including cyberstalking, luring children into offline meetings,
child exploitation and child pornography.

BIBLIOGRAPHY

CHAPTER TWO: A MAN WHO WASN'T THERE
Coleman, Ray, *John Winston Lennon Volume 1 1940–1966* and *John Ono Lennon Volume 2 1967–1980*, Sidgwick & Jackson, 1984.
Jones, Jack, *Let Me Take You Down – Inside the Mind of Mark David Chapman, The Man Who Killed John Lennon*, Virgin Books, London, 1993.
Salinger, JD, *The Catcher in the Rye*, Little Brown & Company, Boston, 1951.

CHAPTER THREE: YOU MADE ME LOVE YOU
Foster, Buddy and Wagener, Leon, *Foster Child*, Mandarin, 1998 and Heinemann, London, 1997.
Kennedy, Philippa, *Jodie Foster – the Most Powerful Woman in Hollywood*, Macmillan London, 1995.

CHAPTER FOUR: THE HERO OF MY OWN LIFE . . .
Rowell, George, *William Terriss and Richard Prince, Two Characters in an Adelphi Melodrama*, The Society for Theatre Research, London, 1987.
Hicks, Seymour, *Between Ourselves*, Cassell and Co., London, 1930.

CHAPTER EIGHT: WILD JUSTICE
Fine, Robert, *Being Stalked, a Memoir*, Chatto & Windus, London, 1997.

GENERAL:
Aftab, Parry, *A Parent's Guide to the Internet and How to Protect Your Children in Cyberspace*, New York SC Press, 1997.
Aftab, Parry, *The Parent's Guide to Protecting Your Children in Cyberspace*, McGraw-Hill, New York, 2000.
de Becker, Gavin, *The Gift of Fear – Survival Signals That Protect Us From Violence*, Little Brown & Company, Boston, 1997.

Meloy, J. Reid, *The Psychology Of Stalking: Clinical and Forensic Perspectives*, The Academic Press, London, 1998.

Orion, Doreen, *I Know You Really Love Me – a Psychiatrist's Journal of Erotomania, Stalking and Obsessive Love*, Macmillan New York, 1997.

Ritchie, Jean, *Stalkers – How Harmless Devotion Turns to Sinister Obsession*, Harper Collins, London, 1994.

Look out for other compelling True Crime titles
from Virgin Books in 2002

Killers on the Loose – Unsolved Cases of Serial Murder

By Antonio Mendoza

Revised and updated edition

According to a recent FBI study of serial murder, it has climbed to an 'almost epidemic proportion'. It is believed that there are currently up to 6000 people a year dying at the hands of serial killers. The FBI and other law enforcement agencies estimate that there are between 35 and 50 serial killers on the loose at any given time. Other estimates put the number of killers closer to 500. In either case, officials expect these numbers to continue their dramatic rise. This is an up-to-date edition of an original in-depth study of serial killers at large, written by one of the world's foremost authorities.

£6.99 ISBN: 07535 0681 5

Crossing to Kill – The True Story of the Serial Killer Playground

By Simon Whitechapel

Since 1993 over 180 women have been raped and brutally murdered in Ciudad Juarez, a Mexican boarder town notorious for its pollution and overcrowding. The police continue to arrest suspects, but the killing won't stop. Authorities suspect that killers are coming from all over Mexico – and even crossing the border from the USA – to rape and kill with impunity.

Is there any way to protect women from this playground for serial killers?

£6.99 ISBN: 07535 0686 6

Jack The Ripper, The Final Chapter
By Paul H Feldman

A haunting journal that came to light in 1991 and was published in 1993 as *The Diary of Jack the Ripper* was believed to be a hoax. Yet no one was able to explain how it was forged, or by whom. The reason, as Paul Feldman explains, is because the journal is genuine. In this exhaustively researched and most extensive Ripper investigation ever undertaken, Paul Feldman cuts through the cover-ups and wild theories surrounding the Ripper mystery to undoubtedly prove that James Maybrick was Jack the Ripper. As well as uncovering crucial new evidence about the murders, Feldman presents sensational revelations from the Ripper's living descendants.

'. . . my own feeling was that Feldman has taken game, set and match.'
Colin Wilson

£6.99 ISBN: 07535 0637 8

Lone Wolf – True Stories of Spree Killers
By Pan Pantziarka
Revised and updated edition

Cases of loner gunmen embarking on slaughter sprees have begun to occur with frightening regularity since the late 1980s. People like Timothy McVeigh, Thomas Hamilton and Michael Ryan. What drives these mass murderers to turn on friends, family and strangers in acts of senseless rage and slaughter? Is there any way to stop this growing tide of violence that devastates entire communities? Pan Pantziarka conducts an in-depth look at the disturbed personalities and the brutal trend of seemingly indiscriminate killing that blights our 'civilised' society.

£6.99 ISBN: 07535 0617 3